Anglican Religious Life

2010-2011

A Year Book of
Religious orders and communities in
the Anglican Communion,
and tertiaries, oblates, associates and companions

Published by
Canterbury Press Norwich
a publishing imprint of Hymns Ancient & Modern Ltd *(a registered charity)*
13-17 Long Lane, London EC1A 9PN
www.scm-canterburypress.co.uk

ARL 2010-2011 published August 2009

ISBN: 978-1-85311-949-1

Agents for Canterbury Press outside the UK:

Australia	Rainbow Book Agency	www.rainbowbooks.com.au
Canada	Novalis Books	www.novalis.ca
Europe (continental)	Durnell Marketing	www.durnell.co.uk
Ireland	Columba Bookstores	www.columba.ie
New Zealand	Church Stores	christianbooksnz.com/churchstores
South Africa	Pearson South Africa	www.pearson.com
USA	Westminster John Knox	www.wjkbooks.com

The Editorial committee of ARLYB and the publishers wish to thank

The Society of the Faith
&
The Confraternity of the Blessed Sacrament

for their financial support, enabling the publication of this *Year Book*.

Original line drawings by Sister Gillian Mary CSP
Additional drawings by Sister Mary Julian CHC
The cover design is by Leigh Hurlock

Printed and Bound in Great Britain by CPI Antony Rowe

Contents

Foreword

by

Most Revd Roger Herft, Archbishop of Perth, Metropolitan of Western Australia

One of the realities that calls me to constant thanksgiving is to know that I live by the prayer of God in Christ for me and for the world *(Romans 8:15-16; Galatians 4:6)*. It is daunting to ask what the glorious Trinity's intentional prayer is for me today. In what ways will I be nourished to make time for true repentance, amendment of life and be refreshed in my soul with grace and comfort? How is this rhythmic, creative, redemptive, sanctifying power at work around us?

Religious communities by their vocation to prayer are a sign of eternal intercession. They point us to the heart of God's being and enable us to be mindful of the Apostle Paul's admonition in I Thessalonians 5:16-18 *"Rejoice always; pray without ceasing; in everything give thanks; for this is the will of God in Christ Jesus"*. In the practice of prayer, Religious communities help us listen for the heartbeat of God in the world.

In silence, in contemplation, they call us to behold God. And as millions of words are spoken, heard, written, typed, read in countless languages, accents and decibels, Religious communities point us with St John of the Cross to the truth that: *"The Father spoke only one Word, it was his Son; and in an eternal silence he never stops saying it; so we too must hear the word in silence"*.

From this silence we are taught to speak a new language as the mind of our hearts are enlightened to discover a new way of being and doing.

May this *Year Book* of Anglican Religious communities across our world keep us mindful of the volume of prayerful intercession that keeps the Church and the world in the love of God, the grace of Jesus Christ and the power of the Holy Spirit.

+ *Roger Perth*

A Prayer for Vocations to the Religious Life

Setting a particular Sunday each year as a Day of Prayer for Vocations to the Religious Life was begun in 1992. This is currently the **Fourth Sunday after Easter**. All are also invited to pray each Friday for the life and work of the Religious communities in the Church, using the following prayer, written by a Little Brother of Francis, originally for communities in Australia and New Zealand.

**Lord Jesus Christ
in your great love you draw all people to yourself:
and in your wisdom you call us to your service.
We pray at this time you will kindle in the hearts of men and women
the desire to follow you in the Religious life.
Give to those whom you call, grace to accept their vocation readily
and thankfully, to make the whole-hearted surrender
which you ask of them, and for love of you, to persevere to the end.
This we ask in your name. Amen.**

A NOVENA OF PRAYER FOR RELIGIOUS LIFE

Day 1: 2 Thessalonians 1: 3
    We give thanks for Religious communities throughout the world.

Day 2: Romans 14: 7-9
    We give thanks for members in our communities who have died.

Day 3: Acts 15: 36-40
    We pray for those who have left our communities.

Day 4: Ephesians 4: 1-6
    We give thanks for our own vocations.

Day 5: 1 Thessalonians 5: 12-14
    We pray for our leaders and for all who make decisions.

Day 6: Titus 2: 7-9
    We pray for novice guardians and all who teach in our way of life.

Day 7: 1 Corinthians 12: 27-31
    We pray that we will be faithful to our vows.

Day 8: Acts 2: 44-47
    We pray for all who seek to know and to do your will and that men and women will be led to join our communities.

Day 9: 2 Corinthians 4: 16-18
    We recognize that the future is in God's hands. We pray that the Holy Spirit will help and support us as we live in the Light of Christ.

We give thanks for the Religious Life *in all its forms*

1 Community of All Hallows *in the UK*
   All Saints Sisters of the Poor *in the UK & the USA*
   Society of the Precious Blood *in Lesotho, South Africa & the UK*
2 Community of the Holy Spirit *in the USA*
   Community of St Mary *in Malawi, the Philippines & the USA*
3 Community of the Resurrection *in the UK*
   Community of the Resurrection of Our Lord *in South Africa*
4 Community of Saint Francis & Society of Saint Francis *in Australia, Brazil,*
       New Zealand, Papua New Guinea, the Solomon Islands, the UK & the USA
   Korean Franciscan Brotherhood *in Korea*
   Little Brothers of Francis *in Australia*
   Society of the Franciscan Servants of Jesus & Mary *in the UK*
   The Third Order SSF *throughout the world*
5 Community of the Servants of the Will of God *in the UK*
   Community of Sisters of the Church *in Australia, Canada, Solomon Islands & UK*
6 Brotherhood of St Gregory *in the USA*
   Christa Sevika Sangha *in Bangladesh*
   Sisterhood of the Epiphany *in the UK*
7 Community of Jesus' Compassion *in South Africa*
   Community of the Holy Name *in Lesotho, South Africa, Swaziland & the UK*
8 Society of the Servants of Jesus Christ *in Madagascar*
   Order of Julian of Norwich *in the USA*
9 Community of St Denys *in the UK*
   Community of the Divine Compassion *in Zimbabwe*
   Society of the Sacred Advent *in Australia*
10 Community of St Laurence *in the UK*
   Chita che Zita Renoyera (Holy Name Community) *in Zimbabwe; and* Chita che
   Zvipo Zve Moto (Community of the Gifts of the Holy Fire) *in Zimbabwe*
11 Order of St Benedict *in independent Abbeys and Priories throughout the world*
   Benedictine Community of Christ the King *in Australia*
   Benedictine Community of the Holy Cross *in the UK*
   Benedictine Community of Our Lady and St John *in the UK*
12 Community of the Holy Transfiguration *in Zimbabwe*
   Community of the Transfiguration *in the Dominican Republic & the USA*
   Oratory of the Good Shepherd *in Australia, north America, South Africa & the UK*
13 Community of the Glorious Ascension *in France & the UK*
   Brotherhood of the Ascended Christ *in India*
   Sisters of Jesus' Way *in the UK*
14 Community of the Servants of the Cross *in the UK*
   Order of the Holy Cross *in Canada, South Africa & the USA*
   Society of the Holy Cross *in Korea*
   Society of the Sacred Cross *in the UK*
15 Community of St Mary the Virgin *in the UK*
   Society of Our Lady St Mary *in Canada*

in the Church, and today we pray especially for:

16 Order of the Teachers of the Children of God *in the USA*
    Community of the Companions of Jesus the Good Shepherd *in the UK*
    Community of the Good Shepherd *in Malaysia*
17 Melanesian Brotherhood *throughout the Pacific region*
    Community of the Sisters of Melanesia *in the Solomon Islands*
18 Companions of St Luke - OSB *in the USA*
    Company of Mission Priests *in the UK*
    Order of the Community of the Paraclete *in the USA*
19 Order of the Holy Paraclete *in Ghana, Swaziland & the UK*
    Community of the Holy Name *in Australia*
20 Society of St Margaret *in Haiti, Sri Lanka, the UK & the USA*
    Community of Nazareth *in Japan*
21 Community of St Clare *in the UK*
    Little Sisters of St Clare *in the USA*
    Order of St Helena *in the USA*
22 Community of the Sacred Passion *in the UK*
    Community of St Mary of Nazareth and Calvary *in Tanzania & Zambia*
23 Community of Celebration *in the UK & the USA*
    Community of St John the Evangelist *in the Republic of Ireland*
24 Community of St John Baptist *in the UK & the USA*
    Worker Brothers & Sisters of the Holy Spirit *in Australia, Canada, Haiti & USA*
25 Community of St Paul *in Mozambique*
    Society of St Paul *in the USA*
    Sisterhood of the Holy Nativity *in the USA*
26 Order of St Anne *in the USA*
    Community of the Sisters of the Love of God *in the UK*
27 Community of St John the Divine *in the UK*
    Sisterhood of St John the Divine *in Canada*
    Society of St John the Divine *in South Africa*
    Society of St John the Evangelist *in the UK & the USA*
    Sisters of Charity *in the UK*
28 Society of the Sacred Mission *in Australia, Lesotho, South Africa & the UK*
    Sisters of the Incarnation *in Australia*
29 Community of St Michael & All Angels *in South Africa*
    Community of St Peter (Woking) *in the UK*
    Community of St Peter, Horbury *in the UK*
    Society of the Sisters of Bethany *in the UK*
30 Community of St Andrew *in the UK*
    Community of the Sacred Name *in Fiji, New Zealand & Tonga*
31 Congregation of the Sisters of the Visitation of Our Lady *in Papua New Guinea*
    Community of the Blessed Lady Mary *in Zimbabwe*
    Sisterhood of St Mary *in Bangladesh*
    Society of Our Lady of the Isles *in the UK*

The Society of the Faith (Incorporated)

Registered charity number 232821

Sponsor of *Anglican Religious Life*

is an Anglican charity founded in 1905 by the Revd Canon John Douglas and his brother, the Revd Charles Douglas. It became a company limited by guarantee in 1926 and moved into its present home, Faith House, Westminster, in 1935. For many years it was well known as a publisher of theology and church music through its subsidiary, the Faith Press, and as a designer and manufacturer of church furnishings through Faith Craft.

Today, The Society of the Faith pursues its objects in a number of imaginative ways. As well as using Faith House proactively and as a base for the distinguished ecclesiastical firm of Watts and Company Ltd, it sponsors publications, holds an annual lecture, grant-aids theological study and makes its fine board room available as a meeting place for associated organisations.

Enquiries should be made to

The Secretary
The Society of the Faith (Incorporated)
Faith House
7 Tufton Street
London SW1P 3QB

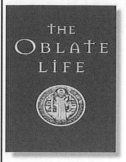

*News
of Anglican
Religious Life*

Cross survives wildfire

Mount Calvary Retreat House and Monastery (**Order of the Holy Cross**), located on a mountain ridge overlooking Santa Barbara, California, was completely destroyed in a sudden and devastating wildfire on 13 November 2008. All twenty-five guests who were on retreat at the time were safely evacuated along with the seven brothers in residence. The fire moved with such speed that less than an hour was available to gather up some common possessions and personal effects before evacuating the site. Though surrounded by destruction on every side, the signature cross in the central courtyard survived unscathed along with the calligraphy and icon studios. The loss was widely reported by the press both in the USA and throughout the world, and elicited many expressions of grief and support.

The center was founded in 1947 and served as the principal West Coast retreat facility for the Order, welcoming thousands of guests each year into a setting of unsurpassed natural beauty and offering a base for the Order's other ministries and enterprises. The brothers are currently residing at St Mary's Convent, Santa Barbara, though the graciousness of the Sisterhood of the Holy Nativity, who came in 1954 to Santa Barbara in part to offer retreat opportunities to women who were not at that time allowed access to Mount Calvary. The Order is now discerning the shape of its future presence in southern California.

Ruins at Mount Calvary Retreat House in California after the wildfire.

Korean Sisters' Project

Following the visit to Korea of Mother Lucy Clare CSP in 2006, the **Society of the Holy Cross** made a great decision at its 2007 Chapter - to send Sisters to the UK for a new mission project. At a rented house in Worcester Park, Surrey, on 25 July 2007, community life began, launched by Mother Lucy Clare and two SHC sisters.

It took about a year for the first Korean Sisters to settle, whilst learning the language and about British culture.

The aim of this project is the renewal of Religious life in contemporary society, as well as strengthening the cross-cultural links between CSP and SHC. The Sisters hope to build up a spiritual centre, with diocesan as well as local links. The house is open to anyone who wants to pray or take a Quiet Time, either individually or in a group. The sisters provide a programme of spiritual direction, Bible study and Prayer Groups, and they visit nursing homes and those who are lonely. There is also mission work with Korean residents in the New Malden area, and, in the near future, with refugees from North Korea, working together with UK aid agencies. Cultural integration and understanding is one of the Sisters' goals.

Building in Prayer

The **Community of the Resurrection** at Mirfield is one of several communities in the UK that have made the decision to build afresh either at their current home or else in a new location. In CR's case, the decision is to stay at Mirfield but develop a new monastery whilst refurbishing the existing buildings. The Superior, Father George Guiver CR, writes:

"Our church is about to undergo a major refurbishment and re-ordering, for which we are launching an appeal for £2m. We are also building a new monastery beside it, to an unusual modern design, cheap and green to run, while our old Community buildings will be turned into flats to generate income from rents. Work should start (God willing) in September 2009. Life for the next two years will be very *ad hoc*, so prayers appreciated!"

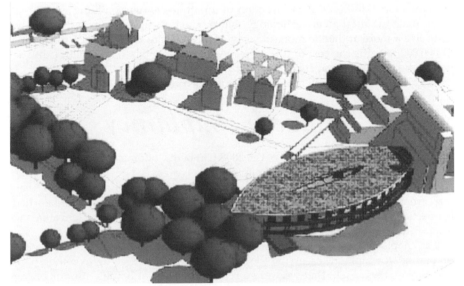

The planned new build at Mirfield.

The **Benedictines of Burford** have decided not only to build afresh but also to move to another county to do it, and have already left behind the stately Burford Priory, and are resident temporarily at Broad Marston. The Superior, Abbot Stuart Burns OSB, explains the reasons behind the community's plans:

"What prompted OSB Burford to sell their beautiful Cotswold monastery, a Grade 1 listed Jacobean manor house, and buy a derelict farm?

"A 'grand' building was very much at odds with the simple life-style we attempt to live; the rambling old house required an increasing fortune to maintain and bring into line with new regulations, let alone try to 'green'; the heavy commitment of labour-intensive formal gardens, woodland and grassland, as well as the large organic kitchen garden and orchards; the Community's desire for a sustainable, carbon-neutral monastery that would support the life we aim to live rather than contradict it ~ these were all elements in the discussion that reached a conclusion in January 2008.

"Mucknell Farm in Worcestershire, built in the 1860s, already had permission to replace the farmhouse and convert the quadrangle of barns. Acanthus Clews Architects of Banbury have produced exciting plans with high-quality insulation, solar energy, biomass heating, rain-water harvesting, a natural filtration system for the sewage and rammed earth walls for the new Oratory, using earth from the site.

"It is hoped that the new monastery will be ready to receive the Community and its guests in the autumn of 2010."

Another community of Benedictines are also moving. They too are concerned about creating a sustainable 'green' home. Mother Mary Luke CHC, Superior of the **Community of the Holy Cross** at Rempstone, writes:

"In 2007, we decided to move from Rempstone, which though beautiful, was never built as a convent. We found a suitable property just two miles away and are now embarking on the construction of an attractive new building which will incorporate the latest green technology, will be much cheaper to run and will allow us to live a more authentic monastic way of life. We are raising funds to provide £1,000,000 towards the cost of this project, which alternately fills us with exhilaration and panic! Your prayers will be much appreciated."

The 2012-13 *Year Book* will hope to report on the progress of these developments.

Lambeth chaplaincy

Father Richard Carter was part of the 2008 Lambeth Conference chaplaincy team, made up primarily of Anglican Religious. He writes:

"Many of the Brothers and Sisters who were asked to form the chaplaincy team were from the Religious communities of Melanesia. Most of the other members had connections with Melanesia. We were also joined by two sisters from Tanzania and Sister Pamela CAH from Norwich.

"The chaplaincy team spent two weeks together before the Conference: praying, preparing worship and discussing the issues we knew were going to come up. It was important, we felt, that we were a real community at home with our prayer together and with one another. It proved a very special time. Melanesian Religious have a gift of friendship and attract others like magnets with their generosity and sense of fun. We also got to know all the young Conference stewards, who came from twenty-six different countries. We prepared a very beautiful space in the Senate Building at the heart of the University of Kent where the Lambeth Conference took place. We called this "The Prayer Place", where we met together for prayer beginning at 6.30 in the morning and ending at 9.45 at night. We knelt around a huge wooden cross we had carried up from Canterbury Cathedral. The first person to come to the Prayer Place was Archbishop Rowan Williams. The Headbrother of the Melanesian Brotherhood asked him if we could pray with him and he looked so grateful. The twenty- two members of our chaplaincy team knelt around him and placed our hands upon him. The Head Brother prayed for God's strength, protection and guidance for him and they sung in their rich harmony of voices: 'Remember all the day long Jesus is in you.'

"At the opening Eucharist, Canterbury Cathedral came alive with the dancing and pan-pipes of the Melanesian Religious communities, completely unfazed by the grandeur of the occasion. Dressed in their traditional bark cloth, they carried the Gospel in a canoe and their dancing broke loose up the steps into the choir, dissolving Episcopal stiffness with energy and joy: Pentecost in sound and movement.

"At the Lambeth Conference our Bishops tried walking together. A love for our Church and for our neighbour came out of hiding - upheld by the prayers of Anglicans from around the world. And at the centre of this longing for unity is prayer. At this Lambeth Conference this was embodied by a simple community of Religious praying together and witnessing to what it means to live in community. Many were drawn to the Prayer Place, so that Morning Prayer and Compline were packed each day. The Office was simple and prayerful, the rich warm Melanesian chants holding prayer and scripture together and grounding us all in a faith of bold humility, which is the mark of Melanesian Religious life. "Remember all day long Jesus is in you."

"At the final Eucharist, the chaplaincy team led a procession up those dramatic steps through the choir, around the High Altar to the chapel of martyrs. It was there that the seven Melanesian Brothers who died in 2003 working for peace were remembered. Seven candles burnt on the altar with an icon painted by a young Brazilian artist in memory of those Brothers. The Archbishop of Canterbury read out their seven names and "Blessed are the peacemakers for they shall be called the children of God." As the Brothers and Sisters sang the litany of martyrs, so many bishops and archbishops - deeply moved - were on their knees in prayer; I was once again struck by this amazing Gospel we follow: where the humble are truly lifted up and where even seeming struggle, disaster and brokenness can lead to the mystery of new life."

Anglican Religious in print

Father Gregory Fruehwirth, the superior of the Order of Julian of Norwich, has published a selection of eloquent and accessible 'chapter talks', arranged according to the liturgical calendar. The book is entitled *Words of Silence* and, as Archbishop Desmond Tutu says in his preface, these contemplative meditations urge us to remember the presence of God in our lives. The result is a profound and thought-provoking book, published in the USA by Paraclete Press (ISBN: 978-1-5572-5601-0) and in the UK by SPCK (ISBN: 978-0-281-016105-1).

The Father Founder of OJN, Father John-Julian, has achieved a significant milestone with *The Complete Julian*, published by Paraclete Press (ISBN: 978-1-5572-5639-3). It is the first book to offer a modern translation of all of Julian's writings (including her complete *Revelations*), plus analysis and copious background material to help us comprehend the depth and profundity of her life and work.

A new book on the Religious Life that combines a coherent and fluent exploration of its meaning with an honest autobiographical narrative can be found in *Together and Apart: a Memoir of the Religious Life*, published by Morehouse (ISBN: 978-0-8192-2315-9). The author is Sister Ellen Stephen OSH and her book provides both understanding of what it means to commit to a life-long seeking of God and also an unsentimental look at the rewards and sacrifices that has brought in her own quest.

One of the best-known communities in the history of Anglican Religious life has been Nashdom Abbey. Published with the support of the Anglo-Catholic History Society by Canterbury Press, *The Labour of Obedience: a history of the Benedictines of Pershore, Nashdom, Elmore* (ISBN: 978-1-8531-1974-3) is scholarly yet accessible, tracing the evolution of the community that came to define Anglo-Papalism in the twentieth century, from its origins at Pershore to its present home at Elmore. Petà Dunstan is the author of this engaging story.

RooT update

The annual conference of RooT took place at St Stephen's House theological college, Oxford, continuing the theme of the contribution of the Religious life to East/West ecumenical relations. Speakers included Bishop Basil of Amphipolis

(Russian Orthodox, Ecumenical Patriarchate), Teresa Burke, Sisters of St Paul (RC Archdiocese of Birmingham) and Jeanne Knights (Anglican, based at Cambridge UK and Diveyevo Convent, Russia). The 2009 September conference will meet at the Community of the Resurrection Mirfield, Yorkshire, to explore:
(1) The currently topical concept of 'Receptive Ecumenism', that is, what gifts Christians might humbly and fruitfully hope to receive from one another, both between the churches and also within each church community.
(2) The 'Deep Church' movement, a desire among some Anglican Charismatic Evangelicals, inspired by C.S. Lewis, to re-appropriate the scriptural, patristic and monastic tradition of the early Church before the division between East and West.

The RooT website is at http://www.forwardinfaith.info/home/root.

DVD on the Religious Life

Anglican Religious life is explored honestly and invitingly on an excellent new DVD called *All for Christ*. Filmed in the early months of 2008, it offers over two hours of material, conveniently divided into sections. A variety of Religious tell the stories of their vocations in a direct and moving way that makes for compelling viewing. The participants share insights into their lives, both about prayer and a variety of work. There is honesty about the struggles experienced in the life but much evidence of the rewards and fulfilment that it can bring. Other sections of the DVD look at communities' interactions with the church and the history of Religious life in the Church of England.

The film is concerned with portraying the unifying values of the Religious life and to encourage vocations to all types of community. Five communities participated: the women's communities at Rempstone (CHC) and Walsingham (SSM), CR brethren from Mirfield and SSF friars, plus the mixed community at Crawley Down (CSWG). It succeeds in showing both the range of community life and a variety of approaches, and challenges the viewer into considering a relationship with this important part of the life of the Church, whether as a visitor, retreatant, associate, oblate or to test a vocation. This is a valuable and informative resource for all Christians.

The DVD can be ordered direct from CSWG (see page 8 or email father.peter@cswg.org.uk) and costs £13.50 including postage and packing. Buyers from outside the UK can email the monastery for details of how to order.

Hermitage in Wales

The Archbishop Rowan Williams Hermitage Trust was set up in 2007. The present Archbishop of Canterbury, the Most Reverend Dr Rowan Williams is the Guardian. Its purpose is to support hermits in recognised vows, who are not supported in any other way, providing a place of spiritual practice and contemplative training and meditation. The Hermitage is located in Wales in the Diocese of St Davids and the building offers a location where it is possible to live out this vocation.

A Te Deum **video** for *RooT –*
Religious of orthodox Tradition

All
for
Christ

– Anglican monks and nuns today

Sections include:
– How It All Began
– Responding to the Call
– Daily Life
– Reaching out to God, Church and World

What do monks and nuns do all day? Why do they live the way they do?

What is the point of their life? Are they contented people? Where do they fit into the Church's life?

Monks and nuns from Communities at
Mirfield, Walsingham, Rempstone & Crawley Down
talk about the life they have chosen

£12.00 + £1.50 P & P (UK only)

Overseas: £12.00 + £3.00 P & P
Please pay either by Sterling cheque;
or by bank payment direct (for details, please e-mail).

The Monastery of the Holy Trinity, Crawley Down,
Crawley. West Sussex RH10 4LH United Kingdom
T: +44 (0) 1342 712074
father.peter@cswg.org.uk

Articles

Hospitality and Difference:
Anglican Religious in a Contentious Communion
by Father Gregory OJN

"Some heretics came to Abba Poemen one day and began to speak evil of the archbishop of Alexandria, suggesting that he had received the laying on of hands from priests. The old man, who had remained silent till then, called his brother and said, 'Set the table, give them something to eat, and send them away in peace.'" *(The Sayings of the Desert Fathers).* Anglican Religious seeking to witness to God in a contentious Communion would do well to follow Abba Poemen's example.

Perhaps Abba Poemen knew beforehand that his guests were 'heretics' and malicious gossipers, perhaps not. In any case, he welcomed them into his home, listened in silence as they talked, fed them with his own food, and sent them away in peace. The corollary here to hospitality in our religious houses is so obvious as to not need much spelling out. We receive everyone into our guesthouses and we give them a place to rest. We welcome them into our prayers, serve them nutritious meals, and offer ourselves for spiritual counsel. Such hospitality, often extremely demanding and exhausting, is as old as monasticism itself.

In a time of ideological polarization and contention in the Church, our houses must continue this tradition of unconditional hospitality. It would be a great tragedy if our houses were to be guarded with careful shibboleths, whether conservative or progressive, implicit or explicit, to make sure only one party is truly welcome.

It is well known that most communities have sisters and brothers with widely varying opinions living side by side - praying, eating, and working together, maturing and growing old together. This is possible because of a commitment to a value that transcends the divisive questions in the Church, this transcendent value being a shared vocation to belong wholly to God through Religious vows professed in a particular community. Sisters and brothers find themselves surprised and perhaps annoyed by a God who brings them forcefully into communion, for the rest of their lives, with sisters and brothers with whom they utterly disagree. Growing through this experience, knowing our own frailty and limitations, we are free to offer an open welcome to our guests,

Father Gregory OJN

receiving them simply as human beings who are loved and sought by God.

In communities where near unanimity has been reached on some issues, where there is no helpful thorn in the side of difference, vigilance must be maintained against the temptation to make the community into a safe haven in the ecclesial storm, a haven that implicitly or explicitly rejects those who hold to different opinions. This requires active restraint of party spirit, prejudice, scorn, and triumphalism, and means remaining able to receive others as human beings loved by Christ rather than primarily as ideological opponents. It is, after all, easy to be triumphant on your own four acres of land with people just like yourself, and assume that you have somehow fully realized the mystery of the Church!

Secondly, and going far beyond hospitality, Abba Poemen practised the ascetical discipline of remaining silent as his guests went from heretical theology, we might assume, to malicious gossip. Instead of arguing with them or rebuking, he fed them with his own food and sent them away in peace.

It is not that the desert fathers did not care about orthodoxy. As lovers of Christ they naturally would have desired the clearest and soundest articulation of the mystery of the faith. Several of them, on different sides of the controversies of their time, were willing to suffer exile and martyrdom for their beliefs. But still, after opening his home to his guests, Abba Poemen chose silence. Why did not he not speak up? Why not defend the faith? Or at least the Archbishop?

The reason for Abba Poemen's silence is found in the conviction that the clearest and soundest articulation of the mystery of the faith is not found in words, and certainly not in the scandalous logomachy of the Church. (Today we might call it 'blogomachy.') Rather, the desert fathers and mothers knew that the clearest articulation of the faith is found in the quality of presence offered by human persons yielded totally to the purging and transforming fire of God. This was what the fathers and mothers sought for in the desert, and they called it by different names: unceasing prayer, purity of heart, humility, and becoming all flame.

Moreover, following the perennial wisdom of spiritual transformation, the desert mothers and fathers knew that they could not have both things - both strident involvement in Church controversy and fidelity to the spiritual path of purgation and transformation in the desert. It might have been good, on one level, for Abba Poemen to argue with his guests, or at least reprove them for their gossip, but too much involvement in such matters would have made Abba Poemen's primary task of yielding to the transforming presence of God impossible. By choosing the lesser good of defending the faith or judging other's morals, he would have lost his very reason for being in the desert in the first place.

The Church does in fact need people willing to engage in the controversies of the day as a deeply self-sacrificial, ascetical path towards self-knowledge and union with God. But not everyone is called to this, just as not everyone is called to monastic or vowed Religious life. It is true that only a few modern-day Religious in the Anglican Communion have actual desert sand in their sandals. Most Orders, even contemplative ones, are more engaged in the regular life of the Church than were the desert mothers and fathers. A good percentage of Religious are ordained priests, some serving in parishes. A few are even Bishops. But no matter how apostolic our charisms might become, no matter how much our work takes us into an active care for the institutional church, each Religious bears at the heart of her or his vocation a seed of that ancient call to living a life that is publicly vowed and offered in the Church for the sake of total transformation in Christ. The fact that such an intention is publicly offered, and offered as our primary gift to the Church, is key. We have vowed, publicly, that such journey into radical transformation is the *sine qua non* of our response to God. This then is our primary, public responsibility in the Church. If we don't give this to the Church, we have not done what we outwardly, visibly, and publicly said we thought was God's will for us. Sometimes the monks will indeed go into the city and the cathedral. Sometimes bishops and theologians will go out to the desert. But the vocations are different, and just as it would be sad for a theologian to lose his vocation by hiding, Jonah-like, in the desert, so it would be sad if Religious lost their vocations by similarly hiding from God in the drama of controversy. It is even more grievous if an entire community loses its vulnerability to God by a perpetually-sustained culture of intrigue and party spirit.

Thus, even for us today, a measure of Abba Poemen's disciplined silence might be necessary so that we, like him, might be able to offer the clearest and most articulate defense of the mystery of our faith. We will offer this not in any point we make, or a brilliant and crushing argument, but in the actual quality of our lives. Such silence means refraining from even "good and helpful speech" as St. Benedict says in his *Rule*. Moreover, if we have truly grown into such silence and suffered the purifying and illumining presence of God through our religious vows, our words, when we do we speak, will emerge as secondary reflections of a depth of love and presence in us, rather than from anxiety-driven egoism.

Finally, notice the last two words of the story: Abba Poemen sent his unpleasant guests away in peace. In peace. It is easy to imagine his guests walking away, not thinking much of the great Abba Poemen, supposing that he wasn't up to their work of reforming the Church or brave enough to partake in the struggle. But maybe, years later, hearing what the good father actually believed, and realizing how much they must have hurt him by their speech, and remembering how he still welcomed and fed them and sent them away in peace, their minds might have been opened to see the full presence of God burning through Poemen's patience, love, and humility, uncomfortably convicting them of their self-righteousness and malicious words.

When Religious keep silence and practise charity with those who differ from them or insult them, not out of timidity or confusion or apathy, but out of finely-developed ability to live on the knife-edge of awareness and spiritual presence, we are doing something extraordinary. With the very substance and full passion of our lives, we are witnessing to a way of being that is totally different than that demanded by our current world and ecclesial environment. We are moreover offering a witness to the depth reality of every human being, a depth that is necessarily beyond all language and controversy, where we learn how to yield ourselves - progressively, slowly, painfully - to the mystery of God. In a contentious communion, embittered by angry rhetoric and divisive controversy, such a witness is like a huge window suddenly thrown open, allowing light and fresh air to flow in, and even the sound, suddenly heard, of birds and the breeze.

'Behold the Handmaid of the Lord':
The Work of Chama Cha Mariamu Mtakatifu

Founded by sisters of the Community of the Sacred Passion (CSP) in 1946, CMM is the only community of women among Anglicans in Tanzania. It was begun by a handful of Sisters living in primitive mud and stick houses in the remote village of Kwa Mkono, where transport was difficult, and there was no running water or electricity. From these small and humble beginnings, there is now a Community numbering well over one hundred, mainly in Tanzania. There are also Sisters in Zambia, and invitations to open houses in Kenya and Uganda once funds become available.

The motto of the Community is *mimi ni mjakazi wa Bwana* (Behold the Handmaid of the Lord) and we aim to be ready to do whatever God asks, and in particular to bring women and children to Christ through helping them attain physical and spiritual wholeness. To do this, we run nursery and Sunday schools, teach in other schools, nurse, run classes in nutrition and family care for women, and also educate about AIDS. We serve the church by making communion wafers - for Lutherans and Moravians as well as Anglicans - candles and vestments. Some Sisters act as secretaries to some of our bishops.

Another ministry is to feed orphans and others who are hungry. The milk from our cows, and the food we grow, helps directly with this, but our farming has a much wider importance. We are working towards becoming self-supporting, and so each house has its own farm and animals, including a cow, with chickens, goats, pigs and ducks where possible. However, we still need some assistance to reach self-sufficiency. In the towns, Sisters have a shamba (small-holding) nearby or in a region outside the town. They lodge there for a few days during the planting and harvesting seasons, and keep an eye on things in between these times. We grow maize, potatoes, rice and vegetables, both for ourselves and to sell to raise money for other work. Another crop is seedling trees, which villagers can buy to replace those used for firewood. To minimise their own use of wood, the Sisters use bio-gas for cooking, derived from the manure produced by our animals. The sludge left behind after the gas has been extracted provides fertiliser for the crops.

In the early days, there was little education for girls, apart from Mission Schools. Since independence in 1964, there has been a rapid expansion in educational opportunities. Many Sisters have now been to, or are at present attending, secondary school. One Sister is on a university course for administration. This education is important for the future work of the community. Besides secular education, our novices receive training in the Religious life. It is very important they grasp the essential elements of our life, so that they retain these even when adapting to the rapid changes in society around them. From being accepted as an aspirant to life profession takes thirteen years.

We still work in Kwa Mkono (but now live in a modern house) and help in the hospital and the polio hostel started by CSP Sisters that caters for children disabled by this disease. Our house at Liuli, on the side of Lake Tanganyika, is even more remote than Kwa Mtono, and has very primitive facilities. In contrast, the house in Dar es Salaam, Tanzania's main port, has modern facilities, good transport and communications. It takes thirteen hours to travel from Liuli to Dar es Salaam on a new rapid bus service.

Just as there are contrasts between the places in which we live, so too in the people with whom we work: fishermen, farmers, office workers, old people with a traditional outlook, younger people anxious to make progress. Similarly in our community: we have older Sisters, venerated for their wisdom and the sacrifices that they made for the growth of the community; then, we have younger Sisters, with a wider education, who struggle to integrate the teaching of Christ and the Religious life with the progressive ideas they encounter. From the outset, the community has welcomed women from all tribes. They have to learn of the traditions of others through our life together. Given that Sisters speak so many different tribal languages, we use the unifying language of Swahili for the Office and other services. Our houses vary greatly in size and facilities. Sisters from cooler areas of the country have to make the difficult transition to working in a house on the hot tropical coasts, and vice versa. Through our life together, we are able to show others how enlarging and liberating it is to cross all these boundaries and learn the diversity of human experience.

Wherever and whoever we are, old or young, we always have a daily celebration of the Eucharist and say a fourfold Office to remind us that all we do is through the power of the Lord. We look to Him to show us each step of the way, so that like Mary, His Mother, we may always say *Tazama, mimi ni mjakazi wa Bwana.*

Journeys in the East
by Father Peter CSWG

The contemplative Community of the Servants of the Will of God at Crawley Down in Sussex has been concerned, as part of its witness, to pray and work for unity between the Churches of East and West. Pursuing links with communities among the Orthodox churches has fostered many contacts and in this article, Father Peter CSWG tells us about some of them and what can flow from them.

Father that they may be one as we are one.
(John 17:22)

Minsk : In November 2008, sisters of a joint monastic-lay community from Minsk in Belarus visited CSWG. Their Community owes its inspiration to a granddaughter of Queen Victoria, St Elisabeth Feodorovna, who married into the Russian royal family. After her husband was assassinated in a bomb attack in 1905, she chose to dedicate her life to the care of the poor and marginalized, founding a Religious community. Her royal status led to her murder by the Bolsheviks in 1918. Heirs to that charism, the Community now in Minsk care for the underprivileged and oppressed, particularly those suffering from mental illness. They run an orphanage, a psychiatric hospital and a TB centre, together with handicraft workshops for the homeless, some of whom are former drug addicts and alcoholics. Their numbers are flourishing: fifty-eight nuns and novices at the last count, meaning three to a cell. The overflow of their vibrant life, their outreach in their need, brings them to our doorstep.

Sisters of the community from Minsk with Brother Andrew CSWG

Tur Abdin : Since September 2008, Father Aho and Father Saliba, two Syrian Orthodox monks from the Diocese of Tur Abdin and Mardin in south-east Turkey have been joining in our life most weekends. This area of Turkey, near to both Iran and Iraq, is dangerous for Christians, and gained notoriety recently when some evangelical missionaries were brutally murdered there.

The arrangement with Tur Abdin is part of an inter-diocesan link with Chichester diocese. From the brothers, we learn an understanding of church that is more familial than usually experienced in the West, where bishops and archbishops mingle freely with priests, deacons and the laity, the result perhaps of a protracted history of being often a victimised minority.

Both of these communities - the Russian and the Syrian - have their Christian faith rooted deeply in history and Tradition. The Syrians in particular make a point of teaching their children Aramaic as a contribution to inculturation. Their national identity is embedded in the chant, prayer and teaching of the Church's liturgy. Yet they are equally able to hold their own with a mobile phone or laptop, and in surfing the web.

The brothers have particularly felt at 'home', participating in the worship of the Divine Office and Eucharist. Over the years, CSWG has made some effort to incorporate traditions of both East and West that bring about a liturgical fullness. Our Eucharist, based on Common Worship, includes modern Orthodox liturgical texts and some chants and selections from the Liturgy of St Basil and St John Chrysostom in the Eucharistic prayer to give emphasis to the epiclesis (the outpouring of the Holy Spirit on the Church) and to the offering of the gifts. There has also been a re-orienting of the liturgy, so that it follows its natural shape and pattern as 'journey' into the Kingdom of God. The liturgy thus conveys the riches and depth from the Tradition whilst remaining contemporary, and at the same time embraces both East and West in its prayer.

A different impetus for unity yet equally strong has come to us through True

Life in God, an ecumenical association of the readers of the divine messages given to Vassula Ryden, a Greek Orthodox lay woman, between 1985 and 2003. Their overriding call is for the unity of the Churches, and especially the two major halves of Christendom: East and West. This is vocalised in the particular call to celebrate Easter on the same day. The resurrection being the unique, distinguishing mark of Christian faith, it is considered important that all Christians celebrate that event on a single day. A two-yearly pilgrimage for Unity is a by-product of all this, swelling in numbers over the years. It began in a small way in Jerusalem in 1998. In 2005, two of us were invited to join the pilgrims in Syria, Lebanon and Jordan; then in 2008 in Turkey, we visited the Seven Churches of Asia. Some 650 pilgrims came from almost sixty different countries and all five continents, with representatives of all mainstream denominations (eighteen in all), including a Roman Catholic Cardinal from India. Although there are, necessarily, ecumenical courtesies and limitations, the sense of oneness at such an event is powerful, even overwhelming. There is, on departure, a conviction that this is the truth of the Church; this is what we are meant to be. One returns home with a sense that it is our separations that now seem the oddity, and so with a longing for unity.

From each of these ecumenical encounters, there comes an experience, not simply of vitality and hope, but of something at work much greater than our limited experience in separated churches. The energy of this we can believe to be divine, whilst the vision and light that inspire the whole are clearly from the same source. None of these encounters takes place outside the mainstream of ecclesial life, since all the participants return to separated churches. Yet they can validly be seen as leaven hidden in the dough that lifts the lump, enabling our vision to transcend the limitations of its horizons. There is no sidestepping of difficulties, but as so often in encounters between East and West, a new and surprising factor can emerge. One important inspiration, rediscovered in recent years in the West, has been the writings of St Maximus the Confessor (580-662). His vision of the world is quite 'modern'; he has much to teach theologically about ecology and care for our world through his clear cosmic vision of the relatedness of everything in creation. Yet he would differ from contemporary views of life in this way: for Maximus, the distinctions and differences in the cosmos are for the purposes of a greater unity, in the same way that the distinctions in the Persons of the Trinity contribute to their greater unity. There is something here for us to learn. So often we treat differences as reasons for separation and division, instead of seeing in them a call to work for something greater.

Maximus' understanding allows for a change of mind, a metanoia, in the way we operate with difference. It is that kind of altered mind-set that characterises these events for unity, and enables participants to work with renewed conviction. They are able to affirm with Gamaliel of old, 'if it is of God, you will not be able to overthrow it'. It is a tenet of creation theology that, what God speaks, he accomplishes. So the impetus depends not on numbers or spectacular achievements, but in the end, on shared prayer, strengthened by a steady conviction that is ready to take the next given step. Meanwhile, new bonds continue to be forged, so that the word may in the end accomplish its purpose: 'that they may be one.'

The Divine Office
An Oblate's Perspective
by Father Simon Jones

There are two places in the *Rule of St Benedict* where monks are urged to hurry to the oratory to celebrate the divine office, the *Opus Dei*, the Work of God. For St Benedict, nothing should delay, obstruct or take priority over this celebration. With its night-time vigil and sevenfold punctuation of the day, the divine office beats at the heart of the community's life. At least four hours of every day are devoted to the *Opus Dei*, which provides a balanced framework into which the monks' other occupations are woven.

How can such a priority be translated into the life of an oblate? The community where we have made our oblation is, in a sense, our spiritual home, and its form and pattern of prayer must be taken into account when considering how and when we should pray. To follow the full pattern of monastic liturgical prayer would be an indigestible and, for most oblates, an unhealthy daily diet. In chapter 50 we see that even the monks themselves are only required to observe the hours 'as best they can'. A generous degree of practical flexibility and realism is built into the *Rule*, just as it should be built into the rule of life of any oblate. It is as true for us as it is for our monastic communities that we each require our own liturgies that take account of our individual lifestyles, work-patterns and responsibilities.

For all oblates, the monastic community will not be the only Religious community to which we belong: our local church communities, a study or cell group, a local school, prison, hospital or homeless shelter. We will have our own denominational allegiances and, not least, our commitment to family and those with whom we share our lives. If there is to be a close correspondence between the Work of God and those who are celebrating it, then our belonging to any one of these communities will have an effect on our celebration of the *Opus Dei*.

Father Simon Jones

For many oblates, it may only be realistic to attempt to pray one office a day, perhaps first thing in the morning, or during a break at work, or once the children have gone to school, or in the stillness of the night. For some, it may be possible for this time of liturgical prayer to be offered with other Christians. For others, it may be a case of retreating to a quiet space, set aside for this purpose. One of Benedict's monks would not have carried an office book when he was working outside the monastery or travelling, so his observance of the prescribed hours would have required the use of his memory to recall the appointed psalms for a particular office. Today, it is unfortunate that the prevailing liturgical culture seems to insist that an office is not an office without a book to read it from. Despite the fact that there are many excellent pocket-sized breviaries available, the discipline of punctuating the day with self-generated excerpts from our liturgical memories is a wonderfully liberating experience. On a train or standing in a queue at a supermarket checkout, in front of a computer screen or walking the dog, sitting in a doctor's waiting room or cooking a meal, we can use our memories to fulfil Benedict's injunction to 'perform the Work of God' wherever we are. What matters here is frequency rather than form. Offer an uncomplicated form of prayer from memory. As a brief act of liturgical prayer, it helps us to live out our vocation to make the Work of God the priority, dipping beneath the surface of our daily routine to be fed by the divine presence which is everywhere, 'but beyond the least doubt we should believe this to be especially true when we celebrate the divine office'. (*Rule of St Benedict*, 19.2)

But what about the relationship between the form of our prayer and that of our monastic community? Benedict's emphasis on obedience and stability leaves no room for individual choice. For some Christians, the repeated use of structured liturgical forms of prayer, with psalms recited and readings chosen according to a pre-determined scheme, stifles the activity of the Holy Spirit. But Benedict does not provide his monks with a liturgical straight-jacket; rather, he enables his community to deepen their relationship with God by being immersed in an unceasing offering of praise and prayer, through the recitation of psalmody, the singing of hymns, and the proclamation of scripture. The Holy Spirit is not silenced by this; instead, he is freed to articulate his own voice beneath the surface of the community's liturgical voice, praying through the heart of the community as the community prays by heart.

Spiritual depth is one reason why Benedict's patterns of prayer should be valued and cherished. Another is that the Work of God is liturgy, not private devotion. It is a celebration of the whole community, presided over by the Abbot, who represents Christ. Oblates belong to that community, and so must retain some liturgical connection. This may be possible by using the same form of office as the monastic community, or following the same liturgical calendar. It may be possible to say at least one office at the same time as it is being celebrated in the oratory. We should try to pray for our communities each day, just as they are praying for us, and to keep a list of the professed and their daily timetable in our office books. Some communities also produce their own prayer diaries or cycles of intercession.

No consideration of Benedict and the daily office would be complete without some attention being given to the importance of psalmody. Benedict's *Rule* is littered with quotations from the Psalms, to the extent that the psalter is quoted more often than the New Testament. Though showing some flexibility in the order in which the psalms might be said in the course of a week, there is no leeway when it comes to quantity.

For oblates, if our minds and hearts are to be transformed by the psalter, we need to make sure that psalmody plays a central part within our celebration of the *Opus Dei*. For this writer, the chief glory of its central position in Benedict's liturgical code is the psalter's ability to allow us to address God, and God to address us. Christian prayer can so often lack honesty and integrity when it fails to reflect the reality of the world in which we find ourselves. The psalms earth us in this reality and enable our prayer to be real. The psalter gives the community which prays it permission to be itself before God, a voice to express itself to God and, not least, an ear to hear the voice of God. This ties in with what we have already said about the Spirit speaking beneath the surface of our liturgical prayer, as well as in and through it. As far back as the third century, in some forms of the office, the community observed a period of silence after the psalmody, which was concluded by a collect - not only to give the psalm a Christological interpretation, but also to draw together the thoughts and prayers of the community which had been triggered by their engagement with the Psalter. It is not by accident that Benedict refers to the Psalmist as the Prophet (for example, 19.3). As well as providing a means of honest spiritual self-expression, the psalter also speaks a prophetic word to the community which points to Christ as well as inviting a response in prayer.

Any insights into the celebration of the Work of God, however, cannot be too prescriptive. It is up to each of us, guided by our communities, to discern how the Rule's teaching concerning the divine office might lead us into a deeper dialogue with God and one another. In the divine conversation, which is the life of discipleship, the *Opus Dei* is both life-giving and life-transforming. It expresses our belonging to a 'school of the Lord's service', but more importantly it opens the ear of our heart to listen to the voice of the God who calls us constantly into union with him.

The article above is a shortened version of an essay published in Gervase Holdaway (editor), The Oblate Life, *Canterbury Press, Norwich, 2008* (ISBN: 9781853118838)

'Alongsiders' and the Religious Life
by Sister Christine CSJD

The Community of St John the Divine in Birmingham, UK, has been a pioneer in developing the opportunity for people to live 'alongside' a Religious community. Here, one of its leaders, Sister Christine, shares her community's experience.

Where did the idea of Alongsiders come from? People have always been attracted to share the life of a Community and today the commitment of Oblates, Associates and Tertiaries speak very clearly of deep relational ties. However, others ask to come and live alongside a Community for periods of up to a year, sharing in its life and worship. The many reasons for these requests all contain the elements of wanting time for spiritual renewal and to discern the way ahead, and also, for many, having 'time out' from the stress of a modern lifestyle.

In this spirit, our Alongsider programme has been running for some eight years now. In order to bring it to birth the Community needed to "be prepared": so that we could allow others to share our life, we had to share our own lives more deeply with each other too. This has not always been easy. It has been as though our relationships with each other, with our Associates and others close to the Community, have needed to become stronger. We have needed to listen to each other much more carefully and be willing to change.

The Guidelines for the Alongsiders evolved out of the experience of those who shared our life in a non-formal way. In our first attempt, the bar was set too high, but it was soon realised we required something more simple and flexible, able to be adapted for a wide range of people. Agreed by the Community, these Guidelines have been reviewed every two years and, although some changes have taken place, the basic document currently remains the same. It defines the commitment of an Alongsider, yet is open-ended enough to be personal for each one. It is available for anyone to see on request.

People have got to know about the Alongsiders through meeting them when visiting, or reading about them in our Annual Report and on the website. Those interested in becoming an Alongsider need to get to know the Community well first of all, and also have the opportunity of talking with a current Alongsider. This means a discernment process can start in considering if time spent in this way might be helpful or not and members of the Community can feel involved in the decision-making, and may be involved in mentoring. A simple application form is completed and references taken. If accepted by the Community, a written Agreement is then signed.

Here are examples of some of the people who have been Alongsiders:

*A young doctor needing time away from a very pressurised job to consider if she would stay in medicine.

*A priest who had been working for L'Arche needing time to pray about the next stage of her priestly ministry.

*Someone having a gap year from university helping with Christian Music Ministries and praying about the future.

*An older person from the USA wanting to use the time for spiritual renewal.

*Two people from Canada who have always wanted to live "community life".

*Recently we have accepted our first male Alongsider, who is needing to recover his health and discern his future.

*Two of our Alongsiders have been full members of the Methodist Church.

One difficulty for the Community was deciding how many Alongsiders could be here at any one time. After lengthy discussions, we decided the maximum would be four. Marking the start and completion of being an Alongsider is considered important and affirming. A special prayer is said for the person concerned, usually at Evening Prayer, asking God's blessing on their time as an Alongsider and a small wooden cross is given to wear. It is hoped this gives a sense of belonging as well as marking the start of this new journey. Alongsiders need to feel welcome and able to share in the life of the Community. Like anyone else they quickly pick up the "vibes" that surround them, and need to feel they are wanted, expected and important members of the team, helping with the ministry of hospitality in the house. A Sister is asked to be their mentor, introducing them to the house and the daily routine. They may also ask for a Sister of their choice to accompany them on their spiritual journey if this would be helpful.

Each Alongsider makes a part-time commitment, as they worship with the Community and offer help in the house or garden for a set number of hours each week. There is a flexible scale for paying for full board and lodging according to the number of hours that can be offered working with the Community. This is clearly negotiated and pre-planned and should mean there is some time for each person to use constructively for prayer, reflection, study and recreation. It is important that Alongsiders are responsible for the safety of any property they own and for the payment of any outgoing expenses from their own bank account.

The experience of being an Alongsider is illustrated by extracts from the written reflections of two of them:

We were warmly embraced into the life of the Community and living alongside the Sisters enabled us to partake fully in the daily rhythm of Community life, so we not only observe the duties and responsibilities of convent life but we had the opportunity to "live it". We began to appreciate the value of silence, time for contemplative prayer, and the intentional balance of work and recreation. We also realised that happiness and peace has nothing to do with the acquisition of material things.

Living as an Alongsider proved to be a life-changing experience for us both, revealing a way of living centred around prayer and ministry of others. Returning home proved to be a real challenge, and significantly demonstrated that the way we were currently living was not how we wanted to continue for the rest of our lives.

The experience of having Alongsiders has been very significant for the Community. It has been mutually a great source of blessing and the starting point and catalyst for considering more wide-ranging change. In 2005, time was spent identifying and studying in greater depth the essence of the Religious life, so that we have wisdom and courage to go on further developing new patterns and sharing them with others. This has led to the development of the Lay Members Programme.

One question now being asked is whether it might be possible for anyone interested in exploring a vocation to the Religious Life to start in the same way as an Alongsider, knowing that for each plans are made with the person concerned to respond to individual need. Two parallel paths could run very closely together, being flexible, interchangeable, being creative as well as challenging. This then opens the possibility of working on a new model for the Religious Life ... but this will be the next chapter!

Sister Christine CSJD

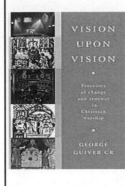

Directory of traditional celibate Religious Orders and Communities

Section 1

Religious communities in this section are those whose members take the traditional vows, including celibacy. For many, these are the 'evangelical counsels' of chastity, poverty and obedience. In the Benedictine tradition, the three vows are stability, obedience and conversion of life, celibacy being an integral part of the third vow.

These celibate communities may be involved in apostolic works or be primarily enclosed and contemplative. They may wear traditional habits or contemporary dress. However, their members all take the traditional Religious vows. In the Episcopal Church of the USA, these communities are referred to in the canons as 'Religious Orders'.

There are an estimated 2,154 celibate Religious in the Anglican Communion, (923 men and 1,231 women).

The approximate regional totals are:

Africa: 343	(Men 47, Women 296)	
Asia: 80	(Men 12, Women 68)	
Australasia & Pacific: 865	(Men 641, Women 224)	
Europe: 566	(Men 129, Women 437)	
North & South America & Caribbean: 299	(Men 94, Women 206)	

International telephoning

Telephone numbers in this directory are listed as used within the country concerned. To use them internationally, first dial the international code (usually 00) followed by the country code (see list below).

Australia	+ 61	Haiti	+ 509	PNG	+ 675
Bangladesh	+ 880	India	+ 91	Solomon Islands	+ 677
Belgium	+ 32	Republic of Ireland	+ 353	South Africa	+ 27
Brazil	+ 55	Japan	+ 81	Spain	+ 34
Canada	+ 1	Korea (South)	+ 82	Swaziland	+ 268
Fiji	+ 679	Lesotho	+ 266	Tanzania	+ 255
France	+ 33	Malaysia	+ 60	UK	+ 44
Ghana	+ 233	New Zealand	+ 64	USA	+ 1

Society of All Saints Sisters of the Poor

ASSP

Founded 1851

All Saints Convent
St Mary's Road
Oxford OX4 1RU
UK
Tel: 01865 249127
Fax: 01865 726547
Email: helenmary@
socallss.co.uk

Website: www.
asspoxford.org

Mattins 6.30 am

Terce or Eucharist
9.00 am

Eucharist 12.00 noon
or Midday Office
12.15pm

Vespers 5.30 pm

Compline 8.00 pm

Variations on Sundays,
Saturdays
& major festivals

Office book
ASSP Office, based on
Anglican Office Book
1980

Registered Charity:
No. 228383

We believe we are called to be alongside the homeless and unemployed, the sick, the dying, the bereaved, the old and lonely. The community has the oversight of St John's Home, a residential home for elderly people. It has pioneered Helen and Douglas House, offering respite and end-of-life care for children and young people with life-shortening conditions and support for their families, and the Porch Steppin' Stone Centre, a day centre for homeless and vulnerably-housed people, which provides support and opportunity for change. These are both independent charities associated with All Saints. Hospitality is central to our life and we offer a warm welcome to guests and visitors for retreat and refreshment. Ordained ministry, spiritual direction and interfaith relations are some of the ways we live out our calling.

At the centre of this activity, and undergirding it, is the daily round of celebrating the liturgy together, with time to set aside for prayer, reading, and waiting upon God. We also give time for one another, respecting and cherishing each other. It is only in being with God and with one another, amidst all our activity, that we come to know the true purpose of our lives.

SISTER HELEN MARY ASSP
(Community Leader, assumed office 9 March 2006)
SISTER JEAN MARGARET ASSP *(Assistant Leader)*

Sister Margaret	Sister Margaret Anne
Sister Helen	*(priest)*
Sister Mary Julian	Sister Jean Raphael
Sister Frances Dominica	Sister Jane
Sister Ann Frances	

Associates
Those in sympathy with the aims of the community are invited to become Associates or Priest Friends.

Community Publication
New Venture, published annually in November. Order from the Society of All Saints.

Community Wares: The Embroiderers make, repair and remount vestments, frontals etc.

Guest and Retreat Facilities
Brownlow House, our guest house with six en-suite rooms, including one double and one twin, and the Upton room offering meeting facilities for up to fifteen people. Both these have self-catering facilities.

Bishop Visitor: Rt Revd Bill Ind

Other Addresses
St John's Home *(for the elderly),* St Mary's Road, Oxford OX4 1QE, UK
Tel: 01865 247725   Fax: 01865 247920   Email: admin@st_johns_home.org

All Saints Embroidery, All Saints Convent, St Mary's Road, Oxford OX4 1RU, UK,
Tel: 01865 248627

Associated Houses
Helen and Douglas House, 14a Magdalen Road, Oxford OX4 1RW, UK
Tel: 01865 794749   Fax: 01865 202702   Email: admin@helenanddouglas.org.uk
Website: www.helenanddouglas.org.uk   Registered Charity No: 1085951

The Porch Steppin' Stone Centre, All Saints Convent, St Mary's Road, Oxford OX4
1RU, UK
Tel: 01865 728545   Email: info@theporch.fsbusiness.co.uk
Website: www.theporch.org.uk   Registered Charity No: 1089612

Community History & Books
Peter Mayhew, *All Saints: Birth & Growth of a Community,* ASSP, Oxford, 1987.
Kay Syrad, *A Breath of Heaven: All Saints Convalescent Hospital,* Rosewell, St Leonard's
on Sea, 2002.
Sister Frances Dominica ASSP, *Just My Reflection: Helping families to do things their own
way when their child dies,* Darton, Longman & Todd, London, 2nd ed 2007, £6.50.
Behind the big red door: the story of Helen House, Golden Cup, Oxford, 2006, £12.00

The Society of All Saints Sisters of the Poor

Founded 1851

Bishop Visitor
The Rt Revd
Donald J Parsons

All Saints is a traditional Community desiring to uphold orthodox Christian faith and morality, and to support the Apostolic tradition in ministry and practice. We are united by our common commitment to the Lord Jesus Christ, and by our desire to live for Him. Within that unity there is great diversity both in our personalities and our talents. In giving these as an offering to the Lord, our communal life is enhanced.

Founded in London, three Sisters came to Baltimore, Maryland, in 1872, at the request of the Rector of Mount Calvary Church. The American sisterhood became an independent House in 1890.

The daily Eucharist is the center of our life. The six-fold Divine Office and our times of personal prayer enable us to pour forth Christ's love to others, in all of our works. Hospitality is an important aspect of our various houses. We also give retreats and missions of various types both at the Convent and elsewhere. Training for a vocation to the sisterhood begins with a month's Observership, then Postulancy and Novitiate. Three years under Junior Vows precede Life Profession.

Community Wares: The Scriptorium produces holy cards and greetings cards, notes and occasional creations by the Sisters.

All Saints Convent
PO Box 3127
Catonsville
MD 21228-0127
USA
Tel: 410 747 4104
Fax: 410 747 3321

Website: www.
asspconvent.org

Meditation
6.00 am

Lauds
6.30 am

Eucharist
7.00 am

Terce   9.30 am

Sext
12.00 noon

None
3.00 pm

Vespers
5.00 pm

Compline
8.30 pm

Office Book
The Monastic Diurnal
adapted to our use

**Most convenient
time to telephone:**
10.00 am - 11.45 am,
2.00 pm - 2.45 pm,
3.30 pm - 4.45 pm
EST/EDT

THE REVEREND MOTHER CHRISTINA OF ALL SAINTS
(Mother Superior, assumed office 2005)
THE SISTER EMILY ANN OF ALL SAINTS *(Assistant Superior)*

Sister Virginia	Sister Elizabeth
(sometime Mother)	Sister Julia Mary
Sister Hannah	Sister Mary Joan
Sister Barbara Ann	Sister Mary Charles
Sister Elaine	Sister Margaret
Sister Catherine Grace	
(sometime Mother)	

EDITOR'S NOTE: *The Community uses no abbreviations of the title of the Society. Sisters put 'of All Saints' after their names.*

Obituaries
28 May 2008   Sister Jane Teresa,
aged 83, professed 32 years

Associates and Fellowship
The All Saints Sisters offer two forms of association. These are *The Associates* and *The Fellowship of All Saints*. Both groups follow a Rule of Life.

Community Publications
   All Saints Convent Scriptorium - a catalog featuring greeting cars for sale and other items.
   The Illuminating Tale of Three Old Monks and a Very Bad Boy - a story to illuminate, more suitable for adults.
   For these, contact The Scriptorium at All Saints Convent.

Addresses
St Gabriel's Retreat House, PO Box 3106,
  Catonsville, MD 21228-0106, USA   *Tel: 410 747 6767*
St Anna's House, 115 North Van Pelt Street,
Philadelphia, PA 19103-1195, USA   *Tel: 215 665 8889*
The Joseph Richey Hospice, 838 North Eutaw Street
Baltimore, MD 21201, USA   *Tel: 410 523 2150*

Guest and Retreat Facilities
While no fees are set, the primary source of income is derived from the donations of those guests who are able to pay, keeping in mind we must buy food, pay staff, etc.

ST GABRIEL'S RETREAT HOUSE - address above.
THE GUEST WING, ALL SAINTS CONVENT - address above.
This is located inside the Convent itself. It is a designated area for female visitors offering nine private bedrooms and shared bathrooms. Meals are in a guest dining room and visitors are encouraged to attend the Eucharist and the Divine Office and enter into the stillness of the Sisters' life.

Brotherhood of the Ascended Christ

BAC

Founded 1877

Brotherhood House
7 Court Lane
Delhi 11054
INDIA
Tel: 11 2396 8515
or 11 2393 1432
Fax: 11 2398 1025

Email:
dbs@bol.net.in

**Morning Worship
& Eucharist**
6.30 am

**Forenoon Prayer
(Terce)**
8.30 am

Midday Prayer (Sext)
12.45 pm

**Afternoon Prayer
(None)**
3.50 pm

Evening Worship
7.30 pm

**Night Prayer
(Compline)**
9.10 pm

Today, the Brotherhood has one bishop, three presbyters, one lay-brother and two lay-probationers who belong to the Church of North India. Since the earliest days, the Brotherhood has had a concern for serving the poor and underprivileged. In 1975, the Delhi Brotherhood Society was set up to organise social development projects in the poorer parts of Delhi. The work and social outreach of the Brotherhood is with and not for the poor of Delhi. The Brotherhood has initiated programmes of community health, education, vocational training and programmes for street and working children.

IAN WEATHRALL BAC
(Head, assumed office 27 March 2004)
COLLIN THEODORE BAC *(Assistant Head)*

Monodeep Daniel   Raju George
Solomon George
                             Probationers: 2

Associates and Companions
There are twenty-three Presbyter Associates and seven Lay Companions who follow a simple Rule of Life adapted to their individual conditions.

Community Publication
Annual Newsletter and Report (free of charge).

Community History
Constance M Millington, *"Whether we be many or few": A History of the Cambridge/Delhi Brotherhood*, Asian Trading Corporation, Bangalore, 1999.
Available from the Brotherhood House.

Guest and Retreat Facilities
The Brotherhood House at Court Lane has a large garden and well-stocked library. It is used as a centre for retreats, quiet days and conferences. The small Guest Wing receives visitors from all over the world.

Most convenient time to telephone:
  7.30 am - 8.30 am, 4 pm - 5 pm   (Indian Standard Time)

Office Book
The Church of North India Book of Worship & Lesser Hours & Night Prayer (BAC)

Bishop Visitor: Rt Revd E W Talibuddin

Chama cha Mariamu Mtakatifu

(Community of St Mary of Nazareth and Calvary)

CMM

Founded 1946

The Convent
Kilimani
PO Box 502
Masasi, Mtwara
TANZANIA
*Tel: 023 2510126
(out of order).*
*Use mobile: 0784
236656 (Mother)*
or 0787 810702
Email:
masasi-cmmsisters
@yahoo.com

Morning Prayer
5.30 am

Mass
6.30 am

Midday Prayer
12.30 pm

Evening Prayer
3.00 pm

Compline
8.30 pm

The Community was founded in 1946 when the first girls took vows, and was under the Community of the Sacred Passion (CSP) until 1968, when they left them and Sister May Elizabeth was elected first Mother Superior CMM.

Bishop Frank Weston is the Grandfather Founder of CMM, while Bishop William Vincent Lucas is the Father Founder CMM. Both were Universities' Missionaries to Central Africa. CMM Sisters are trying their best to keep the aims of the founders: to serve God, His Church and His people.

Since then, there are eleven Houses in Tanzania and one in Zambia. Sisters do different services in the stations where they live, according to the demands and resources. At the time being, the Community is busy to raise up the standard of education of the members, so that it copes with the duties they face.

SISTER GLORIA PRISCA CMM
Revd Mother Superior, assumed office 22 May 2004)
SISTER HELEN CMM *(Sister Superior, Mother House)*
SISTER MARTHA BRIJITA CMM
(Sister Superior, Northern Zone)
SISTER MAGDALENE CMM *(Sister-in-charge, Mother House)*

Sister Rehema	Sister Stella
Sister Cesilia	Sister Agness Margreth
Sister Ethel Mary	Sister Merina Felistas
Sister Neema	Sister Jane
Sister Ester	Sister Rabeca
Sister Christine	Sister Dorothy
Sister Tabitha	Sister Perpetua
Sister Eunice Mary	Sister Jennifer
Sister Joy	Sister Anjelina
Sister Franciska	Sister Julia Rehema
Sister Anjela	Sister Joceline Florence
Sister Anna	Sister Jane Rose
Sister Prisca	Sister Susana Skolastika
Sister Nesta	Sister Anna Beatrice
Sister Bertha	Sister Mariamu Upendo
Sister Aneth	Sister Josephine Joyce
Sister Mary	Sister Skolastika Mercy
Sister Agatha	Sister Mary Prisca
Sister Lucy	Sister Paulina Anna
Sister Berita	Sister Janet Margaret
Sister Mercy	Sister Thecla Elizabeth
Sister Lidia	Sister Janet Elizabeth

Sister Edna Joan
Sister Josephine Brijita
Sister Dainess Charity
Sister Agnes Edna
Sister Jane Felistas
Sister Asnath Isabela
Sister Ethy Nyambeku
Sister Vumilia Imelda
Sister Anna Mariamu
Sister Debora Skolastika
Sister Foibe Edina
Sister Veronika Modesta
Sister Harriet Helena
Sister Hongera Mariamu
Sister Lulu Lois
Sister Martha Anjelina
Sister Lucy Lois

Sister Penina Skolastika
Sister Anet Olver
Sister Roda Rahel
Sister Edith Natalia
Sister Harriet
Sister Victoria
Sister Violet Jaqueline
Sister Debora Dorothy
Sister Nesta Sophia
Sister Lea Felicia
Sister Hongera Elizabeth
Sister Edith Grace
Sister Elizabeth Getrude
Sister Benadeta Jane
Sister Philippa Sapelo
Sister Joan Patricia
Sister Jessie Mary

Sister Imani
Sister Antonia Tereza
Sister Veronica Rita
Sister Violet Minka
Sister Beata
Sister Hope
Sister Erica Mary
Sister Rose Monica
Sister Thecla Leticia
Sister Mariamu
Sister Emma Agatha
Sister Joyce Agnes

Novices: 19
Postulants: 5

Obituaries

25 Jul 2008   Sister May Elizabeth, agd 82, professed 59 years,
                   one of the founding sisters, Revd Mother Superior 1968-71.

Community Wares
Vestments, altar breads, agriculture products, cattle products, crafts, candles.

Office Book: Swahili Zanzibar Prayer Book & The Daily Office SSF

Bishop Visitor: Rt Revd Patrick P Mwachiko, Bishop of Masasi

Other addresses

PO Box 116, Newala,
Mtwara Region,
TANZANIA
Tel: 023 2410222

PO Box 162, Mtwara,
TANZANIA
Tel: 023 2333587

PO Box 45, Tanga
Region, TANZANIA
Tel: 027 2643245

PO Box 195, Korogwe,
Tanga Region,
TANZANIA
Tel: 027 2640643

The Convent, PO Kwa
Mkono Handeni,
Tanga Region,
TANZANIA

Ilala, PO Box 25068,
Dar es Salaam,
TANZANIA
Tel: 022 2863797

PO Box 150, Njombe,
TANZANIA
Tel: 026 2782753

PO Box 6, Liuli, Mbing,
Ruvuma Region,
TANZANIA

Sayuni Msima, PO Box
150, Njombe, TANZANIA
Tel: 026 2782753

Fiwila Mission, PO Box
840112 Mkushi, ZAMBIA

Mtandi, Private Bag,
Masasi, Mtwara
Region, TANZANIA
Tel: 023 2510016

Chita Che Zita Rinoyera (Holy Name Community)

CZR

Founded 1935

St Augustine's
Mission
PO Penhalonga
Mutare
Zimbabwe
Tel:
Penhalonga 22217

Bishop Visitor:
Rt Revd Peter
Hatendi, Bishop of
Manicaland

Our Community was started by Father Baker of the CR Fathers at Penhalonga, with Mother Isabella as the founder. The CZR Sisters were helped by CR Sisters (Liz and Lois), and later by OHP Sisters (especially Lila, Mary Francis, Joyce and Hannah). When they left, Sister Isabella was elected Mother.

Today the CZR Sisters work at the clinic and at the primary and secondary schools. Some do visiting and help teach the catechism. We make wafers for several dioceses, including Harare. Some of the Sisters look after the church, seeing to cleaning and mending of the church linen. We have an orphanage that cares for thirty children, with an age range of eighteen months to eighteen years.

In 1982, half the Sisters and the novices left CZR and created another community at Bonda. Six months later, some of those Sisters in turn went to found Religious Life at Harare. In 1989, some of the Bonda community left to go to Gokwe and begin Religious Life there. So CZR has been the forerunner of three other communities in Zimbabwe. Please pray that God may bless us.

MOTHER BETTY CZR
(Reverend Mother, assumed office 2007)

Sister Stella Mary	Sister Elizabeth
Sister Anna Maria	Sister Emilia
Sister Hilda Raphael	Sister Annamore
Sister Felicity	Sister Sibongile

Community Wares
We sell chickens, eggs, milk, cattle (two or three a year) and wafers.

Community of the Blessed Lady Mary

CBLM

Founded 1982

The Sisters care for orphans on St John's Mission, Chikwaka, and do parish work there and on the two missions of Christ the King, Daramombe, and St Francis Mission, Sherugi, in the diocese of Masvingo.

MOTHER SYLVIA CBLM
(Reverend Mother)

Sister Dorothy	Sister Jasmine
Sister Anna	Sister Praxedes
Sister Faustina	

Address
Shearly Cripps Children's Home,
PO Box 121 Juru, ZIMBABWE

Chita che Zvipo Zve Moto

(Community of the Gifts of the Holy Fire)

CZM

Founded 1977

Convent of Chita che Zvipo Zve Moto
PO Box 138
Gokwe South
ZIMBABWE
Telefax: 263 059 2566

House Prayer   5.00 am

Mattins followed by meditation   5.45 am

Holy Communion
6.00 am

Midday prayers
12 noon

Evensong
followed by
meditation   5.00 pm

Compline   8.30 pm

Office Book
Book of Common
Prayer & CZM Office
Book 2002

Bishop Visitor
Rt Revd Ishmael
Mukuwanda, Bp of
Central Zimbabwe

The Community is a mixed community of nuns and friars, founded by the Revd Canon Lazarus Tashaya Muyambi in 1977. On a visit to St Augustine's Mission, Penhalonga, he was attracted by the life of the CR fathers and the CZR sisters. With the inspiration of the Spirit of the Lord, he believed it was of great value to start a Religious community. The first three sisters were attached to St Augustine's for three months. The first convent was officially opened in 1979 and the initial work was caring for orphans at St Agnes Children's Home.

In January 2000, Canon Muyambi stepped down from leadership, believing the Community was mature enough to elect its own leaders, which it did in March 2000. The Community have a Rule, Constitution and are governed by a Chapter. They take vows of Love, Compassion and Spiritual Poverty. The Community is progressing well with young people joining every year. Each member is qualified or skilled in one trade or another.

SISTER PHOEBE CZM *(Archsister in charge)*
FRIAR JOSHUA CZM *(Archfriar)*
(both assumed office December 2006)

Sister Gladys A	Sister Constance
Sister Eugenia	Sister Tirivatsva
Sister Elizabeth	Sister Lilian
Sister Eustina	Sister Cynthia
Sister Lydia	Friar Costa
Sister Anna Kudzai	Sister Precious
Sister Vongai Patricia	Sister Joyline
Sister Gladys B	Sister Vongai
Sister Teresah	Friar Tapiwa
Sister Martha	Friar Fanai
Sister Alice	Friar Brighton
Sister Tendai A	
Sister Itai	*Novices:* 4 *Postulants:* 1
Sister Juliet	

Obituaries
22 Feb 2009   Novice Friar Bernard, novice since 2006

Other addresses in Zimbabwe
St Patrick's Mission Branch House, P. Bag 9030, Gweru
St James Nyamaohlovu Bulawayo P. Bag, Matebeleland
30 Berwick Road, South Downs, Gweru

Community Wares
Sewing church vestments, school uniforms, wedding gowns; knitting jerseys; garden produce; poultry keeping.

Christa Sevika Sangha
(Handmaids of Christ)

CSS

Founded 1970

Jobarpar
Barisal Division
Uz Agailjhara 8240
BANGLADESH

Oxford Mission,
Bogra Road
PO Box 21
Barisal 8200
BANGLADESH
TEL: 0431 54481

Morning Prayer
Holy Communion
Midday Prayer
Quiet Prayer together
Evening Prayer
Compline

Office Book
Church of Bangladesh
BCP &
Community Office
Book
(all Offices are in
Bengali)

Bishop Visitor
Rt Revd Michael S.
Baroi

The Community was founded in 1970 and was under the care of the Sisterhood of the Epiphany until 1986, when its own Constitution was passed and Sister Susila SE was elected as Superior.

The Sevikas supervise girls' hostels and a play-centre for small children. They also help in St Gabriel's School and supervise St Mary's Asroi (Home) at Barisal. The Community also produces for sale a wide variety of goods and produce.

MOTHER SUSILA CSS
(Mother Foundress, 25 January 1970;
elected Reverend Mother CSS in July 1986)

Sister Ruth	Sister Kalyani
Sister Jharna	Sister Shefali
(House Sister, Jobarpar)	Sister Shalomi
Sister Sobha	Sister Shikha
Sister Agnes	Sister Shipra
Sister Dorothy	
(House Sister, Barisal)	Novices: 1 Postulants: 1
Sister Margaret	

Community Wares
Vestments, children's clothes, embroidery work, wine, wafers, candles. Farm produce: milk, poultry, fish. Land produce: rice, fruit, coconuts & vegetables. Twenty-four books translated into Bengali are for sale.

Community Publication
The Oxford Mission News, twice a year. Write to Oxford Mission, PO Box 86, Romsey, Hampshire SO51 8YD.
Tel: 01794 515004   Annual subscription: £4.00, post free.

Community History
Brethren of the Epiphany, A Hundred Years in Bengal,
ISPCK, Delhi, 1979
Mother Susila CSS, A Well Watered Garden,
(editor: M Pickering), Oxford Mission, Romsey, 2000
available from O. M. address above, £5 including p & p.

Guest and Retreat Facilities
Two rooms for men outside the Community campus. One house (three beds) for women. Donations received.

Fellowship of the Epiphany
The Oxford Mission Fellowship of the Epiphany was founded in 1921 for friends of the Mission in India, Bangladesh, the British Isles and elsewhere.
There is also a Prayer Fellowship group, which so far has ten members with their families.

Community of All Hallows

CAH

Founded 1855

All Hallows Convent
Belsey Bridge Road
Ditchingham
Bungay, Suffolk
NR35 2DT
UK
Tel: 01986 892749
(office)
01986 894607
(Sisters)
Fax: 01986 895838
Email:
allhallowsconvent
@btinternet.com

Lauds 7.30 am

Eucharist
8.00 am (9.30 am Sat,
10.00 am Sun)

Sext   12.15 pm

Evening Prayer
5.30 pm

Compline   8.00 pm

Office Book
Daily Prayer;
we also use BCP & CW
on Sundays.

Registered charity
No 230143

We are a group of women with diverse personalities and gifts called together in a common commitment to prayer and active work under the patronage of the Saints. Central to our life are the daily Eucharist and the Divine Office, combined with time for personal prayer, meditation and spiritual reading. Together they draw us deeper into the desire to "serve Christ in one another and love as He loves us". This overflows into our active works - particularly in our ministry of hospitality, expressed mainly through our Guest Houses, Spiritual Direction, and leading Retreats for individuals and small groups. It also includes some pastoral ministry at our local All Hallows Hospital and Nursing Home, which were founded and developed by us, but now form a separate Charity. In addition we have a large Conference Centre and a Day Nursery within our grounds.

The ministry of hospitality and prayer continues to flourish at our house in Rouen Road, Norwich, which is closely linked with the adjacent Julian Shrine and Centre.

All enquiries about the life and work of CAH should be directed in the first place to the Revd Mother at the Convent.

MOTHER ELIZABETH CAH
(Revd Mother, assumed office 8 July 2004)
SISTER PAMELA CAH *(Assistant Superior)*

Sister Sheila	Sister Winifred Mary
Sister Violet	Sister Edith Margaret
Sister Winifred	Sister Mary
Sister Jean	Sister Rachel
Sister Margaret	Sister Anne

Companions, Oblates, Associates and Contact Members
COMPANIONS, OBLATES, ASSOCIATES and CONTACT MEMBERS offer themselves to God within the community context in a varying degree of 'hands-on' commitment. Apply to the Convent for details.

Community Wares: A wide selection of photography cards.

Community Publication
A newsletter is circulated yearly at All Saints tide. To be included on the mailing list, please write to All Hallows Convent at the address above.

Bishop Visitor
Rt Revd Graham James, Bishop of Norwich

Most convenient time to telephone: 9.00 am - 12 noon, 2.15 pm - 4.30 pm (Mon to Fri); 7.00 pm - 7.55 pm (any day)

Other addresses and telephone numbers
The following all share the same address as All Hallows Convent:
St Gabriel's Conference Centre
                    Tel: 01986 892133 (staff/bookings) 01986 895765 (residents)
Holy Cross Guest House   *Tel: 01986 894092*
All Hallows Guest House   *Tel: 01986 892840*
St Mary's Lodge *(House of silence & retreat)*   *Tel: 01986 892731*
All Hallows House, St Julian's Alley, Rouen Road, Norwich NR1 1QT, UK
Tel: 01603 624738

Community History and books
Sister Violet CAH, *All Hallows, Ditchingham*, Becket Publications, Oxford, 1983.
Mother Mary CAH, *Memories*, privately published 1998.
Sister Winifred Mary CAH, *The Men in my Life*,
                    (reminiscences of prison chaplaincy), privately published 2009

Guest and Retreat Facilities
Enquiries about booking for the Conference Centre should be addressed to the
Convent Secretary at the Convent. Enquiries about staying at one of our guest
houses should be addressed to the sister-in-charge of the relevant house.

Sisterhood of the Epiphany

SE

Founded 1902

All
Hallows Convent
Belsey Bridge Rd
Ditchingham
Bungay, Suffolk
NR35 2DT
UK

Bishop Visitor
Rt Revd
Graham James,
Bishop of Norwich

Registered Charity:
Oxford Mission,
No. 211618

The Oxford Mission Sisterhood of the Epiphany was founded for work in India. The Christa Sevika Sangha *(see separate entry)*, founded in 1970, which works in Barisal and Jobarpar, Bangladesh, was under the guidance of the Sisterhood of the Epiphany for some years.

MOTHER WINIFRED SE
(Revd Mother, assumed office 6 January 1997)

Community Publication
The Oxford Mission News, twice a year. Write to Oxford Mission, PO Box 86, Romsey, Hampshire SO51 8YD, UK
Tel: 01794 515004
Annual subscription costs £4, post free.

Community History and memoirs
Brethren of the Epiphany, *A Hundred Years in Bengal*, ISPCK, Delhi, 1979.
Sister Rosamund SE, *He Leadeth Me: Memoirs of an Oxford Mission Sister of the Epiphany*, Oxford Mission, Romsey, 1999.
Sister Gertrude, *Mother Edith OMSE: A Memoir*, Darwen Finlayson, Beaconsfield, 1964.
Lilian Dalton, *The Story of the Oxford Mission to Calcutta*, SPCK, London, 1947.

Fellowship of the Epiphany
The Oxford Mission Fellowship of the Epiphany was founded in 1921 for friends of the Mission in India, Bangladesh, the British Isles and elsewhere.

Benedictine Community of Christ the King

CCK

Founded 1993

344 Taminick Gap
Road
South Wangaratta
Victoria 3678
AUSTRALIA
Tel/Fax: 3 57257343
Email: cck94
@bigpond.com

**Monastic Mattins
& Prayer Time**
4.30 am

Lauds 6.00 am

Eucharist & Terce
8.00 am

Sext 12 noon

None 1.15 pm

**Vespers & Prayer
Time** 5.00 pm

Compline 7.15 pm

Visitor
Fr Bernard McGrath
OSB

Chaplain
Fr Richard Seabrook
SSC

The Community of Christ the King is a Traditional Anglican Benedictine order, enclosed and contemplative. Its members endeavour to glorify God in a life of prayer under the threefold vow of Stability, Conversion of Life and Obedience. They follow a rhythm of life centred on the worship of God in the Daily Eucharist and sevenfold Office.

The convent nestles at the foot of the Warby Ranges in Victoria, Australia. It is surrounded by attractive flower gardens, a citrus orchard and a kitchen garden. The fruit and vegetables ensure a certain amount of self-sufficiency, and afford the opportunity and privilege of manual labour, essential to the contemplative life.

Hospitality aimed at helping visitors deepen their spiritual lives through prayer is a feature of the life. The property, with its extensive views, bush walks and seclusion, is ideally suited to relaxation, quiet reflection and retreat. It is ringed by fourteen large crosses providing opportunity for meditation on the way of the cross, and for prayer in solitude. We hold silent retreats and hope to develop this outreach.

MOTHER RITA MARY CCK
(*Revd Mother, assumed office 31 July 1997*)
SISTER PATIENCE CCK (*Assistant*)

Obituaries
13 Mar 09   Sister Clare, aged nearly 98, and a few weeks away from her 60th anniversary of profession.

Oblates: An Order of Benedictine Oblates has been established, open to women and men, clerical and lay.

Community Publication
The Community publishes a letter twice a year, sent free of charge to all interested in CCK (approximately 300 copies).

Guest and Retreat Facilities
We cater for those who want to deepen their life in Christ. There is a guest house which can accommodate three people (women or men): a self-contained cottage. There is no charge. A flat is attached to the chapel. A large fellowship room provides for parish quiet days and study groups. The original farmhouse is being renovated for additional accommodation.

Most convenient time to telephone:
10 am - 12 noon, 2 pm - 4 pm, 6.45 pm - 7.40 pm.

Office Book: The Divine Office is based on the Sarum Rite, using AAPB for the Psalms. Whenever the Office is sung, it is in Plainsong using BCP Psalms.

Community of the Companions of Jesus the Good Shepherd

CJGS

Founded 1920

The Priory
2 Spring Hill Road
Begbroke
Kidlington
Oxford OX5 1RX
UK

Tel: 01865 855326
or
01865 855320
Fax: 01865 855336

Email:
cjgs@csjb.org.uk

Lauds 7.30 am

Tierce 9.00 am

Eucharist 9.15 am

Midday Office
12.00 noon

Vespers 5.00 pm

Compline 8.30 pm

When the Community was founded, the first Sisters were all teachers living alone or in small groups but coming together during the school holidays. In 1943, West Ogwell House in South Devon became the Mother House and the more usual form of conventual life was established as well. The work of Christian education has always been of primary concern to the Community, whether in England or overseas, although not all the Sisters have been teachers.

In 1996, the Community moved to Windsor to live and work alongside the Community of St John Baptist, while retaining its own ethos. The Community aims 'to express in service for others, Christ's loving care for his flock.' At present, this service includes involvement in lay and ordained local ministry training; offering companionship to those seeking to grow in the spiritual life through spiritual direction, quiet days and retreats; and especially the befriending of the elderly, lonely, deaf and those in need.

In 2001, the Community moved with the Community of St John Baptist to The Priory, Begbroke.

MOTHER ANN VERENA CJGS
(Mother Superior, assumed office 20 March 1996)
SISTER FLORENCE CJGS *(Assistant Superior)*
Sister Evelyn Theresa
Sister Kathleen Frideswide

Associates
Associates of the Community are members of the Fellowship of St Augustine. They follow a rule of life drawn up with the help of one of the Sisters. They give support to the Community through their prayer, interest and alms, and are remembered in prayer by the Community. They and the Community say the 'Common Devotion' daily. They are truly our extended family.

Community Publication
CJGS News. Contact the Mother Superior.

Guest and Retreat Facilities
See under the entry for the Community of St John Baptist.

Office Book: Common Worship with additions from the old CSJB Office

Bishop Visitor: Rt Revd Dominic Walker OGS,
Bishop of Monmouth

Registered Charity: No. 270317

Community of the Glorious Ascension

CGA

Founded 1960

Brothers:
The Priory
Lamacraft Farm
Start Point
Kingsbridge
Devon
TQ7 2NG
UK

Tel & Fax:
01548 511474

Email:
ascensioncga
@fsmail.net

Registered Charity:
No. 254524

Sisters:
Prasada
Quartier Subrane
Montauroux
83440 Fayenne
Var
FRANCE

Tel & Fax:
04 94 47 74 26

BROTHERS

The life of the Community is shaped through a patterned living of prayer, worship and work. The mission of the Community is to be with and amongst people in daily living.

BROTHER SIMON CGA
(Prior, assumed office 20 May 1993)
Brother David
Brother John

Obituaries
25 Oct 07   Brother Wilfrid, aged 94, professed 33 years

Community Publication
CGA Newsletter, published annually. Write to the Prior.

Guest and Retreat Facilities
The Priory in Devon is not simply a retreat facility, but aims to offer opportunity for relaxation, reflection or holiday by groups, individuals and families. The Community welcomes groups by day and has two rooms in the main house which comfortably accommodate ten people for gatherings and meetings. Self-catering accommodation is also available in cottages set in a converted barn adjacent to the main house.

SISTERS

Prasada is set on the edge of a Provençal hill village, where guests are welcome for a time of rest and refreshment. Many join the Community in their chapel for the Eucharist and Divine Office.
  The Sisters are also involved in various activities with the local English-speaking and French communities.

SISTER JEAN CGA *(Prioress)*
Revd Sister Cécile

Community of the Divine Compassion

CDC

Post Box 214 Nyanga
ZIMBABWE

The Community runs a small hotel, Angler's Rest, as a ministry of Hospitality. They also care for a small number of young men, who have left orphanages, and help them get started in life. They do parish work in the neighbouring parish of St Peter's, Nyanga.

BROTHER BHEKEMPILO CDC
(Guardian)
Brother Peter Chapa
Brother Brian
Novices: 1   *Postulants:* 1

Community of the Good Shepherd

CGS

Founded 1978

Christ Church Likas
PO Box 519
88856 Likas
Sabah
MALAYSIA
Tel: 088 383211

MQ8, Jalan Teluk
Likas
Kota Kinabalu
88400 Likas
Sabah
MALAYSIA

Bishop Visitor:
Rt Revd Albert Vun
Cheong Fui, Bishop of
Sabah

The CGS Sisters in Malaysia were formerly a part of the Community of the Companions of Jesus the Good Shepherd in the UK *(see separate entry).* They became an autonomous community in 1978. Their Rule is based on that of St Augustine and their ministry is mainly parish work. In October 2000, the Sisters moved to Kota Kinabalu, the capital of Sabah, and have settled in at Likas, just opposite to Christ Church. On 25 April 2006, the Venerable Albert Vun Cheong Fui was consecrated and installed as the fifth Diocesan Bishop of Sabah. He has appointed Ven. John Yeo, the Rector of Christ Church, Likas, to be our chaplain. The Diocesan project of building a new Community House has been completed, and occupied in November 2007. It has a spacious ground in front with cool breezes from Likas Bay beyond. There are rooms for visitors and enquirers to Religious Life.

SISTER MARGARET LIN-DIN CGS
(Sister-in-charge, assumed office 1978)

Obituaries
15 Sep 07   Sister Oi Chin, aged 90, professed 44 years

Associates
In Kota Kinabalu, some committed Christian women from the three Anglican Churches join in fellowship with the Community and have become associate members. They follow a simple rule of life to support the Community through prayer and to share in the life and work of the Community. Whenever they can, they come to join the annual retreat.

Community Wares
Stoles and wafers (to supply the Sabah diocese at present).

Benedictine Community of the Holy Cross, Rempstone

CHC

Founded 1857

Holy Cross Convent
Ashby Road
Rempstone
near Loughborough
LE12 6RG
UK

Tel: 01509 880336
Fax: 01509 881812
Email:
chc.rempstone@
webleicester.co.uk

Website: www.
holycrosschc.org.uk

(SOUTHWELL DIOCESE)

Matins 6.15 am

Lauds 7.30 am

Mass 9.30 am
(subject to change)

Terce 9.15 am

Sext 12.15 am
(subject to change)

None 1.30 pm

Vespers 4.30 pm
(4.00 pm Thu & Fri)

Compline 8.00 pm

The Community of the Holy Cross was founded in 1857 by Elizabeth Neale (sister of John Mason Neale, the hymnographer), at the invitation of Father Charles Fuge Lowder. The foundation was intended for Mission work in Father Lowder's parish of London Docks, but succeeding generations felt that the Community was being called to a life of greater withdrawal, and in the twentieth century the Benedictine Office, and later the *Rule of St Benedict*, were adopted.

The Community aims to achieve the Benedictine balance of prayer, study and work. All the work, whether manual, artistic or intellectual, is done within the Enclosure. The daily celebrations of the Eucharist and the Divine Office are the centre and inspiration of all activity.

Apart from worship, prayer and intercession, and the work of maintaining the house, garden and grounds, the Community's works are: the publications and greetings cards described below; providing retreats and quiet days; and dealing with a large postal apostolate.

SISTER MARY LUKE WISE CHC
(Mother Superior, elected 8 November 1991)
SISTER MARY JULIAN GOUGH CHC *(Assistant Superior)*
Sister Mary Michael Titherington
Sister Mary Bernadette Priddin
Sister Mary Joseph Thorpe
Sister Mary Cuthbert Aldridge
Sister Mary Hannah Quark

Novices: 2

Oblates and Associates

The Community has women Oblates who are attached to it in a union of mutual prayers. Each has a rule of life adapted to her particular circumstances. Oblates are not Religious but they seek to live their life in the world according to the spirit of the *Rule of St Benedict*.

There are also Associates who have a much simpler rule.

Community Wares

A great variety of prayer and greeting cards are available for sale. Some are produced by the sisters and others are from a number of different sources.

Community Publications: A *Newsletter* published in the Spring. Available free from the Publications Secretary.

Office Book: CHC Office

Bishop Visitor: Most Revd Dr David Hope

Registered Charity: No 223807

Community History
Alan Russell, *The Community of the Holy Cross Haywards Heath 1857 - 1957: A Short History of its Life and Work,* 1957.

A leaflet: *A short history of the Community of the Holy Cross.*
Available from the Publications Secretary.

Guest and Retreat Facilities
There is limited accommodation for residential, private retreats: main meals are taken at the Convent. The Community also provides for Quiet Days for individuals or groups up to twenty. The Guest House is closed at Christmas.

Community of the Holy Name

CHN

Founded 1888

Community House
40 Cavanagh Street
Cheltenham
Victoria 3192
AUSTRALIA

Tel: 03 9583 2087
Fax: 03 9585 2932
Email: chnmelb
@bigpond.com

Eucharist 7.30 am

Mattins 9.00 am

Midday Office
12.45 pm

Vespers 5.30 pm

Compline 7.30 pm

The Community of the Holy Name was founded in 1888 within the Diocese of Melbourne by Emma Caroline Silcock (Sister Esther). The work of the Community was initially amongst the poor and disadvantaged in the slum areas of inner-city Melbourne. Over the years, the Sisters have sought to maintain a balance between a ministry to those in need and a commitment to the Divine Office, personal prayer and a daily Eucharist.

For many years, CHN was involved in institutions, like children's homes and a Mission house. There were many and varied types of outreach. The Holy Name Girls' High School was established in Papua New Guinea, and the indigenous Community of the Visitation of Our Lady fostered there.

Today, Sisters are engaged in parish work in ordained and lay capacities, and in a great variety of other ministries, including hospital chaplaincies, both general and psychiatric, spiritual companionship and leading of Quiet Days and retreats. The offering of hospitality to people seeking spiritual refreshment or a place away from their normal strains and stresses has become an important part of our life and ministry.

Other Australian Addresses
St Julians, 33 Lorna Street, Cheltenham, VIC 3192
25 Lorna Street, Cheltenham, VIC 3192
68 Pickett Street, Footscray, VIC 3011
48 Charles Street, Lorne, VIC 3232
15 Gisborne Street, East Melbourne, VIC 3002
2/7 James Street, Brighton, VIC 3186
8/7 James Street, Brighton, VIC 3186

Community Wares
Cards are sold at the Community House.

JOSEPHINE MARGARET CHN
(Mother Superior, assumed office 11 April 2005)
CAROL CHN *(Assistant Superior)*

AVRILL CHN, LYN CHN & VALMAI CHN
(Liaison Group)

Andrea	Hilary	Margaret Anne	Ruth
Betty	Hilda	Margot	Sheila
Elizabeth Gwen	Jean	Pamela	Sheila Anne
Felicity	Jenny	Philippa	Shirley
Francine	Maree	Penelope	Winifred Muriel

Obituaries
26 Jan 2008   Gwendoline, aged 82, professed 41 years

Oblates and Associates
The Order of Oblates is for women and men who desire to lead lives of prayer and dedication in close association with the Community. The Oblates have a personal Rule of Life based on the Evangelical Counsels of Poverty, Chastity and Obedience and renew their dedication annually.

The Associates and Priests Associate support and pray for the Community. In some areas they have regular meetings for fellowship. Priests Associate offer the Eucharist with special intention for the Community and seek to promote the Religious Life.

Community Publication
An *Associates Letter* is published four times a year. Write to Sister Avrill, the Associates Sister, for a subscription, which is by donation.

Community History
Sister Elizabeth CHN, *Esther, Mother Foundress*, Melbourne, 1948.
Lynn Strahan, *Out of the Silence*, OUP, Melbourne, 1988.

Guest and Retreat Facilities
Day groups of up to twenty-five people are welcome in the Prayer Group and Gathering Space. There is accommodation for six residential guests at the Community House and a Sister is available for help and guidance if requested. St Julian's Retreat and Spirituality Centre accommodates ten guests in affordable and comfortable surroundings.

Most convenient time for guests to telephone: 10am - 12.30 pm, 2pm - 5pm

Office Book: CHN adaptation of the Anglican Office Book

Bishop Visitor: Most Revd Dr Philip Freier, Archbishop of Melbourne

EDITORS' NOTE: *The Community of the Holy Name in the UK and Africa, which forms several of the* subsequent *entries in this directory, is a community entirely distinct from CHN in Australia. Although sharing the same name, the two communities were founded independently of each other.*

Community of the Holy Name
(UK Province)

CHN

Founded 1865

Convent of
the Holy Name
Morley Road
Oakwood
Derby
DE21 4QZ
UK

Tel: 01332 671716
Fax: 01332 669712

Email: bursarsoffice
@tiscali.co.uk

Website:
www.chnderby.org

Bishop Visitor
Rt Revd
John Inge
Bishop of Worcester

The Sisters combine the life of prayer with service to others in their evangelistic and pastoral outreach and by maintaining their houses as centres of prayer where they can be available to others. They run a small guest house in Derby. In our houses, and from the Convent in Derby, the Sisters are involved in parish work, hospital visiting, retreat-giving and work among the wider community, and with those who come for spiritual guidance.

The members of the Fellowship of the Holy Name are an extension of its life and witness in the world. We encourage those who wish to live alongside for a period of time.

SISTER MONICA JANE CHN
(Provincial Superior, assumed office 10 January 2004)
SISTER EDITH MARGARET CHN *(Assistant Superior)*

Sister Penelope	Sister Elizabeth Clare
Sister Judith	Sister Diana
Sister Ruth	Sister Dorothy
Sister Francesca Mary	Sister Pauline Margaret
Sister Marjorie Jean	Sister Carol
Sister Barbara	Sister Pippa
Sister Joy	Sister Rosemary
Sister Brenda	Sister Irene
Sister Verena	Sister Lynfa
Sister Jean Mary	Sister Elaine Mary
Sister Constance	Sister Julie Elizabeth
Sister Lilias	Sister Linda Frances
Sister Theresa Margaret	Sister Christine
Sister Mary Patricia	Sister Catherine
Sister Lisbeth	
Sister Vivienne Joy	*Novices:* 1
Sister Charity	

Obituaries
7 Oct 07   Sister Beryl, aged 86, professed 43 years
20 Feb 08   Sister Christian, aged 99, professed 61 years
2 May 08   Sister Michael, aged 91, professed 65 years

Fellowship of the Holy Name
The Fellowship is comprised of ecumenically-minded Christians who feel called to share with the Community in their life of prayer and service.

Members have a personal Rule of Life, which they have drawn up in consultation with a particular Sister. This will

Prime
7.45 am

Eucharist
8.00 am
(12.20 pm Tue & Thu)

Mattins
9.15 am
(8.45 am Tue & Thu)

Midday Office
12.45 pm
(12.05 pm Tue & Thu)

Vespers
5.00 pm

Compline
9.15 pm
(8.45 pm Sat)

Office Book
Daily Office CHN

Registered Charity:
No. 250256

include daily private prayer, regular prayer and worship with the local Christian community, as well as time and space for their own well-being and creativity. Each rule varies with the individual. A six-month probation living the rule is required before formal admission to the Fellowship. This usually takes place at the Convent in the context of the Eucharist. There are regional meetings for members living in the same area, and the Community distributes newsletters throughout the year and encourages members to contribute articles for the Community magazine.

Other Addresses
Cottage 5, Lambeth Palace, London SE1 7JU
Tel: 020 7928 5407

64 Allexton Gardens, Welland Estate, Peterborough PE1 4UW
Tel: 01733 352077

Community History
History of the Community of the Holy Name, 1865 to 1950, published by CHN, 1950.
Una C. Hannam, *Portrait of a Community,* printed by the Church Army Press, 1972.

Community Publication
Community magazine - contact the editor

Community Wares
Various cards.

  Booklet of Stations of the Cross, from original paintings by Sister Theresa Margaret CHN, with biblical texts. Can be ordered from the Convent: £5.00 each, or for orders of ten or more £4.50 each. Icons are also available.

Sister Pauline Margaret CHN, *Jesus Prayer,* £3.50.
Can be ordered from the Convent or SLG Press.

Guest and Retreat Facilities
There are opportunities for up to seven individuals to make a private retreat at the guest house, and Sisters would be prepared to give help and guidance if requested. We do not organise group retreats. The guest cottage is closed from Sunday afternoon to Tuesday morning.

Most convenient time to telephone:
10.00 am - 12.30 pm, 2.00 pm - 5.00 pm, 5.30 pm - 9.00 pm

Community of the Holy Name
(Lesotho Province)

CHN

Founded 1865 (in UK)
1962 (in Lesotho)

Convent of the Holy Name
PO Box 22
Ficksburg 9730
SOUTH AFRICA
Tel: 22400249
Email: cohona
@datacom.co.ls

Morning Prayer
6.30 am
(6.45 am Sun)

Terce
7.45 am (Sun only)

Eucharist
7.00 am (8.00 am Sun;
12 noon Wed)

Midday Office 12.15
pm (12.30 pm Sun,
11.45 am Wed)

Evening Prayer
5.00 pm

Compline 8.15 pm

Office Book
South African Prayer
Book, supplemented
by CHN Office Book

Bishop Visitor:
Rt Revd Adam Taaso

The Basotho Community of St Mary at the Cross was founded in Leribe, Lesotho, in 1923, under the Community of St Michael & All Angels, Bloemfontein. In 1959, CHN Sisters were invited to take over this work and started at Leribe in 1962. They had invited the Sisters of S. Mary at the Cross to become members of CHN and the full amalgamation of the two communities was completed in 1964. As a multi-racial community, the witness against racism at a time when apartheid was in the ascendant in South Africa was an important strand of the Community's vocation. New members have joined the Community in succeeding years, and they have continued the evangelistic and pastoral work which is also an important part of the CHN vocation. Sisters are involved in children's work, prison visiting, as well as other outreach in both Lesotho and South Africa. The Sisters in Leribe run a hostel for secondary school students who live too far away to travel daily. Some Sisters are 'Volunteers of Love' for families where there is HIV/AIDS. This work is enabled and strengthened by the daily round of prayer, both corporate and private, which is at the heart of the Community's Rule. A daily Eucharist at the centre of this life of prayer is the aim, but in some houses this is not always possible owing to a shortage of priests. There is a small guest house.

SISTER JULIA CHN
(*Provincial Superior, assumed office April 2007*)
SISTER MPOLOKENG CHN (*Assistant Superior*)

Sister Calista	Sister Ryneth
Sister Alphonsina	Sister Lineo
Sister Hilda Tsepiso	Sister Exinia Tsoakae
Sister Maria	Sister Malineo
Sister Lucia	Sister Malefu
Sister Mary Selina	Sister Molehobeng
Sister Angelina	
Sister Josetta	*Novices:* 3
Sister Gertrude	

Other houses
For other houses, please contact the main house.

Community Wares
Church sewing (including cassocks, albs & stoles); communion wafers; Mothers Union uniforms; mohair and woven goods from the Leribe Craft Centre and the disabled workshop, started by the Community.

Community of the Holy Name
(Zulu Province)

CHN

Founded 1865 (in UK)
1969 (in Zululand)

Convent of the Holy
Name
Pt. Bag 806
Melmoth 3835
Zululand
SOUTH AFRICA
Tel: 3545 02892
Fax: 3545 07564

Email:
chnsisters
@telkomsa.net

Terce 6.30 am

Eucharist
6.30 am (Wed & Fri)
6.45 am (Tue & Thu)
4.30 pm (Mon)

Mattins 8.30 am

Midday Office
12.30 pm

Evening Prayer
4.00 pm (Mon & Wed)
5.00 pm (Tue & Thu)
4.30 pm (Fri)

Compline 7.45 pm

The Community of the Holy Name in Zululand was founded by three Zulu Sisters who began their Religious life with the Community in Leribe. All three Provinces of CHN have the same Rule of life, but there are differences of customary and constitutions to fit in with cultural differences. The daily life of the Community centres around the daily Office, and the Eucharist whenever the presence of a priest makes this possible.

The Sisters are involved extensively in mission, pastoral and evangelistic work. The Zulu Sisters have evangelistic gifts which are used in parishes throughout the diocese at the invitation of parish priests. Several Sisters have trained as teachers or nurses. They work in schools or hospitals, where possible within reach of one of the Community houses. Their salaries, and the handicrafts on sale at the Convent at Kwa Magwaza, help to keep the Community solvent.

MOTHER NOKUBONGWA CHN
(Provincial Superior, assumed office February 2008)
SISTER BENZILE CHN *(Assistant Superior)*

Sister Gertrude Jabulisiwe	Sister Patricia
Sister Claudia	Sister Phindile
Sister Olpha	Sister Nqobile
Sister Nesta Gugu	Sister Fikile Cynthia
Sister Nokuthula Victoria	Sister Sibekezelo
Sister Sibongile	Sister Xolisile
Sister Zodwa	Sister Philisiwe
Sister Mantombi	Sister Ntsoaki
Sister Bonakele	Sister Nomathemba
Sister Nonhlahla	Sister Thandukwazi
Sister Jabu	Sister Zamandla
Sister Thulisiwe	Sister Bongile
Sister Thembelihle	Sister Maureen
Sister Sebenzile	Sister Thembsile
Sister Samkelisiwe	Sister Neliswa
Sister Thandazile	Sister Hlengiwe
Sister Thandiwe	Sister Nkosikhoma
Sister Nondumiso	
Sister Thokozile	*Novices:* 3
Sister Duduzile	

Office Book
Offices are mainly in Zulu, based on the South African Prayer Book & the CHN Office Book.

Community Wares
Vestments, cassocks, albs and other forms of dressmaking to order.

Other Houses
Usuthu Mission, PO Box 8, Luyengo, SWAZILAND

PO Box 175, Nongoma 3950, SOUTH AFRICA

St Benedict House, PO Box 27, Rosettenville 2130, SOUTH AFRICA

Bishop Visitor: Rt Revd Dino Gabriel, Bishop of Zululand

Community of the Holy Transfiguration

CHT

Founded-1982

St David's Bonda Mission
P Bag T 7904
Mutare
ZIMBABWE

House Prayer
5.00 am

Meditation
5.10 am

Mattins   5.45 am

Mid-day Office
12.00 noon

Vespers   6.00 pm

Compline
8.00 pm

The Community started in 1982 with eight members who broke away from the Community of the Holy Name (Chita Che Zita Renoyera). The Community is stationed at St David's Bonda Mission and it is an open community. We assist the Church in evangelistic work and other ministerial duties. Some members are employed by the diocese as priests and some as Evangelists. We run an orphanage with a maximum number of thirty young children. As of now, the age-group is going beyond this age range because of the HIV/AIDS pandemic. We are also a self-reliant community through land tilling and poultry. We look forward to opening branch houses in the near future.

SISTER MILDAH CHT
(Mother, assumed office 2006)

Sister Gloria
Sister Winnie
Sister Francesca
Sister Lucy
Sister Merina
Sister Gloria Mary
Sister Violet
Sister Dorothy

Sister Felicity
Sister Letwin
Rev Friar
            Fungayi Leonard
Evangelist Friar Henry

Bishop Visitor
Rt Revd Peter Hatendi, Bishop of Manicaland

Office Book: Book of Common Prayer

Community of the Holy Spirit

CHS

Founded-1952

621 West 113th
Street
New York
NY 10025-7916
USA

Tel: 212 666 8249
Fax: 801 655 8249

Email: chssisters
@chssisters.org

Website
www.chssisters.org

The daily schedule varies with the seasons.
Please call ahead for current schedule.
Monday is a Sabbath in each house of the Community, during which there is no corporate worship.

Office Book
CHS Office book

Each person is given an invitation to follow Christ. The Sisters of our monastic community respond to that invitation by an intentional living out of the vows of poverty, chastity, and obedience within the structure of a modified Augustinian Rule. Through the vow of poverty, we profess our trusting dependence upon God by embracing voluntary simplicity and responsible stewardship of creation. Through chastity, we profess the sanctity of all creation as the primary revelation of God. Through obedience, we profess our desire to be dependent on God's direction and to live and minister in ways that respect all creation, both now and for generations to come.

Compassionate, respectful love is God's gift to life. Prayer and the worship of God are the lifeblood and heart of our Community and the source of inspiration for all that we undertake. Through our prayer, worship, and creative talents we encourage others to seek God. Through our ministries of hospitality, retreat work, spiritual direction, and education through simple, sustainable, spiritual living, we seek to grow in love and communion with all whose lives touch us and are touched by us. We also provide spiritual support for women and men who wish to be linked with our Community as Associates. By adopting a personal rule of life, they extend the Community's ministry through prayer, worship and service.

SISTER HELÉNA MARIE CHS *(June 2001)*
SISTER FAITH MARGARET CHS *(June 2001)*
SISTER CATHERINE GRACE CHS *(June 2001)*
SISTER LESLIE CHS *(June 2007)*
(Community Council)

Sister Élise
Sister Mary Christabel
Sister Mary Elizabeth
Sister Jerolynn Mary
Sister Dominica
Sister Emmanuel
Sister Maria Felicitas
Sister Donna Martha

Sister Claire Joy
Sister Carol Bernice

Candidates: 1

Resident Companions:
Revd Suzanne Guthrie
William Consiglio

Associates
From the Community's early days, Christian women and men have sought an active association with the Sisters, wishing to live out their baptismal commitments by means of a rule of life.

The Community provides four rules: Fellowship, St Augustine, Confraternity and Priest Associate. Each consists of prayer, reading, self-denial and stewardship. Each provides an opportunity for growth toward God and daily renewal of life in Christ. Each calls for a commitment to pray daily for the Sisters and all others in their life, worship and ministry, using the collect for Pentecost and the Lord's Prayer.

In consultation with the Sister for Associates, they may formulate their own rule if the ones provided cannot be fulfilled as they stand, or if they need to be expanded. As far as is possible Associates support the Community through gifts of time, talents and financial resources. There is an annual fee of $50, if possible.

Other Address
The Melrose Convent - Bluestone Farm and Learning Center
118 Federal Hill Road, Brewster, NY 10509-5307, USA
Tel: 845 278 9777   Fax: 425 944 1085   Email: Melrose@chssisters.org

Community Wares
[From Bluestone Farm]:
Maple syrup, honey, eggs, and other food items as available.

Community Publication
AweWakenings, published twice a year.
There is no charge for this publication; however, donations are always welcomed.
For further information, contact Cheryl Helm, administrator,
Tel: 212 666 8249 extension 312   Email: cheryl@chssisters.org

Community History
The Revd Mother Ruth CHS, *"In Wisdom Thou Hast Made Them"*,
Adams, Bannister, Cox, New York, 1986

Guest and Retreat Facilities
Outpourings ministry at St Hilda's House, New York City: fourteen rooms, total capacity seventeen. Closed irregularly; please call in advance to make reservations. Visit www.chssisters.org - General - Hospitality in NYC for further information.
Tel: 212 932 8098   Email: outpourings@chssisters.org
The Longhouse at Melrose; seven rooms, total capacity eight. Closed irregularly; call in advance to make reservations.
Visit www.chssisters.org - General - Hospitality in Brewster for further information.
Tel: 845 278 9777 ex 30   Email: BFLCreservations@chssisters.org

Most convenient time to telephone:
Generally, phones are staffed irregularly between 9.00 am and 5.00 pm EST Tuesday through Saturday, though you may leave a message at any time.

Bishops Visitor:
Rt Revd Bruce E. Caldwell, Bishop of Wyoming
Rt Revd Mark H. Andrus, Bishop of California
Rt Revd Catherine S. Roskam, Suffragan Bishop of New York

Community of Jesus' Compassion

CJC

Founded 1993

PO Box 153
New Hanover
3230
SOUTH AFRICA
Tel: 033 502 0010

Tel: 033 502 0200
(for second CJC
house in the same
vicinity)

**Morning Prayer,
followed by Terce**
5.30 am

Midday Prayer
12.30 pm

Evening Prayer
4.30 pm

Compline
8.15 pm

Founded in the Diocese of Natal by a sister from the Community of the Holy Name in Zululand, CJC have been based in Newcastle and Ixopo. However, the sisters have now settled at New Hanover, which is half an hour's drive from the cathedral city of Pietermaritzburg.

The main work of the sisters is evangelising in the local parish and children's ministry. The Sisters care for around thirty-five children, which is demanding, but good progress is being made.

On the 19th December 1998, the first professions within the community were received. The Community's formal recognition by the Church of the Province of South Africa followed in 2000 with the first life professions.

In 2006, Sister Thandi became the first nun in the diocese to be ordained to the stipendiary ministry, and she now serves in a parish in Durban. Her priesting followed in June 2007.

MOTHER LONDIWE CJC
(*Mother Superior, assumed office 8 January 2000*)
SISTER THANDI CJC *(Assistant Superior)*
Life professed:
Sister Yeki
Sister Nontombi
Sister Zandile
Sister Jabulile
Sister Nontokozo
Sister Thokozile
Sister Nqobile
Sister Nonhlanhla
Sister Celiwe
Sister Ncebakazi
Sister Mbali

Professed under temporary vows:
Sister Thelma
Sister Ayanda

Novices: 2

Community Wares
Girdles, Prayer Book and Bible covers, vegetables.

Bishop Visitor
Rt Revd Rubin Phillip, Bishop of Natal

Office Book
Anglican Prayer Book 1989 of the Church of the Province of Southern Africa
Midday Office book & Celebrating Night Prayer

Community of Nazareth

CN

Founded 1936

4-22-30 Mure
Mitaka
Tokyo 181-0002
JAPAN

Tel: 0422 48 4560
Fax: 0422 48 4601

Under the guidance of the Sisters of the Community of the Epiphany (England), the Community of Nazareth was born and has grown. The Community is dedicated to the Incarnate Lord Jesus Christ, especially in devotion to the hidden life which he lived in Nazareth.

In addition to the Holy Eucharist, which is the centre and focus of our community life, the Sisters recite a sixfold Divine Office.

We run a Retreat house and make wafers and vestments. We welcome enquirers and aspirants.

SISTER DORCAS MIYOSHI CN
(*Revd Mother, assumed office 4 March 2004*)
SISTER NOBU CN (*Assistant Mother*)

Sister Yachiyo
Sister Chiyo
Sister Haroko
Sister Kayoko
Sister Chizuko
Sister Asako
Sister Setsuko
Sister Yukie
Sister Junko
Sister Sachiko

Morning Prayer
6.25 am

Eucharist
7.00 am

Terce
8.15 am

Sext
12 noon

None
after lunch

Evening Prayer
5.00 pm

Night Prayer
8.15 pm

Associates
Clergy and laity may be associates.

Other Address
81 Shima Bukuro, Naka Gusuku Son, Naka Gami Gun, Okinawa Ken 901-2301, JAPAN

Community Wares
Wafers, vestments, postcards.

Guest and Retreat Facilities
There are twenty rooms available, for men or women, but not children. The suggested donation is ¥6,000 per night, including three meals.

Bishop Visitor
Rt Revd Jintarō Ueda, Bishop of Tokyō

Office Book
BCP of Nippon Seiko Kai Office Book

Benedictine Community of Our Lady & Saint John

Alton Abbey

OSB

Founded 1884

Alton Abbey
Abbey Road, Beech,
Alton, Hampshire
GU34 4AP
UK
Tel: 01420 562145
& 01460 563575
Email: altonabbey@
supanet.com

Website: www.
altonabbey.org.uk

Morning Prayer
6.30 am

Conventual Mass
9.00 am   (10 am Sun)

Midday Office
12.00 noon

Evening Prayer
5.00 pm

Night Prayer
8.30 pm   (7.30 pm Sun)

The monks follow the Rule with its balance of prayer, work and study, supported by the vows of stability, conversion of life and obedience. A wide ministry of hospitality is offered, and visitors are welcome at the daily Mass and Divine Office. The purpose built monastery is built around two cloister garths; the Abbey Church dates from the beginning of the twentieth century. Set in extensive grounds, with contrast between areas that are cultivated and others that are a haven for wildlife, the Abbey is situated about four miles from Alton.

RT REVD DOM GILES HILL OSB
(Abbot, elected 12 September 1990)
VERY REVD DOM WILLIAM HUGHES OSB
(Prior and Novice Master)

Revd Dom Andrew Johnson
Revd Dom Nicholas Seymour (*Guest Master*)
Dom Anselm Shobrook
Rt Revd Dom Timothy Bavin

Oblates
For details of the Oblates of St Benedict, please contact the Oblate Master.

Community Publication
The Messenger, occasional, write to the Abbey.

Community Wares
Altar bread and incense: contact Alton Abbey Supplies Ltd.   Tel: 01420 565977

Guest and Retreat Facilities
Guest house facilities for up to eighteen persons, for both group and individual retreats. There is a programme of retreats each year, available from the Guestmaster.
No smoking in the house.

Most convenient time to telephone: 4.00 pm - 4.30 pm.

Bishop Visitor: Rt Revd Michael Scott-Joynt,
Bishop of Winchester

Office Book: Alton Abbey Office Book

Registered Charity: No. 229216

Community of the Resurrection

CR

Founded 1892

House of the
Resurrection
Mirfield
West Yorkshire
WF14 0BN
UK

Tel: 01924 494318
Fax: 01924 490489
Email:
community
@mirfield.org.uk

Mattins
6.45 am (7.30 am Sun)

Midday Office
12.00 noon

Mass
12.15 pm
On festivals on week
days, the time of Mass
may change.

Evensong
6.30 pm

Compline
9.15 pm

Office Book
CR Office

The Community consists of priests and laymen living a life of worship, work and study within the monastic life. They undertake a wide range of pastoral ministry including retreats, teaching and counselling.

GEORGE GUIVER CR
(assumed office 29 December 2002)
PETER ALLAN CR *(Prior)*

Dominic Whitnall	Antony Grant
Roy France	Nicolas Stebbing
Timothy Stanton	John Gribben
Vincent Girling	Andrew Norton
Zachary Brammer	Philip Nichols
Eric Simmons	Thomas Seville
Aidan Mayoss	Steven Haws
Robert Mercer *(bishop)*	Oswin Gartside
Simon Holden	*Novices:* 1
Crispin Harrison	

Obituaries

3 Sep 07	Benedict Green, aged 83, professed 45 years
19 Jun 08	Anselm Genders *(bishop)*, aged 88, professed 56 years

Oblates
OBLATES, clergy and lay, are those who desire to make a special and permanent offering of themselves to God in association with the Community of the Resurrection.

The Companions of the Community
COMPANIONS seek to live the baptismal vocation of all Christians through a commitment to each community to which they belong and also to the Community of the Resurrection; a commitment to Eucharistic worship, corporate and private prayer and the use of the sacrament of reconciliation; a commitment of time, talents and money. Those who wish to be Companions keep their commitments for at least a year before being admitted, and thereafter, with all Companions, renew their commitment each year. All Companions have a spiritual director or soul friend with whom their commitments are discussed and who undertakes to support them on their journey.

ASSOCIATES have a less demanding relationship with the Community for whatever reason, but do have an obligation of prayer and worship. For more information please contact the Chaplain to the Companions at Mirfield.

Community Publication
CR Quarterly. Write to the Editor. Many subscribe to this who are not Oblates, Companions or Associates. The minimum annual subscription is £10.00.

Community History
Alan Wilkinson, *The Community of the Resurrection: A centenary history,* SCM Press, London, 1992.

Community Wares
Postcards of the buildings, theological and spiritual books, leaflets on prayer, CDs of Community's music, clothes with logo: apply to Mirfield Publications at the House of the Resurrection.

Guest and Retreat Facilities
Retreats are listed on the website.
HOUSE OF THE RESURRECTION
Twenty-four single rooms, two double rooms, nine en-suite rooms, one small flat.

Most convenient time to telephone: 9.00 am - 12 noon, 2.00 pm - 6.30 pm

A further retreat house, owned but not staffed by CR, is:
St Francis' House, Hemingford Grey, Huntingdon, Cambs., PE18 9BJ, UK
Tel: 01480 462185   Email: hemingford@mirfield.org.uk
Seventeen single rooms, three twin rooms. Apply to the Warden.
PLEASE NOTE: This house is closing at the end of 2009.

MIRFIELD CENTRE
The Centre offers a meeting place at the College for about fifty people. Small residential conferences are possible in the summer vacation. Day and evening events are arranged throughout the year to stimulate Christian life and witness.

The Mirfield Centre (College of the Resurrection), Mirfield, West Yorks WF14 0BW, UK
Tel: 01924 481920   Fax: 01924 418921   Email: centre@mirfield.org.uk

COLLEGE OF THE RESURRECTION
The College, founded in 1902 and run by its own independent Council, trains men and women and also provides opportunities for others to study for degrees.

Principal: Revd Joseph Kennedy

College of the Resurrection, Mirfield, West Yorkshire WF14 0BW, UK
Tel: 01924 481900   Fax: 01924 481921   Email: registrar@mirfield.org.uk

Bishop Visitor: Rt Revd Graham James, Bishop of Norwich

Registered Charity: No. 232670

Community of the Resurrection of Our Lord

CR

Founded 1884

St Peter's, PO Box 72
Grahamstown 6140
SOUTH AFRICA
Tel & Fax:
046 622 4210
Email: comres
@imaginet.co.za

Morning Office
6.30 am

Eucharist 7.00 am
(Sun, Tue, Thu & Fri)
(at the Cathedral
Mon & Wed)

Midday Office
followed by silent
intercession
12.30 pm

Evening Office
followed by silent
intercession 5.30 pm

Compline 7.30 pm

Greater Silence: 9 pm

Office Book
Anglican Prayer
Book 1989, CPSA;
Traditional Midday
Office & Compline

This Community was founded in 1884 by Bishop Allan Becher Webb and Cecile Isherwood to undertake pastoral and educational work in Grahamstown. These two types of work, and later Social Welfare work, have predominated in the Community's undertakings throughout its history. The regular life of monastic Offices and personal prayer and intercession has always been maintained, both in the Mother House (Grahamstown) and all branch houses, wherever situated. It is still maintained in Grahamstown, the only centre where the Community life continues, our numbers being now much reduced. The Sisters are involved in various ministries: at the Cathedral and other churches as needed; in the Raphael Centre for people suffering from HIV/Aids etc; in visiting at Old Age Homes and the hospital; soup kitchens; and needlework/banners.

MOTHER ZELMA CR *(priest)*
(Mother Superior, assumed office 24 November 2005)
SISTER KEKELETSO CR *(Assistant Superior)*
Sister Dorianne
Sister Carol *(priest)*
Sister Makhosazana

Obituaries
9 May 2007   Sister Joyce Mary, aged 74,
in community 55 years
1 Oct 2008   Sister Nonie *(priest)*, aged 84,
in community 60 years

Oblates and Associates
OBLATES OF THE RISEN CHRIST live under a Rule drawn up for each individual according to circumstances, on their observance of which they must report monthly to the Oblate Sister.

ASSOCIATES undertake a simple Rule, including regular prayer for the Community. Priest Associates undertake to give an address or preach on Religious Vocation at least once a year.

FRIENDS are interested in the Community and pray for it, and keep in touch with it.

There is a Fellowship Meeting twice a year, after Easter and near the Foundress's birthday on 14 November.

Also there is a Festival gathering of UK Associates at St Peter's Bourne, Whetstone, north London, on the Saturday nearest to St Peter's Day, 29 June, each year, at which two Sisters from South Africa are always present to preserve our links with the UK.

Bishop Visitor: awaiting election

Community Publication
A Newsletter is sent out three times a year to all bishops and Religious communities of CPSA, and also to all the Oblates and Associates of the Community.

Community Wares: Cards, banners and girdles.

Guest and Retreat Facilities
Ten or more guests can be accommodated; though prior consultation is needed. The charge is negotiable. There is also a guest flatlet for two.

Community History and Books
A pictorial record of the Community's history, with commentary, was published in its centenary year, 1984. It was a collaborative work.

Lives of Mother Cecile and her successor, Mother Florence, have been published, in each case written by 'a Sister':

A Sister of the Community (compiler), *Mother Cecile in South Africa 1883-1906: Foundress of the Community of the Resurrection of Our Lord,* SPCK, London, 1930

A Sister of the Community, *The Story of a Vocation: A Brief Memoir of Mother Florence, Second Superior of the Community of the Resurrection of Our Lord,*
The Church Book Shop, Grahamstown, no date.

Guy Butler, *The Prophetic Nun,* Random House, 2000. (Life and art works, with colour illustrations, of Sisters Margaret and Pauline CR, and Sister Dorothy Raphael CSMV.) This is a coffee-table type book available in South Africa and the UK.

Community of the Sacred Name

CSN

Founded 1893

181 Barbadoes Street
Christchurch 8011
NEW ZEALAND
Tel: 03 366 8245
Fax: 03 366 8755

Email: comsacnm
@xtra.co.nz

The Community of the Sacred Name was founded in Christchurch in 1893 by Sister Edith (Deaconess). She was released from the Community of St Andrew in London to establish an indigenous community to respond to the needs of the colonial Church. A wide variety of   teaching, childcare and parish work has been undertaken over the years. Today there are three houses. Since 1966, the Sisters have run a large children's home in Fiji. In 1997, the Sisters undertook work in Tonga, helping in the Church in various ways. The mother house in Christchurch has a small retreat house. The major work is ecclesiastical embroidery. Underpinning all the work is a life of worship.

Other Addresses
St Christopher's Home, PO Box 8232, Nakasi, Suva, FIJI   *Tel: 679 341 0458*

PO Box 1824, Nuku'alofa, TONGA   *Tel: 27998*

Community History
Ruth Fry, *The Community of the Sacred Name - a Centennial History,* PPP Printers, PO Box 22.785, Christchurch, New Zealand, 1993

Morning Prayer
6.40 am

Mass
7.30 am

Terce   9.00 am

Midday Office
12 noon

Vespers   5.15 pm

Compline
7.30 pm

Office Book
Communities
Consultative Council

Community Wares:
Embroidery, cards,
vestments.

Bishops Visitor
Rt Revd
Victoria Matthews
&
Rt Revd Jabez Bryce,
Bishop of Polynesia

MOTHER KELENI CSN
(Mother Superior, assumed office 9 November 2006)
SISTER ANNE CSN *(Assistant)*

Sister Annette	Sister Malaea
Sister Brigid	Sister Manu
Sister Rose Ana	Sister Alena
Sister Lu'isa	Sister Fehoko
Sister Litia	Sister Vutulongo
Sister Mele	Sister Kalolaine
Sister Judith	Sister Sandra

Obituaries
16 Jun 2008   Sister Leona, aged 82, professed 55 years

Oblates and Associates
The Community has Oblates, men and women called by
God to live the contemplative life in the world.
We also have Companions, Associates, Friends of Polynesia
and the Guild of Help. These may be women or men,
priests or lay.

Guest and Retreat Facilities
There is a separate guest/ retreat house with fourteen
single rooms and one double for private or group retreats,
available to both men and women. NZ$25 per person per
night for bed and breakfast.
Write to Reverend Mother re bookings.

Community Publication
Community *Newsletter*, published at Easter, Holy Name
and Christmas.   Write to the Reverend Mother at the
Christchurch address.

Community of the Sacred Passion

CSP

Founded 1911

Convent of the Sacred
Passion
22 Buckingham Road
Shoreham-by-Sea
West Sussex
BN43 5UB
UK
Tel: 01273 453807
Email: communitysp
@yahoo.co.uk

Other Address
725 Wandsworth Road
London SW8 3JF
UK

Community History
Sister Mary Stella CSP,
She Won't Say 'No':
The History of the
Community of the Sacred
Passion
privately published,
1984.

**Most convenient time
to telephone**
4 pm - 7.30 pm.

Bishop Visitor
Rt Revd Ian Brackley
Bishop of Dorking

The Community was founded to serve Africa by a life of prayer and missionary work, bringing to Africans a knowledge of God's love. After the Community of St Mary of Nazareth and Calvary (CMM), which they nurtured, became self-governing, CSP withdrew from Tanzania and now offers encouragement, advice and financial support from England. Among other projects in Tanzania, the Sisters also collect money and goods for the Polio Hostel at Kwa Mkono, which they started, and which still helps disabled children, enabling them to be educated and become self-supporting. At Shoreham, the Sisters offer hospitality for small day events and accommodate various groups from the parish. They are involved in guidance of individuals and have contacts in the local community. The Sister in Clapham is involved in work as a member of the World Community for Christian Meditation, with contacts among people of various faiths. Prayer remains the foundation of the life of the Community.

MOTHER PHILIPPA CSP
(Revd Mother, assumed office 30 August 1999)
SISTER JACQUELINE CSP *(Deputy Superior)*

Sister Etheldreda	Sister Gillian Mary
Sister Dorothy	Sister Rhoda
Sister Thelma Mary	Sister Angela
Sister Mary Joan	Sister Lucia
Sister Joan Thérèse	Sister Mary Kathleen

Obituaries
5 Oct 07   Sister Phoebe, aged 78, professed 34 years
13 Jan 09   Sister Jean Margaret, aged 82,
                                professed 54 years

Oblates: Men and women who feel called to associate themselves with the aims of the community, by prayer and service, and by a life under a Rule. Their own Rule of Life will vary according to their particular circumstances. Oblates are helped and advised by the Oblates' Sister.

Associates: Men and women who share in the work of the community by prayer, almsgiving and service of some kind. They pray regularly for the community.

Priest Associates: Pray regularly for the community and offer Mass for it three times a year, of which one is Passion Sunday (the Sunday before Palm Sunday).

Friends: Pray regularly for the community and help it in any way they can.

All those connected with the community are prayed for daily by the Sisters and remembered by name on their birthdays. They receive the four-monthly intercession paper, and newsletter.

Guest and Retreat Facilities

One room with self-catering facilities in our smaller house, five minutes walk from the main house. Donations. Women only for overnight stay.

Community of St Andrew

CSA

Founded 1861

address for correspondence:
Mother Lillian CSA
34 Reynaud Court
Foxley Lane
Purley, Surrey
CR8 3EN
Tel: 020 8668 8401

Office Book
Common Worship -
Daily Prayer

Bishop Visitor
Rt Revd & Rt Hon
Richard Chartres,
Bishop of London

Registered Charity
No 244321

The founding of our Community was based on the dual vocation of life commitment in community, and in ordained ministry within the life of the Church. Our offering of prayer and worship is expressed in varied aspects of ministry. Our Associates are part of our extended Community family for whom we pray daily.

REVD MOTHER LILLIAN CSA *(deacon)*
(Mother Superior, assumed office 6 November 2000)
Revd Sister Donella CSA *(deacon)*
resident at 34 Reynaud Court, Foxley Lane, Purley, Surrey
CR8 3EN   *Tel: 020 8668 8401*

Revd Sister Teresa CSA *(priest)*
resident at St Andrew's House, 16 Tavistock Crescent,
London W11 1AP   *Tel: 020 7221 4604*
Email: teresajoan@btinternet.com

Sister Dorothy CSA *(deaconess)*
Revd Sister Denzil CSA *(priest) (Tel: 020 8995 1019)*
Revd Sister Patricia CSA *(deacon)*
resident at St Mary's Convent & Nursing Home,
Burlington Lane, Chiswick, London W4 2QE

Sister Pamela CSA *(deaconess)*
resident at 17 War Memorial Place, Harpsden Way,
Henley on Thames, Oxon RG9 1EP   *Tel: 01491 572224*

Community Publications

St Andrew's Review & *St Andrew's Newsletter*. Write to Sister Teresa.   *Distinctive Diaconate News* & *Distinctive News of Women in Ministry*, both edited by Sister Teresa CSA: for UK addresses, £2 each payable to 'Distinctive Diaconate'; for other postal zones, please enquire.

Community History

Henrietta Blackmore (ed), *The Beginnings of Women's Ministry*, Boydell & Brewer, Woodbridge, 2007.
ISBN: 9788433086

Community of St Clare

OSC

Founded 1950

St Mary's Convent
178 Wroslyn Road
Freeland
Witney
OX29 8AJ
UK
Tel: 01993 881225
Fax: 01993 882434

Email: community
@oscfreeland.co.uk

Morning Prayer
7.30 am

Eucharist
8.30 am

Midday Prayer
12.30 pm

Evening Prayer
5.30 pm

Night Prayer
8.00 pm

Office Book
The Daily Office SSF

Bishop Protector:
Rt Revd
Michael Perham,
Bishop of Gloucester

The Community of St Clare is part of the Society of St Francis. We are a group of women who live together needing each other's help to give our whole lives to the worship of God. Our service to the world is by our prayer, in which we are united with all people everywhere. We have a guest house so that others may join in our worship, and share the quiet and beauty with which we are surrounded. We try to provide for our own needs by growing much of our own food, and by our work of printing, wafer baking, writing and various crafts. This also helps us to have something material to share with those in greater need.

SISTER PAULA FORDHAM OSC
(Abbess, elected 30 January 2007)
SISTER ALISON FRANCIS HAMILTON OSC *(Assistant)*

Sister Damian Davies　　　Sister Mary Margaret
Sister Kathleen Marie Staggs　　　　　Broomfield
Sister Mary Kathleen Kearns　Sister Michaela Davis
　　　　　　　　　　　　Sister Susan Elisabeth Leslie

Obituaries
22 Oct 2008　　　Sister Elizabeth Farley,
　　　　　　　　　　aged 72, professed 15 years

Community Wares
Printing, cards, crafts, altar breads:

Guest and Retreat Facilities
Men, women and children are welcome at the guest house. It is not a 'silent house' but people can make private retreats if they wish. Eleven rooms (some twin-bedded). Donations, no fixed charge. Closed for two weeks mid-May and two weeks mid-September, and 16 Dec-8 Jan.
Please write to the Guest Sister at the Convent address.

Most convenient time to telephone:
6.00 pm - 7.00 pm - on Convent telephone: *01993 881225*

Address of the Guest House (for guests arriving)
The Old Parsonage, 168 Wroslyn Road, Freeland,
Witney OX29 8AQ, UK　　　*Tel: 01993 881227*

Community History
P Dunstan, *This Poor Sort*, DLT, London 1997, pp157-167

Community of St Francis

CSF

Founded 1905

UK Houses:

St Francis House
113 Gillott Road
Birmingham B16
0ET
Tel: 0121 454 8302
Email:
birminghamcsf
@franciscans.org.uk

St Francis Convent
Compton Durville
South Petherton
Somerset TA13 5ES
Tel: 01460 240473
Fax: 01460 242360
Email:
comptondurvillecsf
@franciscans.org.uk

Minister Provincial
Email: ministercsf@
franciscans.org.uk

St Matthew's House,
25 Kamloops
Crescent,
Leicester LE1 2HX
Tel: 0116 253 9158
Email: leicestercsf
@franciscans.org.uk

As Franciscan sisters, an autonomous part of the Society of St Francis, our primary vocation is to live the gospel in our time and in the places to which we are called. The setting for this is our life in community, under vows. Our wide range of backgrounds, abilities and gifts contributes to many ways of expressing the three elements of prayer, study and work. Prayer together and alone, with the Eucharist having a central place, is the heart of each house and each sister's life. Five of our sisters are priests; and three live the solitary life. Study nurtures our spiritual life and enables and enriches our ministries. Work includes the practical running of our houses and a wide range of ministries; currently these include hospitality, spiritual direction, prison chaplaincy, parish work and missions, preaching, leading quiet days and retreats, writing, being a presence in poor urban areas, nursing, and work with deaf blind people. Some of this work is salaried, much is voluntary. Each new sister brings her unique gifts, adding a new dimension to our life. As we move on into our second century, we are excited by the challenge of living the Franciscan life in the twenty-first century.

JOYCE CSF
(Minister General, assumed office 8 February 2002)

EUROPEAN PROVINCE

HELEN JULIAN CSF
(Minister Provincial, assumed office 8 February 2002)

Angela Helen	Maureen
Beverley	Moyra
Catherine Joy	Nan
Chris	Patricia Clare
Christine James	Phyllis
Elizabeth	Sue
Gina	Teresa
Gwenfryd Mary	
Hilary	*Novices: 1*
Jannafer	
Jennifer Chan	*Sisters resident in Korea*
Jenny Tee	Frances
Judith Ann	Jemma
Liz	

Obituaries
5 Apr 2008   Jennie, aged 64, professed 14 years

The Vicarage
11 St Mary's Road
Plaistow
London E13 9AE
Tel: 020 8552 4019
Email: stmaryscssf@
franciscans.org.uk

St Alphege Clergy
House, Pocock St
Southwark
London SE1 0BJ
Tel: 020 7928 8912
Email:
southwarkcsf@
franciscans.org.uk

Minister General
Email:
ministergeneralcsf
@franciscans.org.uk

Box 1003
Gumi Post Office
Gumi
Gyeongbukdo
730-021,
REPUBLIC OF KOREA
Tel: (054) 451 2317
Email: koreanfs
@hotmail.com

Website: www.
franciscans.org.uk

Office Book
Daily Office SSF

Bishop Protector
Rt Revd
Michael Perham,
Bishop of Gloucester

Registered Charity
No. 286615

Companions & Third Order
Companions are individual Christians who wish to associate themselves with the Society through prayer, friendship and in seeking to live the spirit of the Gospel in the way of St Francis. For more information about becoming a Companion contact the Secretary for Companions, Hilfield Friary, Dorchester, Dorset DT2 7BE, UK. For the Third Order SSF, see page 170.

Community Publication
franciscan, three times a year. Subscription: £7.00 per year. Write to the Editor of *franciscan*, The Friary of St Francis, Hilfield, Dorset DT2 7BE, UK.

Community History: Elizabeth CSF, *Corn of Wheat*, Becket Publications, Oxford, 1981.

Guest and Retreat Facilities
COMPTON DURVILLE
Guests are welcome, both men and women, in groups or as individuals. There are fourteen single rooms and two twin-bedded. A self-catering cottage, sleeping up to six, and a hermitage for one are also available. Day guests, as individuals or in groups of up to fifty, can also be accommodated. Further information and a programme of events led by sisters are available on request from the Guest Sister. It is also possible to make a longer stay, working alongside the community, as a working guest or Sojourner, for periods from a few days up to six months. For further information, please contact the Guardian.

AMERICAN PROVINCE

The Sisters came to the United States in 1974, and for over thirty years we have engaged in many types of ministry, but with special concern for the poor, the marginalized, and the sick. We can be found in hospitals and nursing homes; among the homeless, immigrants, and people with AIDS; teaching student deacons and serving on diocesan commissions; providing spiritual direction and directing retreats in parishes. In all things we strive to be instruments of God's love.

JEAN CSF
(*Minister Provincial, assumed office June 2004*)

Cecilia	Pamela Clare
Lynne	Ruth
Maggie	

US house:
St Francis House, 3743 Cesar Chavez St, **San Francisco**, CA 94110, USA
Tel: 415 824 0288   *Fax: 415 826 7569*   *Email: csfsfo@aol.com*

Website: www.communitystfrancis.org

Associates: Contact:Yvonne Koyzis Hook TSSF, Secretary for Associates, 37 North Main Street, Stewartstown, PA 17363, USA.

Community Wares: CSF Office Book, home retreat booklets, Franciscan prayer cards.

Community Publication: The Canticle.
Contact St Francis House to subscribe - $5 for two years.

Guest and Retreat Facilities
At the San Francisco house, there is a guest apartment, which has one bedroom (two beds) and a small kitchen.   It has its own entrance. The suggested cost is $40 per night.

Most convenient time to telephone: 9.00 am - 5.00 pm, 7.45 pm - 9.00 pm.

Office Book: CSF Office Book

Bishop Protector: Rt Revd Nedi Rivera, Bishop of Olympia

Community of St John Baptist
(UK)

CSJB

Founded 1852

The Priory
2 Spring Hill Road
Begbroke
Kidlington
Oxford
OX5 1RX
UK
Tel: 01865 855320
Fax: 01865 855336

Founded by Harriet Monsell and Thomas Thelluson Carter to help women rejected by the rest of society, we are now a Community of women who seek to offer our gifts to God in various ways. These include parish and retreat work, spiritual direction, and ministry to the elderly. Two sisters are ordained to the priesthood: one is associate minister in a nearby benefice; the other is chaplain to the homeless community in the centre of Oxford. Both preside regularly at the Community Eucharist. We have links with the Justice and Peace Movement and are specially committed to prayer for peace.

There are close links with the sisters of our affiliated community at Mendham, New Jersey, USA *(see separate entry).*

Daily life centres on the Eucharist and the Divine Office, and we live under the threefold vows of poverty, chastity and obedience. Following the Rule of St Augustine, we are encouraged to grow into 'an ever-deepening commitment of love for God and for each other as we strive to show forth the attractiveness of Christ to the world'.

Email: csjbteam
@csjb.org.uk

Website
www.csjb.org.uk

Morning Prayer
7.30 am

Tierce
9.00 am

Eucharist
9.15 am

Midday Office
12 noon

Evening Prayer
5.00 pm

Compline
8.30 pm (8.15 pm Sun)

Office Book
*Common Worship Daily
Prayer*, with our own
plainsong hymns and
antiphons.

Bishop Visitor
Rt Revd
John Pritchard
Bishop of Oxford

Registered Charity:
No 236939

SISTER MARY STEPHEN CSJB
SISTER ANNE CSJB
SISTER ANN VERENA CJGS *(co-opted)*
(Leadership Team, service of blessing 22 July 2004)

Sister Sheila   Sister Edna Frances
Sister Doreen   Sister Monica
Sister Jane Olive   Sister Elizabeth Jane

Obituaries
6 Oct 07   Sister Zoe, aged 75, professed 39 years

Oblates & Associates
CSJB has women oblates. Men and women may become
Associates or members of the Friends of Clewer - these
answer to a call to prayer and service while remaining
at home and work. This call includes a commitment
to their own spiritual life development and to active
church membership. Oblates, Associates and Friends
support the sisters by prayer and in other ways, and are
likewise supported by the Community, and are part of the
extended family of CSJB.

Community Wares
Cards, books, ribbon markers, Anglican prayer beads,
holding crosses.

Community Publication
Associates' Letter, three times a year. Contact the Leadership
team - payment by donation.

Community History
Books by Valerie Bonham, all published by CSJB:
   A Joyous Service: The Clewer Sisters and their Work (1989),
   A Place in Life: The House of Mercy 1849-1883 (1992),
   The Sisters of the Raj: The Clewer Sisters in India (1997).

Guest and Retreat Facilities
Nine single rooms (two ground floor) and one double
room. Private guests, small residential groups and larger
day groups welcomed. Facilities on the ground floor
have wheelchair access. Disabled guests are welcome if
accompanied by a carer. Details from the guest sister.
Tel: 01865 855327 Email: sisterjane@csjb.org.uk

Most convenient time to telephone:
10 am - 12 noon, 2.30 pm - 4.30 pm, 7 pm-8 pm, Mon to Sat.

Community of St John Baptist
(USA)

CSJB

Founded 1852 (in UK)
1874 (in USA)

PO Box 240 -
82 W. Main Street
Mendham, NJ 07945
USA
Tel: 973 543 4641
Fax: 973 543 0327
Email:
csjb@csjb.org

Website
www.csjb.org

Lauds 8.30 am

Eucharist 8..00 am

Terce 9.30 am

Noonday Office
12 noon

Vespers 5.45 pm

Compline 8.30 pm

Office Book
Our own book based
upon the Book of
Common Prayer of the
Episcopal Church of
the USA

The Community of St John Baptist was founded in England in 1852. The spirit of the Community is to "prepare the way of the Lord and make straight in the desert a highway for our God." We follow the call of our patron through a life of worship, community, and service.

Our Community is made up of monastic women, who share life together under the traditional vows of poverty, chastity and obedience. Our life includes daily participation in the Eucharist and the Divine Office, prayer, and ministry to those in need. We also have married or single Oblates, who commit themselves to a Rule of life and service in the Church, and Associates, who make up the wider family of CSJB.

We live by an Augustinian Rule, which emphasizes community spirit. Those who live with us include Oblates and friends, as well as our pony, dog, and cat. Our Retreat House and guest wing are often full of persons seeking spiritual direction and sacred space. Our buildings are set in a beautiful wooded area.

Our work includes spiritual direction, retreats, hospitality, youth ministry and chaplaincy. The Community participates in a mission in Africa, helps the homeless, and works in parishes.

SISTER BARBARA JEAN CSJB
(Sister Superior, assumed office 2 October 1997)
SISTER ELEANOR FRANCIS CSJB *(Assistant Superior)*
SISTER LAURA KATHARINE CSJB *(Novice Director)*

Sister Suzanne Elizabeth	Sister Deborah Francis
Sister Pamela	Sister Shane Margaret
Sister Mary Lynne	Sister Linda Clare
Sister Margo Elizabeth	Sister Lura Grace

Oblates & Associates
Oblates make promises which are renewed annually. The Rule of Life includes prayer, study, service, spiritual direction, retreats. Associates keep a simple Rule. Membership is ecumenical.

Address of other house
St Mary's Mission House, 145 W. 46th Street, New York, NY 10036, USA.
Tel: 212 869 5830

Community Publication
Michaelmas, Christmas & Easter Newsletters.

Community Wares
Tote bags, mugs, cards, jewelery, candles, ornaments, tapes, prayer beads.

Community History & Books
J. Simpson & E. Story, *Stars in His Crown*, Ploughshare Press, Sea Bright, NJ, 1976.

Books by Valerie Bonham, all published by CSJB:
  A Joyous Service: The Clewer Sisters and their Work (1989); *A Place in Life: The House of Mercy 1849-1883* (1992); *The Sisters of the Raj: The Clewer Sisters in India* (1997).

P Allan, M Berry, D Hiley, Pamela CSJB & E Warrell, *An English Kyriale*.

Guest and Retreat Facilities
ST MARGUERITE'S RETREAT HOUSE
This has twenty-five rooms. The address is the same as for the Convent but the telephone number is: *973 543 4582*

CONVENT GUEST WING
This has six rooms (for women only). The cost is $75.00 for an overnight stay with three meals. Closed Mon and Tue.

Most convenient time for guests to telephone: between 10 am and 4.45 pm.

Bishop Visitor: Rt Revd Herbert A Donovan, retired Bishop of Arkansas

---

Community of St John the Divine CSJD

Founded 1848

St John's House
652 Alum Rock Road
Birmingham B8 3NS
UK

Tel: 0121 327 4174

Email: csjdivine@
btinternet.com

Website
www.csjd.org.uk

The last thirty years have been a time of enormous evolutionary change within our Community. In the last five years, we have been studying in greater depth the essence of the Religious Life, so that we have wisdom and courage to go on further developing new patterns for living our life, that fit the culture of our time, and sharing it with others. Those coming to test their vocation in CSJD need to be women and men not afraid of the Community's exploration. Whilst the essence of Religious life is safeguarded and its intrinsic values remain the same, our lifestyle is changing significantly. We are praying there will be those who feel God calling them to a possible vocation in the Religious Life, who would be interested and challenged and like to know more. We would be delighted to meet you.

We are a centre of prayer within the diocese reflecting older examples of living the Religious life from earlier centuries, when Religious Houses were generous in sharing their life. We are a small Community living in the heart of a multicultural city here in Birmingham. The core Community forms the welcoming centre for a growing number of Associates, Alongsiders and others who share much of our life. Our Associates have a very close relationship with the Community. The programme for Alongsiders, running for some eight years, continues to be valued by those seriously wanting to deepen their spiritual life, or by those who for a variety of reasons need time and space to consider significant issues in their life.

Together our vision is to be: a growing centre of prayer within the Diocese; to exercise a ministry of hospitality to the many who come, either as individuals or as groups; to offer spiritual accompaniment; and to be more open to new ways in which God might use us here. New ministries are opening up such as building friendships with our Muslim neighbours and in complementary therapies such as reflexology. All of our ministries seek to reflect something of the ethos of our Community, which has broadened to cover all aspects of health, healing, reconciliation and pastoral care in its widest context, ministries that all seek in helping people find wholeness.

The underpinning of our life and work is a spirituality based on St John, the Apostle of love.

SISTER CHRISTINE CSJD & SISTER MARGARET ANGELA CSJD
(Leaders of the Community, assumed office April 2007)

Sister Teresa	Sister Elaine	Sister Shirley
Sister Marie-Clare	Sister Ivy	Sister Helen Alison

Obituaries
6 Nov 2008   Sister Dorien, aged 88, professed 51 years

Associates
Associates are men and women from all walks of life who desire to have a close link with the life and work of the Community. They make a simple Commitment to God, to the Community and to one another. Together with the Sisters, they form a network of love, prayer and service. (Guidelines available.)

Alongsiders
Alongsiders come to the Community for varying lengths of time, usually six months to one year. The aim is to provide an opportunity of sharing in the worship and life of the Community, and could be useful for a sabbatical, a time of spiritual renewal, study, to respond to a specific need, or to allow time and space to consider the way ahead. (Guidelines available.)

Community Wares: Various hand-crafted cards for different occasions.

Community Publication: *Annual Report*

Community History
The brochure written for the 150th anniversary contains a short history.

Guest and Retreat Facilities: Quiet Days for individuals and groups. Facilities for residential individual private retreats. Openness to be used as a resource.

Most convenient time to telephone: 9 am, 2.30 pm, 6 pm

Office Book: Celebrating Common Prayer

Bishop Visitor : Rt Revd David Urquhart, Bishop of Birmingham

Registered Charity: No. 210 254

Community of St John the Evangelist

CSJE

Founded 1912

St Mary's Home
Pembroke Park
Ballsbridge
Dublin 4
IRISH REPUBLIC

Tel: 668 3550

Meditation
6.50 am

Lauds
7.30 am

Terce
8.50 am

Mass
10.30 am (Fri only)

Sext & None
12 noon

Vespers
5.00pm

Compline
8.00 pm

Office Book:
Hours of Prayer with
the Revised Psalter

Founded in Dublin in 1912, CSJE was an attempt to establish Religious Life in the Church of Ireland, although it did not receive official recognition. The founder believed that a group of sisters living hidden lives of prayer and service would exercise a powerful influence.

From the 1930s, the Community had a branch house in Wales, which became the Mother House in 1967. In 1996, however, the Sisters returned to Dublin. The remaining Sisters of CSJE continue to live the Religious life to the best of their ability and leave the future in the hands of God.

SISTER ANN DORA CSJE
(*Sister Superior, assumed office February 2000*)
Sister Verity Anne
Sister Kathleen Brigid

Obituaries

14 Feb 2007	Sister Constance Audrey, aged 78, professed 48 years
8 May 2007	Sister Marcella Mary, aged 95, professed 73 years

Associates and Companions
Associates have a simple Rule, Companions a fuller and stricter Rule. Both groups are now much reduced in number.

Bp Visitor: Most Revd John Neill, Archbishop of Dublin

The chapel at St Mary's Home

Community of St Laurence

CSL

Founded 1874

Convent
of St Laurence
4A West Gate
Southwell
Notts, NG25 0JH
UK
Tel: 01636 814800

Registered Charity:
No. 220282

The Community was founded in 1874. The Sisters cared for the 'Treasures' of the Church - those in need of love and care, including elderly ladies. In 2001 the Community moved to a new purpose-built convent in Southwell, adjacent to Sacrista Prebend Retreat House and the Cathedral.

Sister Brenda
Sister Dorothea
Sister Margareta Mary

Associates
Associates pray regularly for the community, and include priests and lay people. We have over one hundred associates.

Guest & Retreat Facilties
None, but the convent is adjacent to the Sacrista Prebend Retreat House.

Office Book: CSL Office & Common Worship

Bishop Visitor
Bishop of Southwell & Nottingham

standing:

Sister Dorothea CSL

Father David Leaning
(Warden)

seated:

Sister
Margareta Mary CSL

Sister Brenda CSL

Community of St Mary
(Eastern Province)

CSM

Founded 1865

St Mary's Convent
242 Cloister Way
Greenwich
NY 12834-7922
USA

Tel: 518 692 3028
Fax: 518 692 3029

Email: compunun@
stmaryseast.org

Website
www.
stmaryseast.org

Matins   6.30 am
(7.30 am Sat & Sun)

Mass   7.00 am
(8.00 am Sat & Sun)

Terce   9.30 am

Sext   12 noon

Vespers   5.30 pm

Compline   7.30 pm

Bishop Visitor
Rt Revd William Love,
Bishop of Albany

The Sisters of St Mary live a vowed life in community, centered around the daily Eucharist and a five-fold Divine Office. Each sister has time daily for private prayer and study. Our way of life is a modern expression of traditional monastic practice including silent meals in common, plainchant in English for much of our corporate worship, a distinctive habit, and a measure of enclosure.

Our ministry is an outward expression of our vowed life of poverty, chastity and obedience. The specific nature of our work has changed over the years since Mother Harriet and our first sisters were asked to take charge of the House of Mercy in New York City in 1865. Being "mindful of the needs of others," as our table blessing says, we have been led in many ways to care for the lost, forgotten and underprivileged. Today our work is primarily hospitality, retreats, and exploration of outreach through the Internet. Sisters also go out from time to time to speak in parishes, lead quiet days and provide a praying community within the Diocese of Albany's Spiritual Life Center and the Diocese of Northern Malawi.

MOTHER MIRIAM CSM
(Mother Superior, assumed office 31 August 1996)
SISTER MARY JEAN CSM *(Assistant Superior)*

Sister Mary Angela
Sister Catherine Clare
Sister Mary Elizabeth
Sister Martha
Sister Monica

Sister Maria Nema

Juniors:
Sister Mary Emily
Sister Jane Chifundo

Novices: 3

Obituaries
15 Aug 2007   Sister Mary Basil, aged 94,
          professed 66 years, Mother Superior 1966-86
15 Sep 2008   Sister Mary Francis, aged 88,
                    professed 33 years
30 Sep 2008   Sister Mary Helen, aged 90,
                    professed 58 years
8 Dec 2008   Sister Anastasia, aged 94,
                    professed 67 years

Associates
Associates of the Community of St Mary are Christian men and women who undertake a Rule of life under the direction of the Community, and share in the support and fellowship of the Sisters, and of one another, whilst living dedicated and disciplined lives in the world. Any baptized, practising Christian who feels called to share in the life and prayer of the Community of St Mary as part of

our extended family is welcome to inquire about becoming an Associate. Each prospective Associate plans his or her own Rule with the advice of a Sister. An outline is provided covering one's share in the Eucharist and the Divine Office; a rule of private prayer; abstinence and fasting; and charity and witness. Individual vocations and circumstances vary so widely in today's world that a 'one size fits all' Rule is no longer appropriate. We do ask Associates to pray specifically for the Community, as we do for them, and, because the Divine Office is central to our way of life, to undertake some form of Daily Office. An Associate is also expected to keep in touch with us, and to seek to bring others to know the Community.

Address of other house: Sisters of St Mary, St Mary's Convent, PO Box 20280, Luwinga, Mzuzu 2, Malawi, South Central Africa

Office Book: The Monastic Diurnal Revised, (The Community of St Mary, New York, 1989): a modern English version of the *Monastic Diurnal* by Canon Winfred Douglas with supplemental texts based upon the American 1979 Book of Common Prayer. Copies are for sale.

Community Publication
St Mary's Messenger. Contact the subscriptions editor. Cost to subscribers in the USA is $5, to those outside the USA $10.

Community History
Sister Mary Hilary CSM, *Ten Decades of Praise,* DeKoven Foundation, Racine, WI, 1965. (*out of print*).

Community Wares: Assorted illuminated greeting cards..

Guest and Retreat Facilities
Accommodations for seven in the Convent Guest wing and a further fifty accommodations on first-come, first-serve basis at adjacent Spiritual Life Center, in Greenwich, NY.
Most convenient time to telephone: 10 am - 7 pm Eastern time

Community of St Mary (Western Province)

CSM

Founded 1865

Website: www.marysmargin.com

The Western Province of the Community of St Mary was set apart as a separate branch of the community in 1904. We share a common Rule, but have separate administration. Our basic orientation is toward a life of prayer, corporate and personal, reaching out to the Church and the world according to the leading of the Holy Spirit. We live singly or in small groups, each sister using her gifts for ministry as she feels led with the support of the whole group. Mary's Margin is the main house of the Western Province. We offer hospitality to individuals for private retreats and to small groups for meetings and quiet days. The sisters are available as spiritual companions on request. Other Margin offerings include Transformation Game workshops, quarterly drum circles, and a unique outdoor labyrinth winding through woods and meadows.

Mary's Margin
S83 W27815
BeaverTrail,
Mukwonago
WI 53149
USA
Tel: 262 363 8489

Email: srstmary@
marysmargin.com
or
CSM@
marysmargin.com

The Farm
S82 W27570
Johnson Ave
Mukwonago, WI
53149
USA
Tel: 262 363 5856

Meditation   7.00 am

Morning Prayer
7.30 am

Eucharist
8.00 am (Sun)

Meditation   5.00 pm

Evening Prayer
8.00 pm

Office Book
Book of Common
Prayer
of the ECUSA

Bishop Visitor:
to be appointed

SISTER LETITIA PRENTICE CSM
(*President, assumed office January 1992*)
SISTER DORCAS BAKER CSM (*Vice President*)
Sister Mary Faith Burgess
Sister Jean Hodgkins
Sister Mary Paula Bush
Sister Mary Grace Rom

Associates
Associates (both men and women) are part of the community family. They follow a Rule of Life and assist the sisters as they are able.

Inner-peace Corps is a program for students or people in transition for whom a year or two of manual labor interwoven with prayer and labyrinthine contemplation would help to go back into the world with more focus and joy. At present we have space for only one candidate at a time (woman or man). (S)he works with the sisters and shares in the life and ministry of the house.

Community Publication
St Mary's Messenger. This is sent out once a year. There is no charge. Write to the community address.

Community History and books
Morgan Dix, *Harriet Starr Cannon,* Longmans, Green & Co, New York, 1896.
Sister Mary Hilary CSM, *Ten Decades of Praise*, DeKoven Foundation, Racine, WI, 1965.
Robert Boak Slocum & Travis Talmadge DuPriest (eds), "*To Hear Celestial Harmonies*", Forward Movement Pubs., Cincinnati, OH, 2002.
All three of these books, and other historical resources, may be accessed via the 'About Us' button on the community's website.

Guest and Retreat Facilities
We welcome both men and women guests. There are 3 single spaces in the main house for overnight guests plus 2 hermitages (with heat, no plumbing). There are also 2 double rooms in the farm house which is a 7-minute walk from Mary's Margin. The cost is $60 per day (3 meals and 1 overnight). Day groups up to 12 can be accommodated at Mary's Margin. The cost is $15 per person. A deposit of $10 per person must accompany group reservations. Day groups up to 20 can be accommodated at the Club House on the farm. No meal service is provided, but there is a full kitchen available or people may bring bag lunches. The cost is $10 per person.

Community of St Mary
(Southern Province)

CSM

Founded 1865

1100 St Mary's Lane
Sewanee
TN 37375
USA

Tel: 931 598 0802
or
931 598 0046
Fax: 931 598 9519

Email: sisofchr@
hotmail.com

**Morning Prayer
& Holy Eucharist**
7.00 am
(8.00 am Holy Eucharist
Sat & Sun)

Noonday Prayer
12 noon
(12.30 pm Sun)

Evening Prayer
5.00 pm

Compline 7.00 pm
(not Sat & Sun)

Office Book
BCP of the ECUSA
plus Plainsong Psalter,
Book of Canticles

The Community of St Mary began in New York in 1865. It was the first women's monastic community founded in the United States, and now has three provinces. The Southern Province has its mother house in Sewanee, Tennessee, and a branch house in the Mountain Province, Philippines.

The primary focus of our life together is prayer and worship. The sisters gather four times a day for corporate prayer. We also nourish ourselves spiritually through meditation, spiritual reading, Bible study and retreats.

The sisters take the three-fold vows of simplicity, chastity and obedience. We live in community and hold all things in common. We choose to live a simple life and endeavour to treat God's creation with care. Hospitality and mission are important components of our community's life.

SISTER LUCY CSM
(Sister-in-charge)
(Election due August 2009)

Sister Elizabeth Grace
Sister Julian Hope
Sister Madeleine Mary   *Sisters in Philippines:*
Sister Mary Martha   Sister Ines
Sister Mary Zita   Sister Evelyn
Sister Miriam
Sister Margaret
Sister Mary Hope

Obituaries
7 Mar 2005   Sister Madeleine, aged 90,
                              professed 21 years
14 Nov 2005   Sister Mary Demetria, aged 75,
                              professed 40 years

Associates and Oblates
ASSOCIATES are a fellowship of men and women who help CSM through friendship, prayer, support and by their dedicated lives in the world. Each associate writes his/her own rule of life, according to guidelines.
We offer associates hospitality, retreats and spiritual companionship.

OBLATES are a fellowship of men and women who pattern their lives on the monastic tradition of prayer and service. Oblates work closely with the sisters.

Other Address
St Mary Convent, Marycroft, Banga'an, 2619 Sagada, Mountain Province, PHILIPPINES

Community wares
Photo cards, hand-painted note cards, rosaries (Anglican & Dominican)

Community publication
The Messenger

Community History
Sister Mary Hilary CSM, *Ten Decades of Praise,* DeKoven Foundation, Racine, WI, 1965

Guest and Retreat Facilities
St Dorothy's guest house

Most convenient time to telephone
Mon-Sat, 9.30 am - 11.30 am, 2 pm - 5 pm

Bishop Visitor: Rt Revd John Bauerschmidt, Diocese of Tennessee

Community of St Mary the Virgin

CSMV

Founded 1848

St Mary's Convent
Challow Road,
Wantage
Oxfordshire
OX12 9DJ
UK
Tel: 01235 763141

Email:
conventsisters
@csmv.co.uk

Website
www.csmv.co.uk

Lauds
7.00 am

Terce   9.45 am
(9.15 am Sun
& principal feasts)

Eucharist   10.00 am
(9.30 am Sun
& principal feasts)

Sext   12.30 pm

Vespers
5.00 pm

Compline
8.30 pm

The Community of St Mary the Virgin was founded in 1848 by William John Butler, then Vicar of Wantage. As Sisters, we are called to respond to our vocation in the spirit of the Blessed Virgin Mary: "Behold, I am the handmaid of the Lord. Let it be to me according to your word." Our common life is centred on the worship of God through the Eucharist, the daily Office and in personal prayer. From this all else flows. For some it will be expressed in outgoing ministry in neighbourhood and parish, or in living alongside those in inner city areas. For others, it will be expressed in spiritual direction, preaching and retreat giving, in creative work in studio and press, or in other forms of ministry. Sisters also live and work among the elderly at St Katharine's House, our Care Home in Wantage.

The Community has had a share in the nurturing and training of a small indigenous community in Madagascar *(see entry for FMJK)*. It was also in India and South Africa for many years. Involvement with these countries remains through 'Wantage Overseas'. Our links with South Africa are maintained by the groups of Oblates and Associates living there.

Other Addresses
St Katharine's House, Ormond Road, Wantage, Oxfordshire OX12 8EA, UK   *Tel: 01235 767380*

366 High Street, Smethwick, B66 3PD, UK
                                                      Tel: 0121 558 0094

116 Seymour Road, Harringay, London N8 0BG, UK
                                                      Tel & fax: 020 8348 3477

Community History
A Hundred Years of Blessing, SPCK, London, 1946.

Community Wares
The Printing Press offers a variety of cards and plainchant music. Orders are not received for cards, which may be purchased at the Convent.   *Email: press@csmv.co.uk*
A variety of other items made by sisters are for sale in the Reception Area.

Office Book: CSMV Office

Bishop Visitor: Rt Revd John Pritchard, Bishop of Oxford

Registered Charity: No 240513

MOTHER WINSOME CSMV
(The Reverend Mother, assumed office 8 December 2006)
SISTER DEIRDRE MICHAEL CSMV *(The Assistant)*

Sister Cecily Clare	Sister Enid Mary	Sister Valerie
Sister Hilda Kathleen	Sister Helen Philippa	Sister Barbara Claire
Sister Margaret Jean	Sister Valeria	Sister Mary Clare
Sister Joan Elizabeth	Sister Phoebe Margaret	Sister Stella
Sister Christiana	Sister Mary Jennifer	Sister Francis Honor
Sister Barbara Noreen	Sister Jean Mary	Sister Patricia Ann
Sister Yvonne Mary	Sister Christine Ann	Sister Anna
Sister Louise	Sister Rosemary	Sister Barbara Anne
Sister Margaret Verity	Sister Bridget Mary	Sister Trudy
Sister Anne Mary	Sister Eileen	Sister Rachel
Sister Anne Julian	Sister Betty	Sister Elizabeth Jane
Sister Ethne Ancilla	Sister Rosemary Clare	Sister Pauline
Sister Catherine Naomi	Sister Sheila Mary	Sister Alison Joy
Sister Honor Margaret	Sister Lorna	

Obituaries

17 Jun 2007	Sister Hilary, aged 82, professed 53 years
17 Apr 2008	Sister Margaret Elizabeth, aged 81, professed 46 years
17 Mar 2009	Sister Margaret Julian, aged 94, professed 60 years

Oblates

The Oblates of the Community respond to their vocation in the same spirit as Mary: "Behold, I am the handmaid of the Lord. Let it be to me according to your word." Oblates may be married or single women or men, ordained or lay. Most are Anglicans, but members of other denominations are also welcomed. There is a common Rule, based on Scripture and the Rule of St Augustine, and each Oblate also draws up a personal Rule of Life in consultation with the Oblates' Sister. There is a two-year period of testing as a Novice Oblate; the Promise made at Oblation is renewed annually. In addition to a close personal link with the Community, Oblates meet in regional groups and support each other in prayer and fellowship.

Associates

Associates are men and women, ordained and lay, who wish to be united in prayer and fellowship with the Community, sharing in the spirit of Mary's 'Fiat' in their daily lives. Each Associate keeps a personal Rule of Life, undertakes regular prayer for the Community, is expected to keep in touch with the Associates' Sister, and to make an annual retreat. The Community sends out a quarterly letter with an intercession leaflet. Every two years an Associates' Day is held at the Convent.

Guest and Retreat Facilities

ST MARY'S CONVENT GUEST WING: The Sisters welcome to the Guest Wing those who wish to spend time in rest, retreat and silence within the setting of a Religious Community. Our particular emphasis is on hospitality to individuals, and where requested we try to arrange individual guidance with a Sister. We are able to accommodate a small number of groups for Retreats and Quiet Days. Guests are welcome to attend the Community's daily Eucharist and Office.

Accommodation: eleven single rooms, one twin, and one ground floor single for the disabled. Facilities include a large Prayer Room, a Library Sitting Room, and an Art Room for the use of guests. There is also a Meeting Room with kitchenette attached, which can accommodate Day Groups of up to fifteen. There is no set charge, but a donation of £29 per night for full board is suggested.

Tel: 01235 763141 / 774075   Email: *guestwing@csmv.co.uk*

Most convenient time to telephone: 11.00 am - 12.15 pm, & 5.45 pm - 6.30 pm

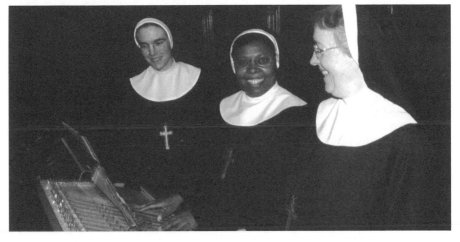

Mother Winsome (centre) and CSMV sisters with a zither

Community of the Servants of the Cross

CSC

Founded 1877

St Katharine's House
Ormond Road
Wantage
Oxfordshire

The Community has an Augustinian Rule and for much of its history cared for elderly and infirm women. In 1997, because of decreasing numbers, the convent at Lindfield (Sussex) was sold and the Mother House moved to the former theological college at Chichester, which had by then become a retirement home. There they continued their pastoral work and used the former college chapel for Mass and Offices. In July 2004, there were only two members of the community left and it was decided that they should move for the last time to be with their 'home community', St Mary the Virgin at Wantage, where they live at St Katharine's House.

MOTHER ANGELA CSC
(Mother Superior, assumed office October 1995)
Sister Jane

Bp Visitor: Rt Revd John Hind, Lord Bishop of Chichester

Warden
Father John Lyon, The Vicarage, 33 Vicarage Lane, East Preston, Littlehampton, BN16 2SP   Tel: 01903 783318

Community of St Michael & All Angels

CSM&AA

Founded 1874

St Michael's House
PO Box 79
9300 Bloemfontein
SOUTH AFRICA

Tel: 051 401 5721

Mass is celebrated
five days a week.

Office Book
Anglican Prayer
Book 1989, of the
Church of the
Province of Southern
Africa

Bishop Visitor
Rt Revd E P Glover,
Bishop of
Bloemfontein

Warden
Rt Revd T S Stanage,
retired Bishop of
Bloemfontein

The Community of St Michael and All Angels was founded by the second Bishop of Bloemfontein, Allan Becher Webb, for pioneer work in his vast diocese, which included the Orange Free State, Basutoland, Griqualand West and into the Transvaal. The sisters were active in mission, nursing and education. Sister Henrietta Stockdale became the founder of professional nursing in South Africa. The South African Synod of Bishops has placed her on the *CPSA Calendar* for yearly commemoration on 6 October. In 1874, the sisters established St Michael's School for Girls in Bloemfontein, which still exists today as one of the leading schools in South Africa.

CSM&AA continues with St Michael's Relief work in the Bloemfontein informal settlements, meeting with the workers, and supporting it with regular financial help.

Today, there is one sister remaining.

Sister Joan Marsh

Associates

The Associates of CSM&AA in South Africa meet four or five times a year. They keep a simple Rule and have an annual residential retreat in the country at a Roman Catholic religious house and farm in the Eastern Free State.

Community History

Margaret Leith, *One the Faith*, 1971.
Mary Brewster, *One the Earnest Looking Forward*, 1991.
Obtainable from St Michael's School, PO Box 12110, Brandhof 9324, SOUTH AFRICA.

Booklets by Sister Mary Ruth:
Dust & Diamonds (on work in Kimberley),
Cave, Cows & Contemplation
                    (on work at Modderpoort Mission)
Ma'Mohau, Mother of Mercy (on Sister Enid CSM&AA)
Medals for St Michael's (CSM&AA in Anglo-Boer War)
Uphill all the Way (on work in Basutoland/Lesotho)
Obtainable from PO Box 79, 9300 Bloemfontein, South Africa

Community Wares

Handmade notelets and greeting cards.

Community of St Peter CSP

Founded 1861

St Peter's Convent
c/o St Columba's
House
Maybury Hill
Woking, Surrey
GU22 8AB
UK

Tel: 01483 750739
(9.30 am - 5 pm
Mon-Thu)
Fax: 01483 766208

Email:
reverendmother@
stpetersconvent.
co.uk

Office Book
Celebrating Common
Prayer

Bishop Visitor:
Rt Revd David Walker,
Bishop of Dudley

Community History
Elizabeth Cuthbert,
In St Peter's Shadow,
CSP, Woking, 1994

Registered Charity:
No. 240675

The Community was founded by Benjamin Lancaster, a Governor of St George's Hospital, Hyde Park, London. He wished his poorer patients to have convalescent care before returning to their homes. The Sisters also nursed cholera and TB patients, and opened orphanages and homes for children and the elderly. They were asked by priests to help in the parish and they were asked to go to Korea in 1892. They have close links with the Society of the Holy Cross in Korea, which was founded by the Community *(see separate entry).*

Since the closure of their Nursing/Care Home, new work is undertaken outside the Community in the way of continued care, using Sisters' abilities, talents and qualifications in nursing, counselling and social work. The Sisters live in houses located where they can carry out their various works and ministry. They recite their fourfold daily Office either together in their houses or individually within their work place.

REVD MOTHER LUCY CLARE CSP
(Mother Superior, assumed office 29 June 2006)
(St Columba's House address)

Sister Caroline Jane *(Assistant Superior)*
(The Flat, St Peter's Church Hall, Laleham Road, Staines, TW18 2DS)

St Mary's Convent & Nursing Home, Burlington Lane, Chiswick, London W4 2QE:
Sister Margaret Paul   Sister Rosamond

41 Sandy Lane, Woking, Surrey, GU22 8BA:
Sister Angela   Sister Georgina Ruth

Obituaries
21 Oct 2007   Sister Constance Margaret,
aged 88, professed 58 years

Associates and Companions
The associates' fellowship meets at St Columba's at Petertide. The associates support the community in prayer and with practical help, as they are able. They have a simple rule and attend the Eucharist in their own Church as their individual commitments permit. Companions have a stricter rule and say the daily Office.

Community Publication
Associates' newsletter at Petertide and Christmas; a quarterly letter sent by Reverend Mother, spring and autumn.

Guest and Retreat Facilities
St Columba's House *(Retreat & Conference Centre)*, Maybury Hill, Woking, Surrey
   GU22 8AB, UK   Director: Revd Owen Murphy
  Tel: 01483 766498   Fax: 01483 740441   Email: director@stcolumbashouse.org.uk
Most convenient time to telephone: 9.30 am - 5.00 pm.
   Twenty-two single bedrooms, four twin bedrooms and a disabled suite. A programme of individual and group Retreats. Also a Conference centre for residential and day use. Complete refurbishment by summer 2009 for retreatants, parish groups, and day/overnight consultations. An outstanding liturgical space with a pastoral, and liturgical programme. A place to retreat and reflect on life's journey.

Community of St Peter, Horbury

CSPH

Founded 1858

St Peter's Convent
Dovecote Lane
Horbury
Wakefield
West Yorkshire
WF4 6BD
UK
Tel: 01924 272181

Email:
stpetersconvent@
btconnect.com

The Community seeks to glorify God by a life of loving dedication to him, by worship and by serving him in others. A variety of pastoral work is undertaken including retreat and mission work, social work and ministry to individuals in need. The spirit of the community is Benedictine and the recitation of the Divine Office central to the life.

MOTHER ROBINA CSPH
(Revd Mother, assumed office 14 Apr 1993)
SISTER ELIZABETH CSPH *(Assistant Superior)*

Sister Gwynneth Mary   Sister Phyllis
Sister Margaret   Sister Jean Clare
Sister Mary Clare *(priest)*

Sister Margaret Ann,
2 Main Street, Bossall, York YO2 7NT, UK
Tel: 01904 468253

Obituary
25 Aug 2008   Sister Monica, aged 84, professed 34 years

Oblates and Associates
The Community has both oblates and associates.

Community Publication: Annual Review: *Keynotes*

Guest and Retreat Facilities: A separate guest wing has four single rooms, with shower room and utility room.

Bishop Visitor: Rt Revd Stephen Platten,
                            Bishop of Wakefield

Lauds	**Midday Office**	
7.30 am	12.00 noon	**Compline**
Mass	**Vespers**	8.30 pm
8.00 am	6.00 pm	

Community of the Servants of the Will of God

CSWG

Founded 1953

The Monastery of
the Holy Trinity
Crawley Down
Crawley
West Sussex
RH10 4LH
UK
Tel: 01342 712074

Email:
(for guests bookings
& enquiries)
brother.andrew@
cswg.org.uk

Vigils	5.00 am
Lauds	7.00 am
Terce	9.30 am
Sext	12.00 noon
None	1.45 pm
Vespers	6.30 pm

Mass
7.00 pm Mon – Fri
11.00 am Sat & Sun

This monastery is set in woodland with a small farm attached. The Community lives a contemplative life, uniting silence, work and prayer in a simple life style based on the Rule of St Benedict. The Community is especially concerned with uniting the traditions of East and West, and has developed the Liturgy, Divine Office and use of the Jesus Prayer accordingly. It now includes women living under the same monastic Rule.

FATHER COLIN CSWG
(Father Superior, assumed office 3 April 2008)

Father Gregory   Brother John of the Cross
Father Brian   Brother Andrew
Brother Martin
Sister Mary Angela
Father Peter
Brother Christopher Mark

Associates
The associates keep a rule of life in the spirit of the monastery.

Community Publication
CSWG Journal: *Come to the Father*, issued Pentecost and All Saints. Write to the Monastery of the Holy Trinity.

Community History
Father Colin CSWG, *A History of the Community of the Servants of the Will of God*, 2002. Available from Crawley Down.

Guest and Retreat Facilities
Six individual guest rooms; meals in community refectory; Divine Office and Eucharist, all with modal chant; donations c.£15 per day.

Most convenient time to telephone: 9.30 am - 6.00 pm.

Community Wares
Mounted icon prints, Jesus Prayer ropes, candles and vigil lights, booklets on monastic and spiritual life.

Office Book
CSWG Divine Office and Liturgy

Bishop Visitor: Rt Revd John Hind, Bishop of Chichester

Community of the Sisters of the Church

CSC

Founded 1870

for the whole people of God

Worldwide Community Website: www. sistersofthechurch .org

ENGLAND
Registered Charity No. for CSC:
271790
Registered Charity No. for CEA:
200240

CANADA
Registered Charity No. 130673262RR0001

AUSTRALIA
Tax Exempt - NPO

Founded by Emily Ayckbowm in 1870, the Community of the Sisters of the Church is an international body of lay and ordained women within the Anglican Communion. We are seeking to be faithful to the gospel values of Poverty, Chastity and Obedience, and to the traditions of Religious Life while exploring new ways of expressing them and of living community life and ministry today. By our worship, ministry and life in community, we desire to be channels of the reconciling love and acceptance of Christ, to acknowledge the dignity of every person, and to enable others to encounter the living God whom we seek.

The Community's patrons, St Michael and the Angels, point us to a life both of worship and active ministry, of mingled adoration and action. Our name, Sisters of the Church, reminds us that our particular dedication is to the mystery of the Church as the Body of Christ in the world.

Each house has its own timetable of corporate worship. The Eucharist and Divine Office (usually fourfold) are the heart of our Community life.

The current houses in England provide different expressions of our life and ministry in inner city, suburban, coastal town and village setting.

LINDA MARY SHUTTLE CSC
(Mother Superior, assumed office July 2009)
Email: lindacsc@ausnet.net.au
29 Lika Drive, Kempsey, NSW 2440, AUSTRALIA

ENGLAND

SUSAN HIRD CSC
(UK Provincial, assumed office September 2008)
Email: susan@sistersofthechurch.org.uk

CATHERINE HEYBOURN CSC *(Assistant Provincial)*

Aileen Taylor	Mary Josephine Thomas
Anita Cook	Rosina Taylor
Ann Mechtilde Baldwin	Ruth Morris
Annaliese Brogden	Ruth White
Beryl Hammond	Scholastica Ferris
Dorothea Roden	Sheila Julian Merryweather
Elspeth Rennells	Sue McCarten
Hilda Mary Baumberg	Teresa Mary Wright
Jennifer Cook	Vivien Atkinson
Judith Gray	
Lydia Corby	*Novices:* 1
Marguerite Gillham	

Addresses in the UK
St Michael's Convent, 56 Ham Common, Richmond, Surrey TW10 7JH
Tel: 020 8940 8711 & 020 8948 2502   Fax: 020 8948 5525
        Email: info@sistersofthechurch.org.uk

82 Ashley Road, Bristol BS6 5NT   *Tel: 01179 413268   Fax: 01179 086620*

St Gabriel's, 27A Dial Hill Road, Clevedon, N. Somerset BS21 7 HL
Tel: 01275 544471

10 Furness Road , West Harrow, Middlesex HA2 0RL   *Tel & Fax: 020 8423 3780*

112 St Andrew's Road North, St Anne's-on-Sea, Lancashire FY8 2JQ
Tel & Fax: 01253 728016

Well Cottage, Upper Street, Kingsdown, near Deal, Kent CT14 8BH
For retreats and holidays, Email: wellcottage@sistersofthechurch.org.uk

CANADA
Arrived in Canada 1890.   Established as a separate Province 1965.

MARGUERITE MAE EAMON CSC
(Provincial, assumed office September 2003)
Email: margueritecsc@sympatico.ca

| Elizabeth Nicklin | Heather Broadwell | Michael Trott |
| (Benedetta) | Margaret Hayward | Rita Dugger |

Obituaries
14 Nov 2008   Mary Adela Carthew, aged 96, professed 65 years

Addresses in Canada
St Michael's House, 1392 Hazelton Boulevard, Burlington, Ontario L7P 4V3
        Tel: 905 332 9240   Email: sistersofthechurch@sympatico.ca

AUSTRALIA
Arrived in Australia 1892.   Established as a separate Province 1965.

LINDA MARY SHUTTLE CSC
(Provincial, assumed office November 1999)
Email: lindacsc@ausnet.net.au

Addresses in Australia
| Audrey Floate | Fiona Cooper | Helen Jamieson |
| Elisa Helen Waterhouse | Frances Murphy | Rosamund Duncan |

Sisters of the Church, 29 Lika Drive, Kempsey, NSW 2440
        Tel: 2 6562 2313   Fax: 2 6562 2314   Email: infoaus@sistersofthechurch.org

PO Box M191, Missenden Road, NSW 2050
        Tel & Fax: 2 9516 2407   Email: francescsc@bigpond.com

Unit 15/75 St John's Road, Glebe, NSW 2037	*Tel & Fax: 2 9660 8020*
Apt 310/99 River Street, South Yarra, Victoria 3141	*Tel & Fax: 3 9827 1658*
PO Box 713, Melton, Victoria 3337	*Tel: 3 9743 6028*

Email: elisacsc@tpg.com.au

SOLOMON ISLANDS

Arrived in Solomon Islands 1970. Established as a separate Province 2001.

KATHLEEN KAPEI CSC
(Provincial, assumed office 26 September 2004)
Email: kkapei@yahoo.com.au
PHYLLIS SAU CSC *(Assistant Provincial)*
Email: phyllissauu@yahoo.co.uk

Agnes Maeusia	Florence Sakua	Priscilla Iolani
Anna Caroline Vave	Florence Toata	Rachel Teku
Anneth Kagoa	Helen Namoi	Rebecca Margaret Sulupi
Annie Meke	Janet Karane	Rose Glenda Kimanitoro
Beglyn Tiri	Jennifer Clare	Rose Houte'e
Belinda Seai	Jessica Maru	Roselyn Tego
Caroline Havideni	Joan Yupe	Roselyn Tengea
Daisy Gaoka	Joanna Suunorua	Ruth Hope Sosoke
Dorah Palmer	Lilian Mary Manedika	Selina Selimaoma
Doreen Awaisi	Lucia Sadias	Sharon Amani
Elenor Ataki	Margosa Funu	Veronica Vasethe
Emily Mary Ikai	Mary Gladis Nunga	Vivian Marie
Esther Teku	Mary Judith Tongisetonu	Von Amevuvlian
Evelyn Yaiyo	Mary Leingala	
Faith Mary Maiva	Muriel Tisafa'a	*Novices: 17 Postulants: 7*
Florence Mola	Patricia Kalali	

Obituaries
14 Mar 2009   Mavis O'Omaea, aged 28, professed 1 year

Addresses in the Solomon Islands
Tetete ni Kolivuti, Box 510, Honiara

PO Box A7, Auki, Malaita   *Tel: 40423*

Patteson House, Box 510, Honiara
Tel: 22413   Fax: 27582   Email: csc@welkam.solomon.com.sb

St Gabriel's, c/o Hanuato'o Diocese, Kira Kira, Makira/Ulawa Province   *Fax: 50128*

St Mary's, Luesalo, Diocese of Temotu, Santa Cruz

St Scholastica's House, PO Box 510, Honiara

Associates
Associates are men and women who seek to live the Gospel values of Simplicity, Chastity and Obedience within their own circumstances. Each creates his/her own Rule of Life and has a Link Sister or Link House. They are united in spirit with CSC in its life of worship and service, fostering a mutually enriching bond.

Community History
A Valiant Victorian: The Life and Times of Mother Emily Ayckbowm 1836-1900 of the Community of the Sisters of the Church, Mowbray, London, 1964.

Ann M Baldwin CSC, *Now is the Time: a brief survey of the life and times of the Community of the Sisters of the Church,* CSC, 2005.

Community Publication:
Newsletter, twice a year, the editor of which is Sister Judith (St Michael's Convent, UK, address, *Email: judith@sistersofthechurch.org.uk*). Information can be obtained from any house in the community and by email.

Community Wares
Books by Sister Sheila Julian Merryweather: *Colourful Prayer; Colourful Advent; Colourful Lent.* All published by Kevin Mayhew, Buxhall, Stowmarket.
Some houses sell crafts and cards. Vestments are made in the Solomon Islands.

Guest and Retreat Facilities
Hospitality is offered in most houses. Ham Common and Tetete ni Kolivuti have more accommodation for residential guests as well as day facilities. Programmes are offered at Ham Common: please apply for details. Please contact individual houses for other information.

Office Book used by the Community
The Office varies in the different Provinces. Various combinations of the Community's own Office book, the New Zealand psalter, the UK *Common Worship* and the most recent prayer books of Australia, Canada and Melanesia are used.

Bishops Visitor
UK   Rt Revd Peter Price, Bishop of Bath and Wells
Australia   *To be appointed*
Canada   Rt Revd Michael Bird, Bishop of Niagara
Solomon Islands Rt Revd Dr Terry Brown, Bishop of Malaita

Address of Affiliated Community: Community of the Love of God (*Orthodox Syrian*) Nazareth, Kadampanad South 691553, Pathanamthitta District, Kerala, INDIA
Tel: 473 4822146

Community of the Sisters of the Love of God

SLG

Founded 1906

Convent
of the Incarnation
Fairacres
Parker Street
Oxford   OX4 1TB
UK
Tel: 01865 721301
Fax: 01865 250798
Email:
sisters@slg.org.uk
Guest Sister:
guests@slg.org.uk

Website
www.slg.org.uk

Matins
6.00 am (6.15 am Sun)

Terce & Mass
9.05 am

Sext   12.15 pm

None
2.05 pm (3.05 pm Sun)

Vespers   5.30 pm

Compline   8.05 pm

Office Book
SLG Office

A contemplative community with a strong monastic tradition founded in 1906, which seeks to witness to the priority of God and to respond to the love of God - God's love for us and our love for God. We believe that we are called to live a substantial degree of withdrawal, in order to give ourselves to a spiritual work of prayer which, beginning and ending in the praise and worship of God, is essential for the peace and well-being of the world.   Through offering our lives to God within the Community, and through prayer and daily life together, we seek to deepen our relationship with Jesus Christ and one another. The Community has always drawn upon the spirituality of Carmel; life and prayer in silence and solitude is an important dimension in our vocation. The Community also draws from other traditions; therefore our Rule is not specifically Carmelite. Another important ingredient is an emphasis on the centrality of Divine Office and Eucharist together in choir, inspired partly by the Benedictine way of life.

SISTER MARGARET THERESA SLG
(Revd Mother, assumed office 24 June 2007)
SISTER CATHERINE SLG *(Prioress)*

Sister Josephine	Sister Helen Columba
Sister Mary Magdalene	Sister Julie
Sister Mary Margaret	Sister Shirley Clare
Sister Benedicta	Sister Avis Mary
Sister Isabel	Sister Alison
Sister Adrian	Sister Tessa
Sister Anne	Sister Raphael
Sister Jane Frances	Sister Barbara
Sister Mary Kathleen	Sister Stephanie Thérèse
Sister Edwina	Sister Clare-Louise
Sister Esther Mary	*(Novice Guardian)*
Sister Barbara June	Sister Freda
Sister Susan	Sister Judith
Sister Edmée	Sister Eve
Sister Christine	Sister Elizabeth
Sister Cynthia	Sister Helen
Sister Rosemary	

Oblates and associates

The Community includes Oblate Sisters, who are called to the contemplative life in the world rather than within the monastic enclosure.   There are three other groups of associates: Priest Associates, Companions, and the Fellowship of the Love of God. Information about all these may be obtained from the Reverend Mother at Fairacres.

Community Publication: *Fairacres Chronicle.*
Published twice a year by SLG Press (see under Community Wares).

Community Wares

SLG Press publishes the *Fairacres Chronicle* and a range of books and pamphlets on prayer and spirituality. Contact details:
The Editor, SLG Press, Convent of the Incarnation, Fairacres, Parker Street, Oxford OX4 1TB, UK
Tel: 01865 241874 Fax: 01865 241889
Best to telephone: Mon-Fri 10.30 am - 12 noon, & Mon-Thu afternoons. A call answering service is in place for voicemail if there is no-one currently in the office.
Email: General matters: *editor@slgpress.co.uk*
      Orders only: *orders@slgpress.co.uk*   *Website: www.slgpress.co.uk*

Guest and Retreat Facilities

There is limited accommodation for private retreats, for both men and women, at Fairacres. Please write to or email the Guest Sister to make a booking.
Email: guests@slg.org.uk   Tel (for guest sister): 01865 258152 (with voicemail)

Most convenient time to telephone:

10.30 am - 12 noon; 3.30 pm - 4.30 pm; 6.00 pm - 7.00 pm
Sunday and Friday afternoons are ordinarily covered by an answer phone, but messages are cleared after Vespers.

Bishop Visitor: Rt Revd Michael Lewis, Bishop of Cyprus & the Gulf

Registered Charity

No. 261722; SLG Charitable Trust Ltd: registered in England 990049

Community of the Sisters of Melanesia

CSM

Founded 1980

KNT/Headquarter
Verana'aso
PO Box 19
Honiara
SOLOMON ISLANDS

**First Office, Mattins
& Mass**
5.45 am

Morning Office
7.45 am

**Mid-day Office
& Intercession**
11.55 am

Afternoon Office
1.30 pm

**Evensong
& Meditation**
5.30 pm

Compline
8.45 pm

Office Book
CSM Office Book
(adapted from
MBH Office book)

The community of the Sisters of Melanesia is a sisterhood of women in Melanesia. It was founded by Nester Tiboe and three young women of Melanesia on 17 November 1980. Nester believed that a Religious community of women in Melanesia was needed for the work of evangelism and mission, similar to the work of the Melanesian Brotherhood, founded by Brother Ini Kopuria.

On 17 November 1980, the four young women made their promises of Poverty, Celibacy, and Obedience to serve in the community. The ceremony took place at St Hilda's Day at Bunana Island and officiated by the Most Reverend Norman Kitchener Palmer, the second Archbishop of the Province of Melanesia.

The community aims to offer young women in Melanesia an opportunity of training for ministry and mission, so that they may serve Christ in the church and society where they live. To provide pastoral care for women and teenage children and uphold the Christian principles of family life. To be in partnership with the Melanesian Brotherhood and other Religious communities by proclaiming the Gospel of Jesus Christ in urban and rural areas in the islands. To give God the honour and glory, and to extend His Kingdom in the world.

Addresses of other houses in the Solomon Islands
Joe Wate Household, Longa Bay, Waihi Parish,
Southern Region, Malaita

Marau Missionary Household, Guadalcanal

NAT Household, Mbokoniseu, Vutu,
Ghaobata Parish, East Honiara, Guadalcanal

Sir Ellison L. Pogo Household, Honiara

Community Wares
Vestments, altar linen, weaving and crafts.

Associates
The supporters of the Community of the Sisters of Melanesia are called Associates, a group established in 1990. It is an organization for men and women, young and old, and has over one thousand members, including many young boys and girls. All promise to uphold the Sisters in prayer, and they are a great support in many ways. The Associates of the Community of the Sisters of Melanesia are in the Solomon Islands, Australia and Canada.

SISTER CATHERINE ROSSER CSM
(*Head Sister, assumed office 26 September 2006*)
SISTER SUSSY LISAGITA CSM (*Assistant Head Sister*)

Sister Lydia Dora	Sister Mary Blessed	Sister Miriam Matena
Sister Phylistus Autedi	Sister Dorothy	Sister Jennifer Forau
Sister Phylistus Pwai	Sister Ireen	Sister Herodias
Sister Kate Collin	Sister Julian	Sister Rogilyn Gaelona
Sister Ella Itopa	Sister Noelyn	Sister June Anu
Sister Naomi	Sister Rachael	Sister Alice Iwa
Sister Mildred	Sister Serah Para	Sister MaryFord Rugu
Sister Elizabeth Olehe	Sister Sandra Mary	Sister Edira Fay
Sister Florence	Sister Mary Lulo	Sister Joyce Buta
Sister Hilda	Sister Unice	Sister Ellen Hiniva
Sister Dora Toke	Sister Elizabeth	Sister Kate Awakeni
Sister Patricia	Sister Sussy Great	
Sister Olivia	Sister Nestar Tetei	*Novices:* 27
Sister Jennifer	Sister Nestar Legala	*Aspirants:* 10
Sister Margaret	Sister Phylistus Sau	
Sister Ellina	Sister Hellen Kolikisi	
Sister Janet Olonia	Sister Lorettalyn	

Bishop Visitor: Most Revd David Vunagi, Archbishop of Melanesia

---

Community of the Transfiguration CT

Founded 1898

495 Albion Avenue
Cincinnati, Ohio 45246
USA
Tel: 513 771 5291
Fax: 513 771 0839
Email: ctsisters@aol.com

Website
www.ctsisters.org

The Community of the Transfiguration, founded in 1898 by Eva Lee Matthews, is a Religious community of women dedicated to the mystery of the Transfiguration. Our life is one of prayer and service, reflecting the spirit of Mary and Martha, shown forth in spiritual, educational and social ministries. The Mother House of the community is located in Cincinnati, Ohio, where our ministries include hospitality, retreats, a school, a retirement/nursing home and a recreation center.

The community also offers a retreat ministry on the West Coast; and in the Dominican Republic, the Sisters minister to malnourished children and their families through medical clinics and a school.

The Sisters live their life under the vows of poverty, chastity and obedience. The motto of the community is Benignitas, Simplicitas and Hilaritas - Kindness, Simplicity and Joy.

Associates
The Community has Associates and Oblates.

Guest and Retreat Facilities: These are available.

Lauds, Morning Prayer
6.30 am

Holy Eucharist 7.00 am

Noon Office 12.30 pm

Evensong 5.00 pm

Compline 8.30 pm

Office Book
CT Office Book
& the Book of Common
Prayer

Bishop Visitor
Rt Revd Christopher
Epting

Other addresses
St Mary's Memorial Home, 469 Albion Avenue,
Cincinnati, Ohio 45246, USA
Bethany School, 555 Albion Avenue,
Cincinnati, Ohio 45246, USA
www.bethanyschool.org
Sisters of the Transfiguration, 1633 "D" Street,
Eureka, California 95501, USA
St Monica's Center, 10022 Chester Road,
Cincinnati, Ohio 45215, USA
Dominican Republic Ministry:
Sister Jean Gabriel CT, DMG # 13174 *or*
Sister Johanna Laura CT, DMG # 13173 *or*
Sister Priscilla Jean CT, DMG # 19105
Agape Flights, 100 Airport Avenue,
Venice, Florida 34285, USA
Email: ct_sisters@yahoo.com

Community Publication: The Quarterly

Fikambanan'ny Mpanompovavin l Jesoa Kristy

(Society of the Servants of Jesus Christ)

FMJK

Founded 1985

Convent Hasina, BP 28
Ambohidratrimo 105
Antananarivo 101
MADAGASCAR

Bishop Visitor
Most Revd Ranarivello
Samoelajaona,
Archbishop of the Indian
Ocean

The FMJK sisters were founded by Canon Hall Speers in 1985. They live in the village of Tsinjohasina, on the high plateau above the rice fields, situated some fifteen kilometres from Antananarivo, the capital of Madagascar. The sisters work in the village dispensary and are active in visiting, Christian teaching and pastoral work in the villages around. They are an independent community but have been nurtured by a connection with CSMV, Wantage, in the UK.

SISTER JACQUELINE FMJK
(Masera Tonia, assumed office 5 June 2002)
SISTER CHAPINE FMJK *(Prioress)*

Sister Ernestine   Sister Voahangy
Sister Georgette   Sister Vololona
Sister Isabelle   Sister Fanja
Sister Odette

Community Wares: Crafts and embroidery.

Office Book: FMJK Office and Prayer Book

Other house
Antaralava, Soamanandray, BP 28,
Ambohidratrimo 105, Antananarivo 101,
MADAGASCAR

Korean Franciscan Brotherhood

KFB

Founded 1994

156 Balsan-Ri,
Nam-Myeon,
Chuncheon
200-922,
REPUBLIC OF KOREA
Tel: 33 263 4662
Fax: 33 263 4048

Email:
kfb1993@
kornet.net

Website
www.francis.or.kr

**Morning Prayer,
Meditation
& Eucharist**
6.00 am

Midday Prayer
12 noon

Evening Prayer
6.00 pm

**Meditation &
Night Prayer**
9.00 pm

The Korean Franciscan Brotherhood is linked by covenant to the Society of St Francis. We are planning to become members of SSF in the near future. Our community aims to contribute to the building up of God's kingdom by a life of witness through prayer, hospitality and service. Our friary is in rural Gangwondo, 90 km northeast of Seoul. We offer hospitality at the friary, manage the nearby diocesan retreat house, take part in some children's and young people's ministry, as well as preaching and leading spirituality and other programmes.

BROTHER STEPHEN KFB
(*Guardian, assumed office 2006*)
Brother Lawrence
Postulants: 1

Associates
We have a Friends' Association with about fifty active members, who make a simple promise to help us by whatever way they can.

Community Publication
A bi-annual English newsletter and a quarterly Korean one are available in printed form (donation appreciated) or on the website.

Community Wares
Block mounted icon prints, candles.

Guest and Retreat Facilities
We have two guest rooms for single or small group use. Guests can share in worship and meals with the community. Larger groups can be accommodated at the nearby diocesan retreat house. There are many walks around the friary and through its mountainous surroundings. As well as regular retreatants, visitors from overseas are welcome, or those making stopovers in Korea. We are about three hours by bus from Incheon International Airport. Accommodation is by donation.

Office Book
The Daily Office SSF (in Korean translation)

Bishop Protector
Rt Revd Paul Kim, Bishop of Seoul

Little Brothers of Francis

LBF

Founded 1987

Franciscan
Hermitage
"Eremophilia"
PO Box 162
Tabulam
NSW 2469
AUSTRALIA

Bishop Visitor
Rt Revd
Godfrey Fryar,
Bishop of
Rockhampton, Qld

We are a community of Brothers who desire to deepen our relationship with God through prayer, manual work, community, and times of being alone in our hermitages. We follow the Rule written by Saint Francis for Hermitages in which three or four brothers live in each fraternity. As others join us we envisage a federation of fraternities with three or four brothers in each.

There are four sources of inspiration for the Little Brothers of Francis. They are:

1. The Gospels

The four Gospels (Matthew, Mark, Luke and John) are central to our spirituality, and the main source material for our meditation and prayer life.

2. St Francis

Francis would recall Christ's words and life through persistent meditation on the Gospels, for his deep desire was to love Christ and live a Christ-centred life.

He was a man of prayer and mystic who sought places of solitude, and hermitages played a central role in his life. Significant events, like the initiation of the Christmas Crib tradition, happened at the hermitage at Greccio, and, of course, he received the stigmata while he was at the hermitage at Mount La Verna.

Though the early brothers embraced a mixed life of prayer and ministry, Francis wanted places of seclusion - hermitages, for the primacy of prayer, in which three or four brothers lived, and for which he wrote a rule.

3. St Francis's Rule for Hermitages

In his brief rule for life within the hermitage, Francis avoided a detailed document and set out the principles that are important.

- Liturgy of the Hours is the focus, and sets the rhythm of the daily prayer.

- Each hermitage was to have at the most four Brothers, which meant they would be both 'little' and 'fraternal'.

- Within this framework, Brothers could withdraw for periods of solitude.

- The hermitages were not to be places or centres of ministry.

4. Desert Fathers

The stories and sayings of the Desert Fathers contain a profound wisdom for any who are serious about the inner spiritual journey. This is why they have held such prominence in monastic circles in both East and West down through the centuries, and why they are a priority source for us.

Brothers have times of Solitude in their hermitage, which vary from a day to weeks or months, where they have their own personal rhythm of prayer and manual work.

Vigil Office
followed by
Lectio Divina
(private)
2.00 am or 4.00 am

Meditation
6.00 am

Angelus and Mattins
7.00 am

Terce
9.00 am

Angelus and Sext
12 noon

None (private)
3.00 pm

Vespers
6.00 pm

Compline
8.00 pm

Office Book
LBF Office book, developed to provide for our needs as a Franciscan Hermitage

Each Brother has responsibility for certain areas of the community's life. Decision-making is by consensus.

Brother Howard LBF
Brother Wayne LBF
Brother Geoffrey Adam LBF

Friends
The Friends of the Little Brothers of Francis are those who feel a spiritual affinity with the Brothers and desire to deepen their prayer life and to support the Brothers in their life and witness. They have an independent organisation, with its own office-bearers and requirements for membership.
Contact:
Australia - Julianne Horsfield
    Email: julianne1000@gmail.com
New Zealand - Ian Lothian
    Email: ianlothian@xtra.com.nz
Or by post, contact the Brothers.

Community Publication: The *Bush Telegraph.*
Contact the Brothers for a subscription, which is by donation.

Community Wares: Hand-carved holding crosses, jam, marmalade, cards, tea-towels and honey.

Guest and Retreat Facilities
There is a guest cottage for one person or possibly two. A fee of $60 per night is negotiable.

The Melanesian Brotherhood

MBH

Founded 1925

Email: mbhches @solomon.com.sb

SOLOMON ISLANDS REGION
The Motherhouse of the Melanesian Brotherhood
Tabalia
PO Box 1479
Honiara
SOLOMON ISLANDS
TEL: +677 26355
FAX: +677 23079

PAPUA NEW GUINEA REGION
Dobuduru Regional Headquarters
Haruro
PO Box 29
Popondetta
Oro Province
PAPUA NEW GUINEA

SOUTHERN REGION
Tumsisiro Regional Headquarters
PO Box 05
Lolowai, Ambae
VANUATU

The Melanesian Brotherhood was founded by Ini Kopuria, a native Solomon Islander from Guadalcanal, in 1925. Its main purpose was evangelistic, to take and live the Gospel in the most remote islands and villages throughout the Solomon Islands, among people who had not heard the message of Christ. The Brotherhood's method is to live as brothers to the people, respecting their traditions and customs: planting, harvesting, fishing, house building, eating and sharing with the people in all these things. Kopuria believed that Solomon Islanders should be converted in a Melanesian way.

Today, the work of the Brotherhood has broadened to include work and mission among both Christians and non-Christians. The Melanesian Brotherhood now has three regions: Solomon Islands, Papua New Guinea, and Southern (Vanuatu plus the Diocese of Polynesia). They have also opened two households and a community centre in the large island of Palawan in the Philippines. There is a Region for Companions and Brothers in Europe.

Following an ethnic conflict in the Solomon Islands 2000-2003, members of the Melanesian Brotherhood have been increasingly called upon as peace makers and reconcilers, work for which they were awarded the United Nations Pacific Peace Prize in 2004.

The Brotherhood has also led missions in New Zealand, Australia, Philippines and UK (2000 and 2005); their missionary approach includes music, dance and a powerful use of drama.

The Brotherhood aims to live the Gospel in a direct and simple way following Christ's example of prayer, mission and service. The Brothers take the vows of poverty, chastity and obedience, but these are not life vows but for a period of three years, which can be renewed. They train for four years as novices and normally make their vows as Brothers at the Feast of St Simon and St Jude.

Community Publications
Spearhead Toktok [Solomon Islands] and *Partnership Toktok* [Philippines] (both occasional)
Companions' Newsletter for the Europe Region (once a year)
 - contact Canon Brian Macdonald-Milne, address under 'Companions' below.

Obituaries
2007   Brother Leonard Vaka, professed 1 year
24 Mar 2008   Brother James Tata, professed 10 years

Timetable of the
Main House

**First Office and
Mattins**
5.50 am
(6.20 am Sun &
holidays)

Holy Communion
6.15 am
(7.15 am Sun &
holidays)

Morning Office
8.00 am

Midday Office
12 noon
(Angelus on Sun
& holidays)

Afternoon Office
1.30 pm
(not Sun & holidays)

Evensong 5.30 pm
(6.00 pm Sun &
holidays)

Last Office
9.00 pm

Office Book
Offices and Prayers
of the
Melanesian
Brotherhood
1996
(not for public sale)

TO BE ELECTED
(Head Brother, assumed office July 2009)
BROTHER ALICK PALUSI *(Assistant Head Brother)*

Professed Brothers: 341
(Solomon Islands: 178; Southern Region: 72; PNG: 91)
Novices: 177
(Solomon Islands: 121; Southern Region: 28; PNG: 28)

SOLOMON ISLANDS REGION
BROTHER LEONARD YANGA MBH *(Regional Head Brother)*
MR ALPHONSE GARIMAE *(Brotherhood Secretary)*
BROTHER ERIC TANO MBH *(Companions Secretary)*
THE MOST REVD DAVID VUNAGI, ARCHBISHOP OF MELANESIA
(Father of the Brotherhood & the Solomon Islands Region)

CENTRAL MELANESIA SECTION
Address for all SI houses in this section:
  PO Box 1479, Honiara, Guadacanal, SOLOMON ISLANDS

BROTHER SIMON PETER MBH *(Section Elder Brother)*
  Central Headquarters, Tabalia, PO Box 1479, Honiara
BROTHER NELSON SELO MBH *(Elder Brother)*
  Norman Kitchener Palmer Household, Honiara
  Tel: 23372 Fax: 23079
BROTHER JAMES PAIKULA MBH *(Brother in charge)*
  St Barnabas Cathedral Working Household, Honiara
  Tel: 24609 Fax: 23079
BROTHER ROBERT CONIEL KAILOU MBH *(Brother in charge)*
  Bishopsdale Working Household, Honiara
  Tel: 27695 Fax: 23079
BROTHER FOX KWANAFIA MBH *(Elder Brother)*
  David Sale Household, Komukama, Guadalcanal

BROTHER ROMEL FRANCISCO MBH *(Brother in charge)*
Iglesia Filipina Independiente (I.F.I.), Delos Reyes Road 2,
Puerto Princesa City, 5300 Palawan, PHILIPPINES

CENTRAL SOLOMONS DIOCESAN SECTION
BROTHER SELWYN SPROTT *(Section Elder Brother)*
  Thomas Peo Section Headquarters, Koloti,
    c/o Central Solomons Diocesan Office, PO Box 52,
  Tulagi, Central Province

Address for other houses in this section:
  c/o Central Headquarters, Tabalia, PO Box 1479, Honiara

BROTHER KENNETH SOAKI MBH *(Elder Brother)*
  Ini Kopuria Household, Kolina, Gela

BROTHER ABRAHAM HUVA MBH *(Elder Brother)*
Olimauri Household, Mbambanakira, Guadalcanal
BROTHER THOMAS WAITARA MBH *(Elder Brother)*
Calvary Household, Surapau, Guadalcanal
BROTHER GEORGE MAHIRA MBH *(Brother in charge)*
Selwyn Rapu Working Household, Guadalcanal
BROTHER COMINS KHAPRI MBH *(Brother in charge)*
Derick Vagi Working Household, Bellona Island

MALAITA DIOCESAN SECTION
Address for houses in this section (except Tasman Working Household):
c/o Malaita Diocesan Office, PO Box 7, Auki, Malaita Province

BROTHER ALFRED FAITA MBH *(Section Elder Brother)*
Airahu Section Headquarters, Malaita
BROTHER DAVIDSON MAEDIANA MBH *(Elder Brother)*
Funakwa'a Household, East Kwaio, Malaita
BROTHER GEORGE TARA MBH *(Brother in charge)*
Wairura Household, Malaita
BROTHER BRIAN DO'ORO MBH *(Brother in charge)*
New Dawn Range Working Household, West Kwaio, Malaita
BROTHER STEPHEN ODO MBH *(Brother in charge)*
Urutao Working Household, North Malaita
BROTHER NATHANIEL ROW *(Brother in charge)*
Kokom Working Household, Auki, Malaita
BROTHER ALLEN KIKOA MBH *(Brother in charge)*
Tasman Working Household, Nukumanu Atoll (PNG), PO Box 1479,
Honiara, Solomon Islands

YSABEL DIOCESAN SECTION
Address for houses in this section:
c/o Isabel Diocesan Office, PO Box 6, Buala, Isabel Province

BROTHER HUBERT UKA MBH *(Section Elder Brother)*
Welchman Section Headquarters, Sosoilo
BROTHER CHRISTIAN AUJARE MBH *(Elder Brother)*
Poropeta Household, Kia
BROTHER ROBERT RAERI MBH *(Brother in charge)*
Alfred Hill Working Household, Jejevo
BROTHER DUDLEY WAITA MBH *(Brother in charge)*
Hulon Working Household, Yandina, Russell Islands
BROTHER NELSON BAIVALE MBH *(Elder Brother)*
John Pihavaka Household, Gizo
BROTHER BEN MEBA MBH *(Brother in charge)*
Noro Working Household, New Georgia Island
BROTHER JUDAH GAVIRO MBH *(Brother in charge)*
Pupuku Working Household, Choisuel Province

HANUATO'O DIOCESAN SECTION
Address for houses in this section:
>   c/o Hanuato'o Diocesan Office, Kirakira, Makira Province

BROTHER ROBERT HENRY MBH *(Section Elder Brother)*
>   Fox Section Headquarters, Poronaohe, Makira

BROTHER JESSIE ARIASI MBH *(Elder Brother)*
>   Simon Sigai Household, Makira

BROTHER NORMAN PARAKO MBH *(Brother in charge)*
>   Johnnie Kuper Working Household, Pamua, Makira

BROTHER IN CHARGE TO BE APPOINTED
>   Star Harbour Working Household, Makira

TEMOTU DIOCESAN SECTION
Address for houses in this section:
>   c/o Temotu Diocesan Office, Luesalo, Temotu Province

BROTHER HENRY MANABIPU MBH *(Section Elder Brother)*
>   Makio Section Headquarters, Santa Cruz Island

BROTHER MOFFAT AU MBH *(Brother in charge)*
>   Lata Working Household, Santa Cruz Island

BROTHER ELLISON VAKETAU MBH *(Brother in charge)*
>   Utupua Working Household, Utupua

SOUTHERN REGION

BROTHER WILFORD TARI MBH *(Regional Head Brother)*
BROTHER FISHER YOUNG *(Regional Secretary)*
TO BE APPOINTED (Regional Companions Secretary)
THE RT REVD JAMES LIGO *(Father of the Southern Region and Vanuatu Section)*

VANUATU SECTION
BROTHER BADDELEY HANGO MBH *(Section Elder Brother)*
>   Tumsisiro Regional Headquarters, Ambae

>   Noel Seu Working Household, South Ambae
>   Hinge Household, Lorevuilko, East Santo
>   Suriau Household, Big Bay, Santo Bush
>   Surunleo Household, Bwatnapni, Central Pentecost
>   Saratabulu Household, West Ambae
>   Canal Household, Santo Town
>   Patteson Household, Port Vila

BANKS & TORRES SECTION
>   THE RT REVD NATHAN TOME *(Section Father)*

BROTHER FRESHER DIN *(Section Elder Brother)*
>   Sarawia Section Headquarters, Vanua Lava Island

POLYNESIA SECTION
>   This section has Companions only at the present time.

PAPUA NEW GUINEA REGION
BROTHER MATTHIAS TOVOTSI MBH *(Regional Head Brother)*
BROTHER KELLIOT BETU *(Regional Secretary)*
BROTHER STANLEY HOKA *(Regional Companions Secretary)*
THE MOST REVD JAMES AYONG, ARCHBISHOP OF PNG *(Father of the PNG Region and of the Aipo Rango Section)*

POPONDOTA SECTION
BROTHER CHILLION MONGAGI *(Section Elder Brother)*
Dobuduru Regional Headquarters, Popondetta

Berubona Working Household
St Christopher's Workshop
Damara Household, Safia
Wanigela Household
Nindewari Household

PORT MORESBY SECTION
BROTHER SAMSON GIS *(Section Elder Brother)*
Port Moresby Section Headquarters, Oro Village

Cape Rodney Household
Morata Working Household
Pivo Household

DOGURA SECTION
BROTHER TONY AREWA *(Section Elder Brother)*
Mawedama Section Headquarters, Sirisiri, Dogura

Iapoa Household
Pumani Household
Samarai Island Working Household
Podagha Project Household

AIPO RONGO SECTION
BROTHER STANFORD GULKUM *(Section Elder Brother)*
Aiome Section Headquarters, Aganmakuk

Kinibong Household
Marvol Household, Ilu Mamusi
Aum Household, Tsendiap
Nambayufa Household, Siane Valley

NEW GUINEA ISLANDS SECTION
BROTHER ALFRED MOGEL *(Section Elder Brother)*
Akolong Section Headquarters

Aseke Household, Au, Gasmata
Hosea Sakira Working Household, Ura, Cape Gloucester

Companions
The Melanesian Brotherhood is supported both in prayer, in their work and materially by the Companions of the Melanesian Brotherhood (C.O.M.B.).

For more information about becoming a Companion, please contact:

Revd Canon Brian Macdonald-Milne   or   Companions Chief Secretary
39 Way Lane, Waterbeach,   PO Box 1479
Cambridge CB25 9NQ, UK   Honiara
   Email: bj.macdonaldmilne@homecall.co.uk   SOLOMON ISLANDS

Alongside Companions, the Brotherhood also has associates whose ministry is more closely associated with the community, except that they do not take the threefold vow. They work voluntarily without wages just like the brothers.

Community History and other books
Brian Macdonald-Milne, *The True Way of Service: The Pacific Story of the Melanesian Brotherhood, 1925-2000*, Christians Aware, Leicester, 2003.

Richard Carter, *In Search of the Lost: the death and life of seven peacemakers of the Melanesian Brotherhood*, Canterbury Press, Norwich, 2006.

Charles Montgomery, *The Shark God: Encounters with myth and Magic in the South Pacific*, Fourth Estate/Harper Collins, London, 2006.

Guest and Retreat Facilities
CHESTER RESTHOUSE, PO Box 1479, Honiara, SOLOMON ISLANDS, offers a Christian welcome. Eight twin-bedded rooms, self-catering, £15 per room per night.

All the Brotherhood's headquarters, and also section headquarters, can provide simple accommodation for visitors. Retreats can be made by prior arrangement with the relevant Chaplain at Central, Regional or Section headquarters.

Women are not allowed to enter the Brotherhood Square (St Simon & Jude), which is usually outside the chapel of every Brotherhood station (not in Honiara). Women are not allowed to enter brothers' dormitories.

Father of the Brotherhood in the European Region
The Most Revd Dr Rowan Williams,
                  Archbishop of Canterbury

Advisors to the Brotherhood
Revd Canon Brian Macdonald-Milne
Revd Dr Keith Joseph *(Administrative Advisor)*

Order of the Holy Cross

OHC

Founded 1884

Holy Cross
Monastery
PO Box 99
(1615 Rt. 9W)
West Park
NY 12493
USA
Tel: 845 384 6660
Fax: 845 384 6031

Email: superior@
hcmnet.org

Website: www.
holycrossmonastery.
com

Mattins 7.00 am

Holy Eucharist
9.00 am

Midday Prayer
12 noon

Vespers 5.00 pm

Compline 8.30 pm

Mondays are observed
as a sabbath day on
which there are no
scheduled liturgies.

The Order of the Holy Cross is a Benedictine monastic community open to both lay and ordained. The principles governing the Order's life are in those of the *Rule of St Benedict* and The Rule of the Order of the Holy Cross, written by its founder James Otis Sargent Huntington.

The liturgical life of each house centers around the corporate praying of the Divine Office and the celebration of the Holy Eucharist. Members also expected to spend time in private prayer and meditation.

The work of the Order is varied, depending on the nature of the household and the gifts and talents of its members. Houses vary from traditional monastic centers with active retreat ministries to urban houses from which brothers go forth to work. A small number of brothers live independently as Monks Not In Residence.

Members are engaged in preaching, teaching, counseling and spiritual direction, parish and diocesan support work, the arts, evangelism, hospice care, and ministry with the homeless and those with HIV/AIDS. The South African community administers educational and scholarship programs for local children and youth.

Other Addresses
Mount Calvary Retreat House, PO Box 1296,
Santa Barbara, CA 93102, USA
Tel: 805 962 9855

Holy Cross Priory, 204 High Park Avenue, Toronto,
Ontario M6P 2S6, CANADA
Tel: 416 767 9081Fax: 416 767 4692

Mariya uMama weThemba Monastery, PO Box 6013,
Grahamstown 6141, SOUTH AFRICA
Tel: 46 622 8111   Fax: 46 622 6424

Community History
Adam Dunbar McCoy OHC, *Holy Cross: A Century of Anglican Monasticism,* Morehouse-Barlow, Wilton, CT, 1987.

Community Wares: Incense and Publications (West Park).

Office Book: *A Monastic Breviary* (OHC)
or *Lauds and Vespers* (Camaldolese Monks OSB)

Bishop Visitor: Rt Revd Mark S Sisk
Deputy Bishop Visitor: Rt Revd Ann E Tottenham

ROBERT LEO SEVENSKY OHC
(Superior, assumed office 2008)
SCOTT WESLEY BORDEN OHC *(Assistant Superior)*

Thomas Schultz	James Robert Hagler
Christian George Swayne	Leonard Abbah
Laurence Harms	Reginald-Martin Crenshaw
Samuel DeMerell	Richard Paul Vaggione
Rafael Campbell-Dixon	Cecil Couch
Bede Thomas Mudge	Lary Pearce
Ronald Haynes	Andrew Colquhoun
Brian Youngward	John Forbis
Nicholas Radelmiller	Bernard Jean Delcourt
Roy Parker	James Randall Greve
Adrian Gill	Daniel Ludik
David Bryan Hoopes	Robert Magliula
Adam McCoy	James Dowd
Carl Sword	
William Brown	*Novices:* 2
Timothy Jolley	

Obituaries

22 Sep 2007	Anthony-Gerald Stevens, aged 95, professed 56 years
10 Jun 2008	Michael Stonebraker, aged 78, professed 52 years
14 Jun 2008	Bernard Van Waes, aged 87, professed 27 years
14 Oct 2008	William Sibley, aged 74, professed 37 years

Associates

The Associates of Holy Cross are men and women of many different Christian traditions affliated to the Order through a Rule of Life and annual retreats and reports.

Community Publication

Holy Cross, published annually.
Mundi Medicina (West Park, NY) published thrice yearly
Uxolo (Grahamstown, South Africa), published thrice yearly
Mount Calvary (Santa Barbara, CA) published thrice yearly
Cost - by donation.

Guest and Retreat Facilities

WEST PARK: 39 rooms at US$70 per day ($80 weekends).
Accommodations for couples and individuals. Closed Mondays, for two weeks in January and for the month of August.
SANTA BARBARA: Facility destroyed by wildfire in November 2008. Alternative arrangements pending.
TORONTO: 1 double room; 2 singles. Canadian $60 per day for couples, $40 for singles.
GRAHAMSTOWN: 19 rooms (doubles and singles). Closed on Mondays, Christmas and the month of January.

Order of the Holy Paraclete

OHP

Founded 1915

St Hilda's Priory
Sneaton Castle,
Whitby
North Yorkshire
YO21 3QN
UK
Tel: 01947 602079
Fax: 01947 820854
Email:
ohppriorywhitby
@btinternet.com
Website: www.
ohpwhitby.org

Morning Prayer
7.15 am
(7.30 am Sat & Sun)

Eucharist
7.45 am (Mon, Wed
& Fri)
8.00 am (Sat)
9.30 am (Sun)
12.30 pm (Tue & Thu)

Midday Office
12.40 pm
12.15 pm (Tue & Thu)
12 noon (Sat)

Vespers   6.00 pm
(4.30 pm Sun)

Compline   9.00 pm
(8.30 pm Fri)

Founded as an educational order, the sisters have diversified their work in UK to include hospitality, retreats and spiritual direction, hospital chaplaincy, inner city involvement, preaching and mission, and development work overseas.

The Mother House is at St. Hilda's Priory, Whitby. Some sisters work in the adjacent Sneaton Castle Centre, which caters for a wide variety of day and residential groups. Other houses are in York, Hull and Sleights (near Whitby).

Overseas, the Order's long-standing commitment to Africa has been extended in exciting new developments: raising awareness of AIDS and providing a home for abused girls in Swaziland, and fostering vocations to Religious life in Ghana, where, in response to perceived local interest and support, a new convent has been built in Jachie, Ashanti. An eye clinic is also run by OHP. The Order withdrew from their work in Johannesburg in May 2008.

Central to the Order's life in all its houses are the Divine Office and Eucharist, and a strong emphasis on corporate activity.

Houses in the UK
Beachcliff, 14 North Promenade, Whitby, North Yorkshire YO21 3JX
Tel: 01947 601968   Email: ohpbeaccliff@hotmail.co.uk

St Oswald's Pastoral Centre, Woodlands Drive, Sleights, Whitby, North Yorkshire YO21 1RY
Tel: 01947 810496   Email: ohpstos@globalnet.co

1A Minster Court, York YO7 2JJ
Tel: 01904 620601   Email: ohpyork@onetel.com

OHP Hull, 9 Cranbourne Street, Spring Bank, Hull HU3 1PP   *Tel: 01482 586816   Fax: 01482 213114
Email: ohphull@karoo.co.uk*

Houses in Africa
Jachie, Convent of the Holy Spirit, PO Box AH 9375, Ahinsan, Kumasi Ashanti, GHANA, West Africa
Tel: 233 242 or 203432   Email: ohpjac@yahoo.com

The Sisters OHP, Box 523, Piggs Peak, SWAZILAND
*Tel: 437 1514
Emails: srkaran@bulembu.org   & carole@bulembu.org*

Bishop Visitor: Most Revd John Sentamu,
                                        Archbishop of York

Office Book: OHP Office
Registered Charity: No. 271117

SISTER DOROTHY STELLA OHP
(Prioress, assumed office 15 July 2005)
SISTER HEATHER FRANCIS OHP *(Sub-Prioress)*

Sister Kathleen	Sister Margaret Shirley	Sister Barbara Ann
Sister Ursula	Sister Nancye	Sister Carole
Sister Barbara Maude	Sister Patricia	Sister Mavis
Sister Sophia	Sister Gillian	Sister Rachel
Sister Olive	Sister Hilary Joy	Sister Linda
Sister Marjorie	Sister Grace	Sister Aba
Sister Rosa	Sister Janette	Sister Pam
Sister Constance	Sister Janet Elizabeth	Sister Helen
Sister Janet	Sister Betty	Sister Karan
Sister Alison	Sister Benedicta	Sister Margaret
Sister Michelle	Sister Caroline	Sister Alberta
Sister Mary Nina	Sister Margaret Elizabeth	Sister Sabina
Sister Stella Mary	Sister Marion Eva	Sister Katherine Therese
Sister Lucy	Sister Judith	
Sister Heather	Sister Erika	*Novices*: 2
Sister Muriel	Sister Maureen Ruth	*Postulants*: 1
Sister Mary Margaret	Sister Margaret Anne	
Sister Anita	Sister Jocelyn	

Obituaries

21 Jul 2007	Sister Catherine, aged 78, professed 52 years
11 Nov 2007	Sister Margaret Irene, aged 81, professed 57 years
20 Jan 2008	Sister Philippa, aged 87, professed 51 years
19 Dec 2008	Sister Maureen, aged 70, professed 43 years

Tertiaries and Associates
THE OHP TERTIARY ORDER is a fellowship of women and men, united under a common discipline, based on the OHP Rule, and supporting one another in their discipleship. Tertiaries are ordinary Christians seeking to offer their lives in the service of Christ, helping the Church and showing love in action. They value their links with each other and with the Sisters of the Order, at Whitby and elsewhere, and when possible they meet together for mutual support in prayer, discussion and ministry. The Tertiary Order is open to communicant members of any Trinitarian Church.

THE OHP ASSOCIATES are friends of the Order who desire to keep in touch with its life and work while serving God in their various spheres. Many have made initial contact with the Sisters through a visit or parish mission, or via another Associate. All are welcome, married or single, clergy or lay, regardless of religious affiliation.

Community Publication: OHP Newsletter, twice a year. Write to The Publications Secretary at St Hilda's Priory. Annual subscription: £4.50 for the UK, £5.50 for the rest of Europe and £7.00 for the rest of the world.

Community History
A Foundation Member, *Fulfilled in Joy*, Hodder & Stoughton, London, 1964.

Rosalin Barker, *The Whitby Sisters*, OHP, Whitby, 2001.

Community Wares
Cards and craft items. St Hilda's Priory has a shop selling books, cards, church supplies and religious artefacts.   *Email: sneatonshop@btinternet.com*

Guest and Retreat Facilities
ST HILDA'S PRIORY: six rooms (four single; one double; one twin) available in the Priory or nearby houses. Individuals or small groups are welcome for personal quiet or retreat, day or residential. If requested in advance, some guidance can be provided. There is no programme of retreats at the Priory. Contact the Guest Sister with enquiries and bookings.

SNEATON CASTLE CENTRE: seventy-one rooms (one hundred and twenty beds). The Centre has conference, lecture and seminar rooms with full audio-visual equipment, and recreational facilities. There is a spacious dining room and an excellent range of menus. Guests are welcome to join the community for worship or to arrange their own services in the Chapel.
Contact the Bookings Secretary, Sneaton Castle Centre, Whitby YO21 3QN.
Tel: 01947 600051   See also the website: *www.sneatoncastle.co.uk*

ST OSWALD'S PASTORAL CENTRE: 13 rooms (16 beds). 3 self-catering units.

Most convenient time to telephone:: 9 am - 5 pm, Mon-Fri; 10 am - 12 noon Sat

Order of Julian of Norwich

OJN

Founded 1985

2812 Summit Avenue Waukesha WI 53188-2781 USA Tel: 262 549 0452

Email: ojn@ orderofjulian.org

Website www. orderofjulian.org

The Order of Julian of Norwich is a contemplative semi-enclosed Religious order of nuns and monks in the Episcopal Church, living together in one house. We profess traditional vows of poverty, chastity, and obedience, with the added vow of prayer 'in the spirit of our Blessed Mother Saint Julian', the fourteenth-century English anchoress and our patron.

The ministry of the Order to the Church is to be a community of prayer and contemplative presence, expressed in communal liturgical worship in chapel and in the silence and solitude of the cell. Gregorian Chant is used for most of the four-fold Divine Office of the Book of Common Prayer. The Eucharist is the centre of our life, the genesis of our work of contemplative and intercessory prayer. This primary apostolate supports a limited exterior apostolate of the teaching of classical contemplative spirituality by retreats, spiritual direction, study and writing.

Founded in 1985 by the Revd John Swanson, the Order was canonically recognized by the Episcopal Church in 1997, and is affiliated with the Conference of Anglican Religious Orders in the Americas. For further information on the Order or its affiliates, please address the Guardian.

Guest and Retreat Facilities: Two guest rooms. There is no charge.

Morning Prayer
5.00 am

Mass
7.00 am

Noonday Office
12 noon

Evensong
5.00 pm

Compline
7.50 pm

Office Book
The Book of
Common Prayer
of the Episcopal
Church of the USA
for Morning Prayer;
OJN Chantbook for
other Offices.

Bishop Visitor
Rt Revd
Edwin Leidel,
retired Bishop of
Eastern Michigan

THE REVD FATHER GREGORY FRUEHWIRTH OJN
(Guardian, assumed office 14 April 2003)
REVD MOTHER HILARY CRUPI OJN *(Warden)*

Revd Father
John-Julian Swanson
Sister Cornelia Barry
Sister Monica Clark
Sister Therese Poli

Brother Barnabas Leben
Sister Mary Jude Vorhees

Novices: 2
Sister Sarah Janeks
Brother Jonathan Galliher

Associates and Oblates

ASSOCIATES

Friends of the Order, desiring a spiritual bond with the Julian Community who keep a simple Rule (one daily Office, Sunday Mass, annual reports to the Warden of Associates) and pledge financial support for the Order.

OBLATES

Persons committed to live the Order's spiritual and contemplative charism in the world under an adaptation of regular vows. They have a Rule of: two BCP Offices daily; three per cent of their tithe to the Order; three hours contemplative prayer a week; a four-day silent retreat annually; Sunday Mass and seven Holy days of Obligation, etc. They make a semi-annual report to the Warden of Oblates.

Community Publication

JuliaNews (newsletter) & *Julian Jottings* (essays), both quarterly. Subscription free. Contact Sister Monica OJN.

Community History and other books

Teunisje Velthuizen, ObJN, *One-ed into God: The first decade of the Order of St Julian of Norwich,* The Julian Press, 1996.

Gregory Fruehwirth OJN, *Words for Silence,* Paraclete, Orleans, MA, 2008.

John Julian Swanson OJN, *The Complete Julian,* Paraclete, Orleans, MA, 2009.

Other publications (Liturgical works) - see the website.

Community Wares

The Julian Shop has books, religious articles, many pamphlets written by members.
Email: julianshop@orderofjulian.org

Earthing the Religious life!

Order of
St Anne
at Bethany

OSA

Founded 1910

25 Hillside Avenue
Arlington
MA 02476-5818
USA
Tel: 781 643 0921
Fax: 781 648 4547
Email: bethany
convent@aol.com

Morning Prayer
7.00 am

Eucharist
8.00 am (Tue-Fri)
7.30 am (Sun)

Midday prayers
12 noon

Evensong 5.00 pm

Compline 7.30 pm

Office Book
SSJE Office Book

Community Wares
Communion altar
bread.

Bishop Visitor
Rt Revd M. Thomas
Shaw SSJE, Bishop of
Massachusetts

We are a small multi-cultural community of women committed to witnessing to the truth that, as Christians, it is here and now that we demonstrate to the Church and the world that the Religious Life lived in community is relevant, interesting, fulfilling and needed in our world and our times.

We strive to recognize and value the diversity of persons and gifts. We believe that God has a vision for each one of us and that opportunities to serve the Church and the world are abundant. For this to become real, we know that our spirits and hearts must be enlarged to fit the dimensions of our Church in today's world and the great vision that God has prepared for our Order. We are especially grateful for our continuing ministry within the Diocese of Massachusetts.

The Rule of the Order of St Anne says our houses may be small, but our hearts are larger than houses. Our community has always been 'people-oriented' and we derive a sense of joy and satisfaction in offering hospitality at our Convent, at the Bethany House of Prayer and in our beautiful chapel.

Always constant in our lives are our personal prayer and our corporate worship, our vows of Poverty, Celibacy and Obedience, our commitment to spiritual growth and development of mind and talents, and our fellowship with one another and other Religious communities, as friends and sisters.

SISTER ANA CLARA OSA
(Superior, assumed office 1992)

Sister Olga   Sister Maria Agnes
Sister Felicitas   Sister Maria Teresa

Associates
We have an associate program and continue to receive men and women into this part of our life.

Community History
Sister Johanna OSA (editor), *A Theme for Four Voices,* privately printed, Arlington, Mass., 1985

Guest and Retreat Facilities
The Bethany House of Prayer, 181 Appleton Street, on the grounds of the Convent and Chapel, sponsors, coordinates and offers a variety of programs and events including Quiet Days, Special Liturgies, contemplative prayer, spiritual direction, day-retreats, hospitality and workshops. For more information call 781 648 2433.

Order of St Benedict

ex-Burford

OSB
Founded 1941

Broad Marston Manor
Broad Marston
Stratford-upon-Avon
CV37 8XY

Email: information
@burfordosb.org.uk

Website: www.
burfordosb.org.uk

*Timetable
under review*

Office Book
Burford Office

Bishop Visitor
Rt Revd
Stephen Oliver,
Bishop of Stepney

Registered Charity:
No. 221617

After sixty years at Burford Priory, the community of Benedictine nuns and monks are 'in transit' to a new monastery near Worcester. In 2008, they sold Burford Priory and bought a derelict farm. As that is being transformed into their new monastery, they are renting Broad Marston Manor, parts of which were built by the Cistercians in the thirteenth century. The new monastery should be ready during the autumn of 2010, and will be a model of 'sustainable ' design.

During this period of transition, the Community is unable to exercise its normal ministry of hospitality, and is using this sabbatical time as a period of retreat and an opportunity to review its way of life in the hope that it can be 'fit for service' in the world of the twenty-first century.

The Community hopes to continue to provide a place of ecumenical encounter and reconciliation, enjoying, as it does, links with Baptist, Lutheran, Orthodox and Roman Catholic communities. Its ecumenism has broadened to include dialogue with people of other faiths and those who are seeking a spiritual way, either within or outside an established religious tradition.

RT REVD BROTHER STUART BURNS OSB
(Abbot, elected 14 October 1996)

Sister Scholastica Newman	Brother Anthony Hare
Sister Mary Bernard Taylor	Brother Philip Dulson
Sister Gabriel Allatt	Sister Mary Kenchington
Brother Thomas Quin	*Novices:* 1

Friends: There is a Friends' Association.
Contact: *friends@burfordosb.org.uk*

Community Wares: Incense, hand-written icons using traditional materials, block mounted icon prints, and Chinese brush painted cards.
Contact: *craftsales@burfordosb.org.uk*

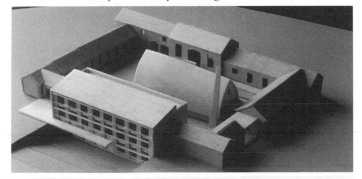

A model of the proposed new monastery in Worcestershire.

Order of St Benedict

Busan

OSB

Founded 1993

810-1 Baekrok-ri
Habuk-myon
Yangsan-shi
Kyungnam 626-860
SOUTH KOREA

Tel: 55 384 1560

Mobile: 010 9335 1560

Email: bundo1993
@hanmail.net

Morning Prayer
6.20 am

Eucharist
7.00 am (Wed only)

**Day Office
(Intercessions)**
12 noon

Evening Prayer
5.30 pm

Compline
8.00 pm

Office Book
Korean Common
Prayer Book

There has been an Anglican community in Seoul for many years, but it was the wish of Bishop Bundo Kim to establish a community in Busan - in the south of Korea. Thus it was that in 1993, the Order of St Benedict was founded in Busan City. In four years, sufficient money was raised by the Diocese to buy a more spacious, rural accommodation in Yangsan (to the north of Busan), offering more room for retreats, and for community and parish work.

SISTER MARTHA HAN OSB
(Senior Sister, assumed office 1998)
Sister Michaela

Associates
There is an informal group of Associates.

Community Publication
Summer and Christmas Newsletters. Contact Sister Martha re donations.

Guest and Retreat Facilities
There are three guest rooms for private retreats, with good kitchen and bathroom facilities. For larger groups, Korean-style accommodation is used. There are no restrictions on length of stay, and both men and women are welcome. There is no set charge but by donation only.

Most convenient time to telephone: 9.30 am - 7.00 pm

Bishop Visitor
Rt Revd Solomon Yoon, Bishop of Busan

Labouring in the garden

Order of St Benedict

Camperdown

OSB

Founded 1975

Benedictine
Monastery
PO Box 111
Camperdown
Victoria 3260
AUSTRALIA

Tel: 3 5593 2348
Fax: 3 5593 2887

Email: benabbey@
dodo.com.au

Website
www.
benedictineabbey
.com.au

Abbot Visitor
Rt Revd Dom
Bruno Marin OSB

Confessor
Very Revd Graeme
Lawrence OAM

Diocesan Bishop
Rt Revd
Michael Hough,
Bishop of Ballarat

The community was founded in the parish of St Mark, Fitzroy, in the archdiocese of Melbourne on 8 November 1975, when the first two monks were clothed. In 1980, after working in this inner city parish for five years, and after adopting the *Rule of Saint Benedict*, they moved to the country town of Camperdown in the Western District of Victoria. Here the community lives a contemplative monastic life with the emphasis on the balanced life of prayer and work that forms the Benedictine ethos.

In 1993, the Chapter decided to admit women and to endeavour to establish a mixed community of monks and nuns. To this end, two nuns came from Malling Abbey (UK) and one has transferred her stability to Camperdown.

The community supports itself through the operation of a printery, icon reproduction, manufacture of incense, crafts and a small guest house. A permanent monastery has now been built and the monastery church was consecrated by the diocesan bishop in February 1995. On July 11th 2002, the community elected the founder, Dom Michael King, as the first Abbot and he was blessed by the Bishop Visitor in the Abbey Church on the Feast of the Transfiguration, August 6th 2002.

In 2005, the Chapter petitioned the Subiaco Congregation of the Benedictine Confederation for aggregation to the Congregation. After a period of probation this was granted on the Feast of SS Peter and Paul 2007. This is an historic step for our community, giving us the opportunity to live our life in association with the Subiaco Congregation, thereby receiving the benefits of such a world-wide body but retaining our Anglican ethos - a great step in ecumenism. Abbot Michael was able to attend the General Chapter of the Congregation held at Subiaco in September 2008 and the Abbot President, assisted by the Abbot of Pluscarden, conducted a Visitation in January 2009. The fruits of our association are already being shown forth.

THE RT REVD DOM MICHAEL KING OSB
(*Abbot, elected 11 July 2002*)

Dom Placid Lawson
Sister Mary Philip Bloore
Sister Raphael Stone
Sister Mary Emmanuel Massy-Greene

Monk Postulants: 1

Vigils
4.30 am

Lauds
6.30 am

Terce &
Conventual Mass
8.15 am

Sext
11.45 am

None
2.10 pm

Vespers
5.00 pm

Compline
7.30 pm

Oblates
There is a small group of clerics and lay people who form the Oblates of St Benedict attached to the community. The group numbers seventy persons from Australia, New Zealand and Canada following the Benedictine life according to their individual situations. Oblates usually visit the monastery once a year and keep in regular contact with the parent community.

Community Publication: The Community produces a newsletter yearly in December.

Community Wares
Printing, icons, cards, incense, devotional items.

Guest and Retreat Facilities
There is a small guest house (St Joseph's), which can accommodate six people, open to men and women, for private retreats and spiritual direction. Guests eat with the community and are welcome to attend the services in the church. A donation of $50.00 per day is suggested.

Office Book: Camperdown breviary with a two-week cycle of the Psalter and seasonal and sanctoral variations.

Order of St Benedict

Community of St Mary at the Cross, Edgware

OSB

Founded 1866

With its dedication to St Mary at the Cross, this community has a special vocation to stand with Christ's Mother beside those who suffer. From its earliest days in Shoreditch, where Mother Monnica Skinner and Revd Henry Nihill worked together as co-founders, the sisters were drawn to the desperately poor and sick people around them. Awareness of the needs of many 'incurable children', led to the building of a hospital, marking the beginning of the community's life work.

Time passes and needs change; over the years the community's work has evolved to meet the present needs of elderly frail people for nursing or residential care. This care provision continues in Henry Nihill House at Edgware Abbey, where Residents enjoy close links with the community, its worship and its life.

From its foundation, the heart of the community's vocation lay in prayer; the Divine Office and the Eucharist were and are central to its life, love finding its expression in a care for those in need. Today many people are welcomed at the abbey, finding there a place of peace; all are offered Benedictine hospitality and given space for rest and renewal, with the opportunity to share in the community's worship.

Edgware Abbey
Priory Field Drive
Hale Lane
Edgware
Middlesex HA8 9PZ
UK
Tel: 020 8958 7868
Fax: 020 8958 1920
Email:
nuns.osb.edgware
@btclick.com

Website: www.
edgwareabbey.
org.uk

Readings and Lauds
7.00 am   (7.30 am Sun)

Midday Office
11.55 am (except Sun)

Vespers   5.30 pm
(4.40 pm Fri)

Compline   7.30 pm

Mass
7.45 am weekdays
11.00 am once a week
11.00 am Sun &
feast days

Holy Hour:
4.40 pm on Fri (Vespers
and Benediction)
First Fri of month:
11.55 am
Exposition and prayer,
ending in Holy Hour.

Office Book
The Divine Office.
with own form of
Compline

Bishop Visitor
Rt Revd Peter
Wheatley,
Bishop of Edmonton

RT REVD DAME MARY THÉRÈSE ZELENT OSB
(Abbess, elected 30 March 1993)
VERY REVD DAME MARY EANFLEDA BARBARA JOHNSON OSB
(Prioress)
Dame Ruth Mary Catherine Campbell
Intern Oblate: Raili Lappalainen

Ethiopian Orthodox: Sister Atsede Bekele
Sister Tirsit Eguale

CZM sisters: Sister Patricia   Sister Tendai

Oblates: Our Oblates are part of our extended Community
family: living outside the cloister; following the spirit of
the Holy Rule of St Benedict; bonded with the Community
in prayer and commitment to service.

Community Publication
Abbey Newsletter, published yearly. There is no charge but
donations are welcome. Obtainable from the Convent.

Community Wares
CLOISTER CRAFTS   Small Convent Craft Shop. Goods
available include printed and hand-crafted cards for many
occasions, devotional items, attractive hand-crafted goods,
a good range of books, including new publications.

Guest and Retreat Facilities
The Abbey conference and guest facilities include the
Thérèse Centre, Loreto and St Raphael's guest areas, and
the Emmaus Dining Room.
THE THÉRÈSE CENTRE contains a large airy room and
conservatory with views onto the garden. The main room
can hold up to fifty people and there is also space for small
group work. It is fitted with a sound and loop system.
It also has a small kitchenette with facilities for tea and
coffee. The Thérèse Centre has good disabled access.
ABBEY GUEST AREAS contain single rooms, with a washbasin
in each room, a kitchenette where tea and coffee can be
made at any time and sitting areas with views out onto
the garden. There is also a room suitable for a disabled
person. The abbey guest areas contain seventeen guest
rooms. There is also a small chapel in each area for guest
use.
THE EMMAUS ROOM is the dining room and also contains
the Library area which guests are welcome to use. Guests
are also welcome to spend time in our tranquil garden.
The Abbey has ample parking within the Abbey grounds.
Registered Charity: No. 209261

Order of St Benedict

Elmore Abbey

OSB

Founded 1914

Elmore Abbey
Church Lane
Speen, Newbury
Berkshire RG14 1SA
UK

Tel: 01635 33080
Email: elmore.
abbey
@virgin.net
Website: www.
elmoreabbey.org

Vigils   5.30 am

Lauds   8.00 am

Terce   10.00 am

Sext   12.00 noon

None   4.00 pm

Vespers   6.00 pm

Compline 8.30 pm

Mass
8.00 am Mon – Sat
(with Lauds)
10.00 am Sun

The monastery aims to provide an environment within which the traditional monastic balance between worship, study and work may be maintained with a characteristic Benedictine stress upon corporate worship and community life. To this end, outside commitments are kept to a minimum.

VERY REVD DOM SIMON JARRATT OSB
(Conventual Prior, elected 13 December 2005)
(RT REVD) DOM KENNETH NEWING OSB *(Sub-Prior)*
Dom Francis Hutchison
Dom Bruce De Walt
Brother Hugh Kelly

Oblates
An extended confraternity of oblates, numbering over 300 men and women, married and single, seek to live according to a rule of life inspired by Benedictine principles. From the start, the community has believed in the importance of prayer for Christian unity and the fostering of ecumenism. Details can be obtained from the Oblate Master.

Community History
Petà Dunstan, *The Labour of Obedience*, Canterbury Press, Norwich, 2009

Community Publications
Elmore Abbey Record, yearly, write to the Cellarer.

Books:
Augustine Morris, *Oblates: Life with Saint Benedict* £4.25.
Simon Bailey, *A Tactful God: Gregory Dix*, £12.99.

Guest and Retreat Facilities
There is a small guest house with accommodation for up to four wishing to stay for a personal retreat or period of quiet. Guests are admitted to the Oratory, the Guests' Common Room, the Refectory and the front garden.

Most convenient time to telephone
9.30 am - 9.50 am; 10.30 am - 11.45 am; 2.30 pm - 3.45 pm; 5.00 pm - 5.30 pm
Tel & answerphone: 01635 33080

Bishop Visitor:
Rt Revd Dominic Walker OGS, Bishop of Monmouth

Office Book: Elmore Abbey Office books

Registered Charity:
Pershore Nashdom & Elmore Trust - No. 220012

Order of St Benedict

Malling Abbey

OSB

Founded 1891

St Mary's Abbey
52 Swan Street
West Malling, Kent
ME19 6JX
UK
Tel: 01732 843309

Vigils 4.30 am
(5.00 am Sun)

Lauds 6.50 am
(8.10 am Sun)

Eucharist 7.30 am
(9.00 am Sun)

Terce 8.45 am

Sext 12.00 noon

None 3.00 pm

Vespers 4.45 pm

Compline 7.30 pm

Office Book
Malling Abbey Office

Bishop Visitor
Rt Revd John Waine

Our community was founded in 1891 and became Benedictine in 1906. The Rule of Saint Benedict provides a structured community life within the enclosure for those whose priority is seeking God. Our framework is a balanced day with pride of place given to worship and prayer (the Eucharist and seven-fold sung office, personal prayer and *lectio divina*), work in the house and large gardens and hospitality to our many guests. Times for recreation, study, literary and artistic work and various crafts complete a full and satisfying day. A newcomer who wishes to explore her vocation here is welcomed, first for several weeks as an aspirant, then for at least six years of training and discernment before she makes her solemn life vows. Each novice is encouraged to make her own unique contribution to the common life while also inheriting the community's traditions. These include our concern for the well-being of God's creation, our work for Christian unity and interfaith dialogue, and the cherishing of the legacy of the life, work and remaining medieval buildings of the original Benedictine nuns of Malling Abbey.

MOTHER MARY DAVID BEST OSB
(Abbess, elected 16 September 2008)
SISTER MARY STEPHEN PACKWOOD OSB *(Prioress)*
SISTER MARY MARK BROOKSBANK OSB *(Sub-Prioress)*

Sister Macrina Banner	Sister Bartimaeus Ives
Sister Mary John Marshall	Sister Seonaid Crabtree
Sister Mary Ignatius Conklin	Sister Mary Michael Wilson
Sister Mary Simon Corbett	Sister Miriam Noke
Sister Ruth Blackmore	Sister Mary Owen DeSimone
Sister Mary Cuthbert Archer	Sister Margaret Joy Harris
Sister Mary Gundulf Wood	
Sister Felicity Spencer	*Novices:* 1 *Postulants:* 1

Sister Jean CHF

Obituaries
26 Jul 2007   Sister Mary Francis Tillard,
aged 88, professed 34 years

Oblates
Oblates are men and women who feel called by God to follow the Benedictine way in their lives outside the cloister. After a two-and-a-half-year period of training and discernment they make a promise of the conversion of their life during the Eucharist and are then welcomed into the oblate family. Their commitment is expressed in a personal Benedictine rule of life, which balances their personal prayer, worship and *lectio divina* with their responsibility to family and work.

Community Wares
Cards and booklets printed and painted at the abbey are on sale at the Guest House.

Guest and Retreat Facilities
At the Abbey Guest House we can welcome ten individuals at a time. Our guests come to share in the worship and God-centred quiet, and to have the space and time for spiritual reflection and refreshment. Some choose to make a private retreat.

Monastic Experience
We welcome women who wish to deepen their spiritual lives by spending six to twenty-four months living alongside the community within the enclosure. This enables them to experience something of the common life according to the Rule of St Benedict and the traditions of our community. Further details may be obtained from the Mother Abbess.

Most convenient time to telephone: 9.30 am - 11.30 am

Order of
St Benedict

Servants of Christ
Priory

OSB

Founded 1968

28 West Pasadena
Avenue
Phoenix
AZ 85013 2002
USA
Tel: 602 248 9321
Email:
cderijk@cox.net

Morning Prayer
6.00 am

Mass 6.30 am

Midday Prayer
12 noon

Evening Prayer
4.30 pm

Compline 8.00 pm

A community united in love for God and one another following the Benedictine balance of prayer, study and work reflects the life of the monks. Outside engagements are accepted as long as they do not interfere with the monastic routine.

THE VERY REVD CORNELIS J. DE RIJK OSB
(*Prior, assumed office November 1985*)
The Revd Lewis H. Long

Oblates
Oblates follow a rule of life consistent with the Rule of St Benedict adapted to their lifestyle. Those in the metropolitan Phoenix area meet once a month at the monastery.

Community Wares
We have a gift shop which stocks prayer books, Bibles, hymnals, religious books and jewelry. We also supply altar bread and candles to numerous parishes. Through the sale of home-made bread, marmalade and jam, we raise funds for Navajo Indians, especially the seniors on the Reservations.

Guest and Retreat Facilities
We have two single rooms and two double rooms for individuals who wish to come and participate in our life. Day guests are also welcome. Guests have use of the grounds, the library, and share meals with the community. We are closed in August. there is a separate guest house with two double beds, sitting room, fireplace, kichen and bahroom.

Bishop Visitor: Rt Revd Kirk Stevan Smith, Bp of Arizona

Office Book: The BCP of ECUSA

St Gregory's Abbey

Three Rivers

OSB

Founded 1939

St Gregory's Abbey
56500 Abbey Road
Three Rivers
Michigan 49093-9595
USA
Tel: 269 244 5893
Fax: 269 244 8712
Email: abbot@
saintgregorys
threerivers.org

Website
saintgregorys
threerivers.org

Matins 4.00 am
(5.30 am Sun &
solemnities, with
Lauds)

Lauds 6.00 am

Terce & Mass
8.15 am (8.30 am Sun
& solemnities)

Sext 11.30 am
(12 noon Sun &
solemnities, with
None)

None 2.00 pm

Vespers 5.00 pm

Compline 7.45 pm

St Gregory's Abbey is the home of a community of men living under the Rule of St Benedict within the Episcopal Church. The center of the monastery's life is the Abbey Church, where God is worshipped in the daily round of Eucharist, Divine Office, and private prayer. Also offered to God are the monks' daily manual work, study and correspondence, ministry to guests, and occasional outside engagements.

RIGHT REVD ANDREW MARR OSB
(*Abbot, elected 2 March 1989*)
VERY REVD AELRED GLIDDEN OSB (*Prior*)

Father Benedict Reid*   Brother Martin Dally
Father Jude Bell   Brother Abraham Newsom
Father William Forest   Brother Cuthbert Donehue

*resident elsewhere

Community Publications and History
Abbey Newsletter, published four times a year. A subscription is free. To be added to the mailing list, write to the Abbey Business office.

The book *Singing God's Praises* was published in the Fall of 1998. It includes articles from community newsletters over the past sixty years and also includes a history of St Gregory's. Copies can be bought from the Abbey, price $20 a copy, postpaid.

Community Wares: The Abbey sells a calendar each year featuring photographs taken by one of the monks.

Guest and Retreat Facilities
Both men and women are welcome as guests. There is no charge, but $30 per day is 'fair value for services rendered' that is not tax-deductible. For further information and arrangements, contact the guest master by mail, telephone or e-mail at *guestsga@net-link.net.*

Associates
We have a Confraternity which offers an official connection to the Abbey and is open to anyone who wishes to join for the purpose of incorporating Benedictine principles into their lives. For further information and an application form, please write the Father Abbot.

Office Book: The community uses home-made books based on the Roman Thesaurus for the Benedictine Office.

Bishop Visitor: Rt Revd Arthur Williams,
suffragan Bishop of Ohio (retired)

Order of St Helena

OSH

Founded 1945

Convent of
St Helena
3042 Eagle Drive,
Augusta
GA 30906
USA
Tel: 706 798 5201
Fax: 706 796 0079

Email:
augofficemgr
@comcast.net

Website
www.osh.org

Matins
7.30 am

Eucharist
8.00 am

**Diurnum
and intercessions**
noon

Vespers
5.00 pm

Compline
7.00 pm

The Order of St Helena witnesses to a contemporary version of traditional monasticism, taking a threefold vow of Poverty, Celibate Chastity and Obedience. Our life in community is shaped by the daily Eucharist and fourfold Office, plus hours of personal prayer and study, and from this radiates a wide range of ministries.

As an Order, we are not restricted to any single area of work but witness and respond to the Gospel, with individual sisters engaging in different ministries as they feel called by God and affirmed by the community. Our work is thus wonderfully varied: sisters work in parishes as priests or as pastoral assistants; they lead retreats, quiet days and conferences; work with the national Church and various organizations; offer spiritual direction; are psychotherapists; teach; serve in hospital chaplaincies and community service programs. Seven sisters are ordained priests.

In 1997, the Order adopted a new style of governance and no longer has a superior or single sister as head. Instead, the Order was led by a four-member Leadership Council, with responsibility and ultimate authority vested equally in all four members. Since 2007, the Council has had three members.

In 2008, the sisters closed both their New York convents and consolidated into one house in Augusta, Georgia.

Leadership Council:
REVD SISTER DEBORAH MAGDALENE OSH
(Minister of Vocations)
SISTER MARY LOIS MILLER OSH
SISTER LINDA JULIAN OSH

Revd Sister Mary Michael	Sister June Thomas
Sister Ruth Juchter	Sister Ann Prentice
Sister Cornelia Ransom	Sister Veronica Aryeequaye
Sister Ellen Stephen	Revd Sister
Revd Sister Jean Campbell	Ellen Francis Poisson
Revd Sister Carol Andrew	Sister Linda Elston
Sister Barbara Lee	Revd Sister Sophia Woods
Sister Benedicta	Sister Faith Anthony
Sister Cintra Pemberton	
Sister Elsie Reid	*Novices:* 1
Revd Sister Rosina Ampah	

Associates
ASSOCIATES - open to all women and men. Write to the Secretary for Associates at the Augusta Convent.

Community Publication: saint helena, published quarterly, free of charge. Write to the Convent of St Helena for a subscription. Also available online at www.osh.org.

Community Wares and Books
Hand-made rosaries - *write to* Sister Mary Lois.
Hand-done copper enamels with religious themes -
> *write to* Sister Ellen Stephen.

Sister Cintra Pemberton OSH, *Soulfaring: Celtic Pilgrimage then and now,*
> SPCK, London, & Morehouse, Harrisburg, PA, 1999.

Doug Shadel and Sister Ellen Stephen OSH, *Vessel of Peace: The voyage toward spiritual freedom*, Three Tree Press, 1999.

Sister Ellen Stephen OSH, *Together and Apart: a memoir of the Religious Life*,
> Morehouse, Harrisburg, PA, 2008.

Community History: A history is in process, being written by Sister Mary Michael.

Office Book
The Saint Helena Breviary, Monastic Edition, which includes all the music in plainchant notation, is now published. It follows closely the BCP of the Episcopal Church of the USA. The focus is on inclusive language and expanded imagery for God, following principles set forth by the Standing Commission for Liturgy and Music of the Episcopal Church, USA. The *Saint Helena Psalter*, extracted from the Breviary, was published in November 2004, *The Saint Helena Breviary, Personal edition*, in July 2006, both by Church Publishing Co., Inc.

Bishop Visitor: Rt Revd Neil Alexander, Bishop of Atlanta

Registered Charity No: US Government 501 (c)(3)

Sisterhood of the Holy Nativity

SHN

Founded 1882

Website
www.
episcopalian.org/shn

Ours is a mixed life, which means that we combine an apostolic ministry with a contemplative lifestyle. The Rule of the Sisterhood of the Holy Nativity follows the model of the Rule of St Augustine of Hippo. As such, we strive to make the love of God the motive of all our actions. The four 'charisms', which undergird our life, are Charity, Humility, Prayer, and Missionary Zeal. Each of these spiritual gifts we desire to develop in our lives both for the fraternal unity they foster among us, and for the power they provide for the work of evangelistic ministry.

We are a small community, but continue to do whatever God gives us to do in local parishes or travelling to conduct retreats and teaching or preaching missions. We built a smaller Convent and moved here in December 1999.

Bethlehem-by-the-Lake
W1484
Spring Grove Road
Ripon
WI 54971-8655
USA

Tel: 920 748 5332

Email: srboniface
@hotmail.com

Matins
7.30 am

Eucharist 8.00 am

**Diurnum
(Noonday Prayer)**
12 noon

Vespers
5.30 pm

Compline
8.00 pm

Office Book
The Monastic Breviary,
published by the Order
of the Holy Cross

Bishop Visitor
Rt Revd
Russell E Jacobus,
Bishop of
Fond du Lac

SISTER BONIFACE SHN
(Revd Mother, assumed office March 2007)
SISTER MARGARETTA SHN *(Assistant Superior)*

Sister Elsbeth   Sister Charis
Sister Columba   Sister Abigail
Sister Kathleen Marie

Obituaries
20 Dec 2008   Sister Mary Frances,
                              aged 83, professed 50 years

Associates and Oblates
ASSOCIATES are men and women who connect themselves to the prayer life and ministry of the community, and keep a Rule of Life. Membership is open to adult (lay and clerical) members of the Episcopal Church.

OBLATES can be men or women who desire a closer connection with the Community and are able to commit to spending at least three weeks each year living and working with the Sisters at one of our Houses. We have fourteen Oblates and have seven Novice Oblates.

Other Addresses
St. Mary's Retreat House, 505 East Los Olivos Street, Santa Barbara, CA 93105 USA   *Tel: 805 682 4117*

St Mary's Retreat House is now being administered by the Order of the Holy Cross. The Brothers from Mount Calvary Retreat House will continue their ministry of hospitality at St Mary's for a time.

Community Publication
We put out an occasional newsletter, *Sisters of the Holy Nativity*. If interested contact: Bethlehem-by-the-Lake, W1484 Spring Grove Road, Ripon, WI 54971-8655, USA *(Email: srboniface@hotmail.com).*
There is no charge, though we occasionally make an appeal for donations.

Guest and Retreat Facilities
The Mother House can accommodate one or two guests. An offering is accepted.

Sisterhood of St John the Divine

SSJD

Founded 1884

St John's Convent
233 Cummer Ave
Toronto
Ontario M2M 2E8
Canada
Tel: 416 226 2201
ext. 301
Fax: 416 222 4442

Emails:
convent@ssjd.ca
guesthouse@ssjd.ca

Website
www.ssjd.ca

Morning Prayer
8.30 am

Holy Eucharist
12 noon (8.00 am Sun)

Praise at Mid-day
12 noon (when
Eucharist not at noon)

Evening Prayer
5.00 pm

Compline 8.10 pm

Office Book
Book of Alternative
Services 1985

The Sisterhood of St John the Divine is a contemporary expression of the Religious life for women within the Anglican Church of Canada. Founded in Toronto in 1884, we are a prayer- and gospel-centred monastic community, bound together by the call to live out our baptismal covenant through the vows of poverty, chastity and obedience. Living as we do in a time of change, these vows anchor us in the life of Jesus and in the transforming experience of the Gospel. Nurtured by our founding vision of prayer, community and ministry, we are open and responsive to the needs of the Church and the contemporary world, continually seeking the guidance of the Holy Spirit in our life and ministry.

St John's Convent is a centre of prayer, community, and mission, which nurtures and supports the life of the whole Sisterhood. The Convent's mission includes: a guest house where individuals and groups are welcomed, and share in the community's prayer and liturgy; regularly scheduled retreats; availability of Sisters to preach, teach, speak, lead retreats and quiet days; programs which help people to build bridges between our secular culture, the Church, and the monastic tradition; discernment programs for those seeking guidance in their life and work; the offering of spiritual direction; embroidered white church linens; music and liturgical leadership for the Church; ecumenical outreach; and partnership with St John's Rehab Hospital.

The Sisterhood supports St John's Rehab Hospital through membership in the Hospital Corporation and Board of Directors, and through its presence on the Hospital staff. The Sisters advocate for a vision of health care which expresses SSJD's mission and values in a multi-faith, multi-cultural setting, and provides spiritual and pastoral support for patients, staff and volunteers.

Other address
ST JOHN'S HOUSE, BC,
3937 St Peter's Rd, Victoria, British Columbia V8P 2J9
Tel: 250 920 7787   Fax: 250 920 7709
E-mail: bchouse@ssjd.ca
A community of Sisters committed to being a praying presence in the Diocese of British Columbia. Prayer, intentional community, hospitality, and mission are at the heart of our life in the Diocese and beyond.

Community Publication
The Eagle (newsletter). Contact the Convent Secretary. Published quarterly. $10.00 suggested annual donation.

SISTER ELIZABETH ANN ECKERT SSJD
(Reverend Mother, assumed office 13 April 2005)
SISTER ELIZABETH ROLFE-THOMAS SSJD *(Assistant to the Reverend Mother)*

Sister Constance Murphy	Sister Anitra Hansen
Sister Joyce Bodley	Sister Margaret Mary Watson
Sister Helena Ward	Sister Jessica Kennedy
Sister Wilma Grazier	Sister Constance Joanna Gefvert
Sister Thelma-Anne McLeod	Sister Brenda Jenner
Sister Jean Marston	Sister Anne Norman
Sister Beryl Stone	Sister Peta-Ann Jackson
Sister Merle Milligan	Sister Helen Claire Gunter
Sister Doreen McGuff	Sister Susan Elwyn
Sister Patricia Forler	Sister Louise Manson
Sister Madeleine Mary Salter	Sister Dorothy Handrigan
Sister Jocelyn Mortimore	Sister Amy Hamilton
Sister Margaret Ruth Steele	Sister Patricia Marion
Sister Sarah Jean Thompson	

Novices: 1

Obituaries

22 Sep 2007	Sister Margaret Ann Macfarlane, aged 80, life professed 53 years
1 Sep 2008	Sister Philippa Watson, aged 85, life professed 55 years

Associates and Oblates
Our approximately nine hundred associates are women and men who follow a Rule of Life and share in the ministry of the Sisterhood. The Sisterhood of St John the Divine owes its founding to the vision and dedication of the clergy and lay people who became the first Associates of SSJD. A year of discernment is required before being admitted as an Associate to see if the Associate Rule helps the person in what she/he is seeking; and to provide the opportunity to develop a relationship with the Sisters and to deepen the understanding and practice of prayer. The Associate Rule provides a framework for the journey of faith. There are three basic commitments: belonging in a parish; the practice of prayer, retreat, study of scripture, and spiritual reading; and the relationship with SSJD. Write to the house nearest you for further information.

We have a small but growing number of Oblates. Oblate are women who wish to make a promise of prayer and service in partnership with the Sisterhood. Each Oblate develops her own Rule of Life in partnership with the Oblate Director, her spiritual director, and a support group. A year of discernment is also required, as well as an annual residency program. Write to Sister Constance Joanna at the Convent in Toronto for more information.

Community Wares
A variety of cards made by Sisters or Associates. Good selection of books on spiritual growth for sale at the Convent (not by mail) and a few CDs. Anglican rosaries made by the sisters and some knitted items.

Bishop Visitor: Rt Revd Colin Johnson

Community History and Books

Sister Eleonora SSJD, *A Memoir of the Life and Work of Hannah Grier Coome, Mother-Foundress of SSJD, Toronto, Canada*, OUP, London, 1933 (out of print).

The Sisterhood of St John the Divine 1884-1984, published 1931 as *A Brief History*; 4th revision 1984, (out of print).

Sister Constance Joanna SSJD, *From Creation to Resurrection: A Spiritual Journey*, Anglican Book Centre, Toronto, 1990.

Sister Constance SSJD, *Other Little Ships: The memoirs of Sister Constance SSJD*, Patmos Press, Toronto, 1997.

Sister Thelma-Anne McLeod SSJD, *In Age Reborn, By Grace Sustained*, Path Books, Toronto, 2007

Guest and Retreat Facilities

Guest House has thirty-seven rooms (forty-two people) used for rest, quiet time and retreats. Contact the Guest Sister at the Convent for details about private accommodation, scheduled retreats, quiet days and other programs.

The Sisters in Victoria also lead quiet days and retreats and have room for one guest. Please contact St John's House, BC, for detailed information.

Sisterhood of St Mary

Founded 1929

St Andrew's Mission
PO Haluaghat
Mymensingh
BANGLADESH

(Morning) Prayer
6.30 am

Meditation 8.00 am

(Mid-morning) Prayer
9.00 am

(Mid-day) Prayer
11.30 am

(Afternoon) Prayer
3.00 pm

(Evening) Prayer
6.00 pm

Compline 8.00 pm

The community is located on the northern border of Bangladesh at the foot of the Garo hills in India. The community was formed in Barisal at the Sisterhood of the Epiphany, and was sent here to work among the indigenous tribal people, side by side with St Andrew's Brotherhood already working in the area. The membership of the Sisterhood has always been entirely indigenous. The first sisters were Bengalis. The present sisters are the fruit of their work - all are Garo. They take the vows of Poverty, Purity and Obedience and live a very simple life. They lead a life of prayer and formation of girls. They also look after the Church and do pastoral work among women and children in the Parish.

SISTER MIRA MANKHIN
(Sister Superior, assumed office 2002)
SISTER ANITA RAKSAM *(Assistant Superior)*
Sister Bregita Doffo
Sister Mala Chicham
Novices: 2

Community Wares
Some handicrafts and vestments for church use and sale.

Bishop Visitor
Rt Revd Michael Baroi, Bishop of Dhaka

Sisters of Charity

SC

Founded 1869

237 Ridgeway
Plympton
Plymouth
PL7 2HP
UK

Tel: 01752 336112

Email:
plymptonsisters
@tiscali.com.uk

Morning Prayer
8.00 am

Vespers
5.00 pm

Compline
7.00 pm

Office Book
Daily Prayer

Registered Charity:
No. X33170

A Community following the Rule of St Vincent de Paul and so committed to the service of those in need. The Sisters are involved in parish work and the Community also has a nursing home in Plympton.

MOTHER ELIZABETH MARY SC
(Revd Mother, assumed office 21 April 2003)
SISTER CLARE SC *(priest) (Assistant)*

Sister Faith Mary
Sister Theresa
Sister Angela Mary
Sister Rosamund
Sister Hilda Mary
Sister Mary Joseph
Sister Gabriel Margaret
Sister Mary Patrick

Obituaries
8 Jul 2008   Sister Margaret Veronica, aged 93,
                              professed 54 years
9 Nov 2008   Sister Faith Nicolette, aged 94,
                              professed 55 years

Oblates and Associate Members
The Community has a group of Oblates and Associate Members, formed as a mutual supportive link. We do not provide a rule of life; instead we ask our Oblates and Associate Members to add to their existing rule the daily use of the Vincentian Prayer.

Oblates are also asked to use the Holy Paraclete hymn and one of the Daily Offices, thereby joining in spirit in the Divine Office of the Community. Oblates are encouraged to make an annual retreat.

Associate Members support us by their prayers and annual subscription.

Other addresses
Saint Vincent's Nursing Home,
Fore Street, Plympton, Plymouth PL7 1NE
Tel: 01752 336205

Guest and Retreat Facilities
We welcome individuals for Quiet Days.

Most convenient time to telephone: 4.00 pm - 6.30 pm

Bishop Visitor: Rt Revd Robert Evens, Bishop of Crediton

Sisters of the Incarnation

SI

Founded 1981

The House of the
Incarnation
6 Sherbourne Terrace
Dover Gardens
SA 5048
AUSTRALIA
Tel: 08 8296 2166

Email: sisincar
@chariot.net.au

Office Book
A Prayer Book for
Australia (1995 edition)
for
Morning and Evening
Prayer, and Compline;
Midday Prayer is from
another source

The sisters live under vows of poverty, chastity and obedience in a simple life style, and seek to maintain a balance between prayer, community life and work for each member and to worship and serve within the church. They combine the monastic and apostolic aspects of the Religious Life. The monastic aspects include prayer, domestic work at home, community life and hospitality. The sisters are engaged in parish ministry and with priestly responsibility for two parishes.

The community was founded in the diocese of Adelaide in 1981 as a contemporary expression of the Religious Life for women in the Anglican Church. In 1988, the two original sisters made their Profession of Life Intention within the Sisters of the Incarnation, before the Archbishop of Adelaide, the Visitor of the community. One member was ordained to the diaconate in 1990 and the priesthood in 1993. The governing body of the community is its chapter of professed sisters, which elects the Guardian, and appoints an Episcopal Visitor and a Community Advisor. The community is not endowed; the sisters work to earn sufficient for their needs.

SISTER PATRICIA SI
(*Guardian, assumed office 1981*)
Sister Juliana (*priest*)

Friends
The community has a group of Friends who share special celebrations and significant events, many of whom have supported the community from the beginning, while others become Friends as we touch their lives. There is no formal structure.

Bishop Visitor: Rt Revd Dr K Rayner

Sisters of Jesus Way

Founded 1979

Redacre
24 Abbey Road
West Kirby
Wirral
CH48 7EP

Two Wesley deaconesses founded the Sisters of Jesus Way. There have been many strands that have been instrumental in the formation of the community but primarily these have been the Gospels, the Charismatic Renewal, the teaching and example of the Pietists of the 17th and early 18th centuries as practised in some German communities and the lives of saints from many denominations.

Our calling is to love the Lord Jesus with a first love, to trust the heavenly Father as his dear children for all our needs both spiritual and material and to allow the Holy Spirit to guide and lead us. Prayer, either using the framework of a simple liturgy or informal, is central to all

Tel: 0151 6258775
Email:
sistersofjesusway
@redacre.org.uk

Morning Prayer
8.00 am

Intercessory prayer
(community only)
2.00 pm

Evening Prayer
7.00 pm

Bishop Guardian
Rt Revd
Dr Peter Forster,
Bishop of Chester

Registered Charity
No 509284

that we do. We make life promises of simplicity, fidelity and chastity.

Our work for the Lord varies as the Holy Spirit opens or closes doors. We welcome guests, trusting that as the Lord Jesus lives with us, they will meet with him and experience his grace. Music, some of which has been composed by the sisters, is very much part of our life. We work together, learning from the Lord to live together, as a family in love, forgiveness and harmony.

SISTER MARIE
(Little Sister, assumed office 1991)
SISTER SYLVIA *(Companion Sister)*

Sister Hazel   Sister Beatrice
Sister Lynda   Sister Susan
Sister Florence   Sister Louise

Associates
The Followers of the Lamb are a small group of women following a simple Rule of Life and committed to assisting the Sisters.

Guest and Retreat Facilities
8 single rooms, 4 double rooms. Several rooms for day visitors and small groups.

Most convenient time to telephone: 9.30am-12.30pm; 2.30pm-6pm; 7.30pm-9pm

Community Publication
Twice-yearly teaching and newsletter. Contact Sister Louise.

Community History
Published by the Sisters of Jesus Way and available from the Community:
The Beloved Community - Beginnings; A Time to Build;
Circles of Love - the Life and Work of the Sisters of Jesus Way

Society of the Holy Cross

SHC

Founded 1925

3 Jeong-dong
Jung-ku
Seoul 100-120
KOREA
Tel: 2 735 7832
or 2 735 3478
Fax: 2 736 5028
Email: holycross25
@yahoo.com

Website
www.sister.or.kr

Morning Prayer
6.15 am

Holy Eucharist
6.45 am

Midday Prayer
12.30 pm
(12 noon Sun & great
feast days)

Evening Prayer
5.00 pm

Compline   8.00 pm

Office Book
Revised Common
Prayer for MP & EP
and Compline; & SHC
material for Midday
Office

The community was founded on the feast day of the Exaltation of the Holy Cross in 1925 by the Rt Revd Mark Trollope, the third bishop of the Anglican Church in Korea, admitting Postulant Phoebe Lee and blessing a small traditional Korean-style house in the present site of Seoul.   The Community of St Peter, Woking, Surrey in England, sent eighteen Sisters as missionaries to Korea between 1892 and 1950, who nourished this young community for a few decades.   Sister Mary Clare CSP, who was the first Mother Superior of this community, was persecuted by the North Korean communists and died during the 'death march' in the Korean War in 1950. This martyrdom especially has been a strong influence and encouragement for the growth of the community.

Our spirituality is based on a modified form of the Augustinian Rule harmonized with the Benedictine one. Bishop Mark Trollope, the first Visitor, and Sister Mary Clare CSP compiled the Divine Office Book and the Constitution and Rule of the Community. The activities that are being continuously practised even now include pastoral care in parishes, running homes for the elderly and those with learning difficulties, teaching English, and counselling people.

We run a programme for vocation one weekend each month, and a spiritual prayer meeting and workshop monthly with people who want to improve their spiritual life. We also conduct Quiet Hours and Retreats individually or in groups. We lead contemplation based on Ignatian Spirituality.

SISTER ANGELA SHC
(Reverend Mother, assumed office 1 Jan 2007)
SISTER HELEN ELIZABETH SHC *(priest) (Assistant Superior)*

Sister Monica	Sister Martha Joanna
Sister Phoebe Anne	Sister Theresa
Sister Edith	Sister Grace
Sister Cecilia	Sister Helen Juliana
Sister Maria Helen	Sister Lucy Edward
Sister Etheldreda	
Sister Catherine *(priest)*	*Juniors:*
Sister Maria Clare	Sister Martha
Sister Pauline	Sister Prisca
Sister Monica Alma	
	Novices: 2

Friends and Associates

FRIENDS are men and women from all walks of life who desire to have a close link with the community.   They follow a simple Rule of Life, which includes praying for the Sisters and their work. Friends also form a network of prayer, fellowship and mutual support within Christ's ministry of wholeness and reconciliation. About one hundred members come together for the annual meeting in October at the Motherhouse. The committee members meet bi-monthly at the convent.

ASSOCIATES: thirty-eight friends have been trained for admission and vow-taking for full membership since 2005.

Other Addresses

St Anne's Convalescent Home for Elderly People,
619-28 Onsuri, Kilsang, Kangwha, Inch'on, 417-840 South Korea
Tel: 32 937 1935 Fax: 32 937 0696   Email: anna1981@kornet.net
Website: www.oldanna.or.kr

St Bona House for Mentally Retarded People,
2-4 Neamni, Kadok, Chongwon, Chungbuk 363-853, South Korea
Tel: 82 43 297 8348   Fax: 82 43 298 3156   Email: sralma@chollian.net
*   Website: www.bona.or.kr*

Community Publication

Holy Cross Newsletter, published occasionally, in Korean.
Sister Catherine SHC, *Holy Vocation* (booklet for the SHC 75th anniversary, 2000)

Community History

Jae Joung Lee, *Society of the Holy Cross 1925-1995*, Seoul, 1995 (in Korean).
Sisters Maria Helen & Catherine, *The SHC: the First 80 Years*, 2005

Community Wares

Wafers and wine for Holy Eucharist, vestments and church linen, and the following items: prayer books, Bibles, hymnals, cards, crosses, candles, candle-stands, bells, cruets, Anglican rosaries etc.

Guest and Retreat Facilities

The Community occasionally organizes retreats and quiet days for Christians.

Bishop Visitor: Rt Revd Paul Kim, Bishop of Seoul

Society of the Precious Blood
(UK)

SPB

Founded 1905

Burnham Abbey
Lake End Road
Taplow, Maidenhead
Berkshire SL6 OPW
UK
Tel & Fax:
01628 604080
Email:
burnhamabbey@
btinternet.com

Website: www.
burnhamabbey.org

Lauds 7.30 am

Eucharist 9.30 am

Angelus & Sext
12.00 noon

Vespers 5.30 pm

Compline 8.30 pm

Office Book
SPB Office Book

Bishop Visitor
Rt Revd
Stephen Cottrell,
Bishop of Reading

Registered Charity
No. 900512

We are a contemplative community whose particular work within the whole body of Christ is worship, thanksgiving and intercession. Within these ancient Abbey walls, which date back to 1266, we continue to live the Augustinian monastic tradition of prayer, silence, fellowship and solitude. The Eucharist is the centre of our life, where we find ourselves most deeply united with Christ, one another and all for whom we pray. The work of prayer is continued in the Divine Office, in the Watch before the Blessed Sacrament and in our whole life of work, reading, creating, and learning to live together. This life of prayer finds an outward expression in welcoming guests, who come seeking an opportunity for quiet and reflection in which to deepen their own spiritual lives, or to explore the possibility of a religious vocation.

SISTER MARY BERNARD SPB
(Reverend Mother, assumed office 30 January 2003)

Sister Margaret Mary	Sister Mary Benedict
Sister Dorothy Mary	Sister Victoria Mary
Sister Jane Mary	Sister Miriam Mary
Sister Mary Laurence	Sister Elizabeth Mary
Sister Mary Philip	Sister Grace Mary

Companions and Oblates
Oblates are men and women who feel drawn by God to express the spirit of the Society, united with the Sisters in their life of worship, thanksgiving and intercession. They live out their dedication in their own situation and make a yearly Promise.

Men and women who desire to share in the prayer and work of the Society but cannot make as full a commitment to saying the Office may be admitted as Companions.

Community History
Sister Felicity Mary SPB, *Mother Millicent Mary*, 1968.
Booklets and leaflets on the history and life of the Abbey.

Community Wares: The Sisters find a creative outlet in producing cards, rosaries, holding crosses and other crafts (for sale in the Guest House).

Community Publications: *Newsletter*, yearly at Christmas. *Companions/Oblates Letter*, quarterly.

Guest and Retreat Facilities: We have a small guest house with four single rooms for individual (unconducted) retreats.
Most convenient time to telephone: 10.30 am - 12 noon, 3.00 pm - 4.30 pm, 7.00 pm - 8.00 pm

Society of the Precious Blood
(Lesotho)

SPB

Founded 1905

Priory of Our Lady
Mother of Mercy
PO Box 7192
Maseru 100
LESOTHO
Tel: 00266 58859585
00266 270002605

Morning Prayer 7.00 am

Eucharist 7.30 am

Terce 10.00 am

Midday Office
12 noon

Evening Prayer 5.30 pm

Compline 8.00 pm

Office Book
Daily Prayer & An
Anglican Prayer Book
1989, CPSA

St Monica's
House of Prayer
46 Green St, West End
Kimberley, 8301
SOUTH AFRICA
Tel: 053 832 7331

Bishop Visitor
Rt Revd Adam Taaso,
Bishop of Lesotho

Five Sisters of the Society of the Precious Blood at Burnham Abbey came to Masite in Lesotho in 1957 to join with a community of African women, with the intention of forming a multi-cultural contemplative community dedicated to intercession. In 1966, this community at Masite became autonomous, although still maintaining strong ties of friendship with Burnham Abbey. In 1980, a House of Prayer was established in Kimberley in South Africa, which has developed a more active branch of the Society.

SISTER ELAINE MARY SPB
(*Prioress, assumed office 24 September 1997*)

Sister Josephine Mary	Sister Cicily Mary
Sister Theresia Mary	Sister Camilla Mary
Sister Magdalen Mary	*Intern Oblates: 2*
Sister Lucia Mary	
Sister Diana Mary	*Novices: 1*

Obituaries
4 Apr 2008   Sister Mary Dominic, aged 92,
professed 42 years

Oblates and Companions
The Community has thirteen oblates (in Lesotho, South Africa, Zambia, New Zealand and the UK), and eighty-six Companions and Associates (in Lesotho, South Africa and the UK). All renew their promises annually. Oblates are sent prayer material regularly. Companions and Associates receive quarterly letters and attend occasional quiet days.

Community History and books
Sister Theresia Mary SPB, *Father Patrick Maekane MBK*, CPSA, 1987
Evelyn Cresswell (Oblate SPB), *Keeping the Hours*, Cluster Pubs, Pietermaritzburg, 2007

Community Publication
Annual *Newsletter;* apply to the Prioress. No charge.

Community Wares: Cards, crafts, religious booklets.

Guest and Retreat Facilities
Small guest house with three bedrooms. There is no fixed charge. It is closed in winter (June to mid-August). Both men and women are welcome for retreats, which may be private or accompanied by a Sister. We also welcome anyone who wishes to share our life for a few months, to live with us in the Priory.

Society of the Sacred Advent

SSA

Founded 1892

Community House
34 Lapraik Street
Albion
QLD 4010
AUSTRALIA
Tel: 07 3262 5511
Fax: 07 3862 3296

Email:
sistersofssa@
stmarg.qld.edu.au

eunice@
stmarg.qld.edu.au

Quiet time
6.00 am

Morning Prayer
6.30 am
(7.00 am Sun & Mon)

Eucharist 7.00 am
(7.30 am Sun)

Midday Prayer
12 noon

Evensong 5.30 pm

Compline 7.30 pm
(8.00 pm Wed & Sat)

The Society of the Sacred Advent exists for the glory of God and for the service of His Church in preparation for the second coming of our Lord and Saviour Jesus Christ.

Members devote themselves to God in community under vows of poverty, chastity and obedience. Our life is a round of worship, prayer, silence and work. Our Patron Saint is John the Baptist who, by his life and death, pointed the way to Jesus. We would hope also to point the way to Jesus in our own time, to a world which has largely lost touch with spiritual realities and is caught up in despair, loneliness and fear.

As part of our ministry, Sisters may be called to give addresses, conduct Retreats or Quiet Days, or to make themselves available for spiritual direction, hospital chaplaincy and parish work. The aim of the Community is to grow in the mind of Christ so as to manifest Him to others. The Society has two Schools, St Margaret's and St Aidan's and two Sisters are on each of the School Councils.

SISTER EUNICE SSA
(Revd Mother, assumed office 21 March 2007)

Sister Dorothy   Sister Gillian
Sister June Ruth   Sister Moira-Grace
Sister Sandra   *Novices:* 1
Sister Beverley

Fellowship and Company

THE FELLOWSHIP OF THE SACRED ADVENT
Since 1925, the work of the Community has been helped by the prayers and work of a group of friends known as the Fellowship of the Sacred Advent. They have a simple Rule of Life.

THE COMPANY OF THE SACRED ADVENT began in 1987. This is a group of men and women, clergy and lay, bound together in love for Jesus Christ and His Church in the spirit of St John the Baptist. It seeks to proclaim the Advent challenge: 'Prepare the Way of the Lord.' Members have a Rule of Life and renew their promises annually.

Members of the Fellowship and Company are part of our extended Community family. The Sisters arrange Retreats and Quiet Days and support them with their prayers, help, or spiritual guidance, as required.

Other address:

Society of the Sacred Advent, 261 Anduramba Road, Crows Nest, Q'ld 4355, AUSTRALIA

Community Publication
There is a Newsletter, twice yearly. For a subscription, write to Sister Sandra SSA. The cost is A$5 per year.

Community History: Elizabeth Moores, *One Hundred Years of Ministry,*
published for SSA, 1992.
Community Wares: Cards and crafts.

Bishop Visitor: Rt Revd Godfrey Fryar, Bishop of Rockhampton

Guest and Retreat Facilities
There are twenty single rooms. Both men and women are welcome. The facilities are closed over Christmas and in January.

Office Book
A Prayer Book for Australia; *The Daily Office SSF* is used for Midday Prayer.

Society of the Sacred Cross

SSC

Founded 1914
(Chichester);
moved to Wales in
1923

Tymawr Convent
Lydart, Monmouth
Gwent NP25 4RN
UK

Tel: 01600 860244
or 860808

Email:
tymawrconvent
@btinternet.com

Website: www.
churchinwales.org.
uk/tymawr/index.
html

The community, part of the Anglican Church in Wales, lives a monastic, contemplative life of prayer based on silence, solitude and learning to live together, under vows of poverty, chastity and obedience, with a modern rule, Cistercian in spirit. At the heart of our corporate life is the Eucharist with the daily Office and other times of shared prayer spanning the day. All services are open to the public and we are often joined by members of the neighbourhood in addition to our visitors. Our common life includes study, recreation and work in the house and extensive grounds. It is possible for women and men, married or single, to experience our life of prayer by living alongside the community for periods longer than the usual guest stay. Hospitality is an important part of our life at Tymawr and guests are most welcome. We also organise and sponsor occasional lectures and programmes of study for those who wish to find or develop the life of the spirit in their own circumstances. The community is dedicated to the crucified and risen Lord as the focus of its life and the source of the power to live it.

SISTER MARY JEAN SSC
(Revd Mother, assumed office 2 July 1998)
SISTER GILLIAN MARY SSC *(Assistant)*

Sister Anne   Sister Heylin Columba*
Sister Veronica Ann   Sister Emma Joy
Sister Lorna Francis*
                                Novices: 1   *Postulants:* 1

* *Living the contemplative life away from Tymawr.*

Obituaries
20 Aug 2008   Sister Laurie, aged 53, professed 3 years
11 Jan 2009   Sister Cara Mary, aged 83, professed 51 years

Morning Prayer
7.00 am

Terce 8.45 am

Eucharist
12.00 noon

Evening Prayer
5.30 pm

Silent Corporate Prayer
8pm

Compline 8.30 pm

Office Book
CCP, with additional SSC material.

Most convenient time to telephone:
6.45 pm – 8.00 pm only,
except Mondays,
Fridays and Sundays.

Community History
Sister Jeanne SSC,
A Continuous Miracle,
(privately printed).

Bishop Visitor
Rt Revd
Dominic Walker OGS,
Bishop of Monmouth

Registered Charity:
No. 1047614

Oblates and Associates
There are forty-eight Oblates, living in their own homes, each having a personal Rule sustaining their life of prayer. One hundred and twelve Associates, women and men, have a simple commitment. Three Companion Brothers, who are priests, live a life of prayer as a 'cell' under a Rule inspired by SSC's Rule. One Companion Sister lives a solitary life of prayer under vow. Three months are spent annually with SSC. There are also two residents who live alongside the community.

Community Wares
The Border series of books, co-published by Tymawr Convent & Canterbury Press. Authors: Una Kroll, John Polkinghorne, Esther de Waal & Jane Williams. Obtainable from Tymawr at £3 each.
Colour photographs cards of Tymawr available at 60p each (including envelope).

Community Publication
Tymawr Newsletter, yearly at Advent. Write to the above address.

Guest and Retreat Facilities
The community offers facilities for individual guests and small groups. There are five rooms (one double) in the guest wing of the Main House for full board. Michaelgarth, the self-catering guest house offers facilities for individuals or groups (five singles and two doubles), and also for day groups. The Old Print House offers full facilities for day groups of up to eight. Individuals may have private retreats with guidance from a member of the community. The community occasionally organises retreats and study days. Pilgrimages round the grounds, on a variety of themes, can be arranged. Please write with a stamped addressed envelope for details.

Society of the Sacred Mission

SSM

Founded 1893

Office Book
Celebrating
Common Prayer

Bishops Visitor
Rt Revd
Tom Butler,
Bishop of
Southwark
(PROVINCE OF
EUROPE)

Most Revd
Philip Freier,
Archbishop of
Melbourne
(SOUTHERN
PROVINCE)

Most Revd
Thabo Makgoba,
Archbishop of Cape
Town
(SOUTHERN AFRICAN
PROVINCE)

Founded in 1893 by Father Herbert Kelly, the Society is a means of uniting the devotion of ordinary people, using it in the service of the Church. Members of the Society share a common life of prayer and fellowship in a variety of educational, pastoral and community activities in England, Australia, Japan, Lesotho, and South Africa.

PROVINCE OF EUROPE
JONATHAN EWER SSM
(Provincial, assumed office April 2001)

Frank Green
Ralph Martin
Andrew Muramatsu
Edmund Wheat
Colin Griffith
Mary Hartwell
Elizabeth Macey
Michael Maasdorp

Associates:
Linda Bosworth
David Bosworth
Margaret Moakes
Paul Golightly
Elizabeth Baker
Robin Baker
Marcus Armstrong
Joan Golightly

Obituaries
26 Feb 08   Clement Mullenger, aged 92, professed 67 years
4 Apr 08   Andrew Longley, aged 82, professed 51 years

Addresses
Provincial & Administrator:
The Well, Newport Road, Willen MK15 9AA, UK
Tel: 01908 241974   Email: ssmlondon@yahoo.co.uk

St Antony's Priory, Claypath, Durham DH1 1QT, UK
Tel: 0191 384 3747   Email: durham.ssm@which.net

1 Linford Lane, Milton Keynes, Bucks MK15 9DL,
UK
Tel: 01908 663749

Community History
Herbert H Kelly SSM, *An Idea in the Working*, SSM Press, Kelham, 1908.
Alistair Mason, *SSM: History of the Society of the Sacred Mission*, Canterbury Press, Norwich, 1993.

Community Publication
SSM News (newsletter of the Province of Europe)
The Secretary, SSM Newsletter, The Well, Newport Road, Willen MK15 9AA, UK

SOUTHERN PROVINCE
MATTHEW DOWSEY SSM
(Provincial, assumed office November 2004)

Laurence Eyers	Steven de Kleer	*lay members:*
Henry Arkell	Gregory Stephens	Geoff Pridham
David Wells		Stuart Smith
Dunstan McKee		Lynne Rokkas
Christopher Myers		Joy Freier
Margaret Dewey		John Lewis

Obituaries
22 Jul 07   Francis Horner, aged 80, professed 50 years

Addresses
St John's Priory, 14 St John's Street, Adelaide, SOUTH AUSTRALIA 5000
Tel: 8 8223 1014   Fax: 8 8223 2764   Email: ssm.adelaide@bigpond.com

St Michael's Priory, 75 Watson's Road, Diggers Rest, Victoria 3427,
AUSTRALIA
Tel: 03 9740 1618   Fax: 03 9740 0007   Email: ssm.melbourne@bigpond.com

Community Publication:
Sacred Mission (newsletter of the Southern Province): Editor, St John's Priory, 14 St John's Street, Adelaide, SOUTH AUSTRALIA 5000

SOUTHERN AFRICAN PROVINCE
(re-founded September 2004)
MICHAEL LAPSLEY SSM
(Provincial, assumed office September 2004)

William Nkomo	Moeketsi Motojane	Samuel Monyamane
Robert Stretton	Moeketsi Khomongoe	Thato Tjakata
Tanki Mofana	Moiloa Mokheseng	Mosuoe Rahuoane
Mosia Sello	Keketso Sebotsa	*Novices: 2*

Addresses
33 Elgin Road, Sybrand Park, Cape Town, SOUTH AFRICA, 7708
Tel: 21 696 4866 Email: michael.lapsley@attglobal.net

SSM Priory, PO Box 1579, Maseru 100, LESOTHO
Tel: 22315979   Fax: 22310161   Email: priorssm@ilesotho.com

Associates and Companions (applicable to all provinces)
ASSOCIATES: are men and women who share the life and work of a priory of the Society.

COMPANIONS: are men and women who support the aims of the Society without being closely related to any of its work. They consecrate their lives in loving response to a vocation to deepen their understanding of God's will, and to persevere more devotedly in commitments already made: baptism, marriage or ordination.

Society of St Francis

SSF

Founded 1919 (USA)
1921 (UK)

Minister General
Email: clark.berge@
s-s-f.org
**Minister Provincial
(European
Province)**
Email: ministerssf
@franciscans.org.uk

**European Province
Website:** www.
franciscans.org.uk

Office Book
The Daily Office SSF

Bishop Protector
Rt Revd
Michael Perham,
Bishop of Gloucester

**European Province
SSF
Registered Charity:**
No. 236464

Community History
Petà Dunstan
This Poor Sort
DLT, London, 1997
£19.95 + £2 p&p

The Society of St Francis has diverse origins in a number of Franciscan groups which drew together during the 1930s to found one Franciscan Society. SSF in its widest definition includes First Order Brothers, First Order Sisters (CSF), Second Order Sisters (OSC) and a Third Order. The First Order shares a common life of prayer, fraternity and a commitment to issues of justice, peace and the integrity of creation. In its larger houses, this includes accommodation for short-term guests; in the city houses, the Brothers are engaged in a variety of ministries, chaplaincies and care for poor people. The Brothers are also available for retreat work, for counselling and for sharing in the task of mission in parishes and schools. They also undertake work in Europe and there are houses in America, Australasia and the Pacific, and are supportive to incipient communities in Zimbabwe and Korea.

CLARK BERGE SSF
(Minister General, assumed office 1 November 2007)

EUROPEAN PROVINCE
SAMUEL SSF
(Minister Provincial, assumed office 1 July 2002)
BENEDICT SSF *(Assistant Minister)*

Alan Michael	John
Amos	Julian
Andrew	Kentigern John
Angelo	Kevin
Anselm	Malcolm
Arnold	Martin
Austin	Maximilian
Bart	Nathanael
Benjamin	Nicholas Alan
Christian	Paschal
Colin Wilfred	Paul Anthony
Damian	Philip Bartholomew
David Jardine	Raphael
Desmond Alban	Raymond Christian
Donald	Reginald
Edmund	Ronald
Edward	Thomas Anthony
Giles	Vincent
Hugh	Wilfrid
James Anthony	
James William	*Novices: 6*
Jason Robert	

Companions: Companions are individual Christians who wish to associate themselves with the Society through prayer, friendship and in seeking to live the spirit of the Gospel in the way of St Francis. For more information about becoming a Companion contact: The Secretary for Companions at Hilfield Friary.

Third Order: See page 170 for the Third Order SSF.

Addresses   *All email addresses are @franciscans.org.uk*

The Friary, **Alnmouth**, Alnwick, Northumberland NE66 3NJ
  Tel: 01665 830213   Fax: 01665 830580   Email: alnmouthssf

Bentley Vicarage, 3a High Street, **Bentley**, Doncaster DN5 0AA
  Tel: 01302 872240

St Matthias's Vicarage, 45 Mafeking Rd, **Canning Town**, London E16 4NS
  Tel: 020 7511 7848

The Master's Lodge, 58 St Peter's Street, **Canterbury**, Kent CT1 2BE
  Tel: 01227 479364   Email: canterburyssf

St Mary-at-the-Cross, **Glasshampton**, Shrawley, Worcestershire WR6 6TQ
  Tel: 01299 896345   Fax: 01299 896083   Email: glasshamptonssf

The Friary of St Francis, **Hilfield**, Dorchester, Dorset DT2 7BE
  Tel: 01300 341345   Fax: 01300 341293   Email: hilfieldssf

The Vicarage, **Holy Island**, Berwick-upon-Tweed, Northumberland TD15 2RX
  Tel: 01289 389216   Email: holyislandssf

25 Karnac Road, **Leeds** LS8 5BI. *Tel: 0113 226 0647   Email: leedsssf*

House of the Divine Compassion, 42 Balaam St, **Plaistow**, London E13 8AQ
  Tel: 020 7476 5189   Email: plaistowssf

The Vicarage, 11 St Mary's Road, **Plaistow**, London E13 8AQ
  Tel: 020 8552 4019   Email: stmarycssf

Our Lady of the Angels, 8 Knight Street, **Walsingham**, NR22 6DA
  Tel: 01328 820762   Email: walsinghamssf

Community Publications: franciscan, three times a year - annual subscription is £7.00. Write to the Subscriptions Secretary at Hilfield Friary. Books available from Hilfield Friary book shop include: *The Daily Office SSF,* £10 + £2 p&p.

Community Wares: Hilfield Friary shop has on sale 'Freeland' cards, SSF publications and books of Franciscan spirituality and theology, as well as traidcraft goods.

Guest and Retreat Facilities

HILFIELD   The Friary has eight bedrooms (one twin-bedded) for men and women guests. Individually-guided retreats are available on request. There are facilities for day guests and for groups of up to forty. The Hilfield project *(www.hilfieldproject. co.uk)* is an initiative at the Friary to work for peace among people of different faiths and to care for the environment. It offers facilities in three self-catering houses for families and groups to meet, pray and focus on issues of justice, peace and the integrity of creation. The friary is normally closed from Sunday afternoon until Tuesday morning.

ALNMOUTH   The Friary has twelve rooms (including one twin-bedded) for men or women guests. Some conducted retreats are held each year and individually-guided retreats are available on request. The recently-innovated chalet is available

Addresses for
ANZ Province

The Hermitage
PO Box 46
Stroud
NSW 2425
AUSTRALIA
Tel: 2 4994 5372
Fax: 2 4994 5527

Email: ssfstrd@
bigpond.com

The Friary
PO Box 6134
Buranda
Brisbane
QLD 4102
AUSTRALIA
Tel: 7 3391 3915
Fax: 7 3391 3916

Email: BrDonald@
franciscan.org.au

Friary of the
Divine
Compassion
PO Box 13-117
Hillcrest
Hamilton
AOTEOROA NEW
ZEALAND
Tel: 7 856 6701

Email: friary
@franciscan.org.nz

Office Book
The Daily Office SSF

for families and groups in particular need referred by churches and social services. The Friary is closed for twenty-four hours from Sunday afternoon.

GLASSHAMPTON   The guest accommodation, available to both men and women, comprises five rooms. Groups can visit for the day, but may not exceed fifteen people. The friary is closed from noon on Mondays for twenty-four hours.

AUSTRALIA/NEW ZEALAND PROVINCE

SSF friars went from England to Papua New Guinea in the late 1950s and the first Australian house was established in 1964. The first New Zealand house followed in 1970. In 1981, the Pacific Province was divided into two: Australia/ New Zealand and the Pacific Islands.

ALFRED BOONKONG SSF
(Minister Provincial, assumed office 1 May 2003)
CHRISTOPHER JOHN SSF *(Assistant Minister)*

Brian	Donald Campbell	Lionel
Bruce-Paul	Gabriel Maelasi	Nathan-James
Damian Kenneth	James Andrew	Noel-Thomas
Daniel	Joseph	William

Community Publication
Franciscan Angles, New Zealand, & *Franciscan Angles*, Australia, published three times a year. To be put on the mailing list, write to the Hamilton or Brisbane address. Subscription is by donation.

Community Wares: Holding Crosses (Stroud and Brisbane)

Guest and Retreat Facilities
There is limited accommodation for short stay guests available in the Brisbane and Hamilton friaries, and the Hermitage at Stroud. Payment is by donation. The old monastery of the Clares at Stroud is also available for accommodation. For bookings tel: 2 4960 7100.

Websites: www.franciscan.org.au
www.franciscan.org.nz

Bishops Protector
Most Revd Roger Herft, Archbishop of Perth
(Protector General)
Most Revd David Moxon, Archbishop of the New Zealand Dioceses & Bishop of Waikato
(Deputy Protector for New Zealand)

Little Portion Friary
PO Box 399
Mount Sinai
NY 11766/0399, USA
Tel: 631 473 0533
Fax: 631 473 9434
Email: mtsinaifriary
@s-s-f.org

San Damiano
573 Dolores Street
San Francisco
CA 94110, USA
Tel: 415 861 1372
Fax: 415 861 7952
Email: judehillssf
@aol.com

St Clare's House
1601 Oxford Street
Berkeley
CA 94709, USA
Tel: 510 705 1591

Divine Providence
Friary
Rua Acurua 180
- Vila Ipojuca
05053-000 Sao
Paulo-SP, BRAZIL
Tel: (11) 3672 5454
Email: freicezar@
hotmail.com

Minister Provincial
Tel: 415 861 7951
Fax: 415 861 7952
Email: judehillssf
@aol.com

Province Website
www.s-s-f.org

Office Book
SSF Office Book

PROVINCE OF THE AMERICAS

The Province of the Americas of SSF was founded as the Order of St Francis in 1919 by Father Claude Crookston, who took the name Father Joseph. Under his leadership the community developed, based first in Wisconsin and then on Long Island, New York. The Order originally combined a monastic spirituality with a commitment to missions and evangelizing. In 1967, the OSF friars amalgamated with the Society in the UK and became the American Province of SSF.

Our lives are structured around our times together of formal prayer and the Eucharist, which give our lives a focus. Brothers engage in a wide variety of ministries: community organizing, missions, work in parishes and institutions, counselling and spiritual direction, study, the arts, serving the sick and infirm and people with AIDS, the homeless, workers in the sex industry, political work for the rights of people who are rejected by society. We come from a wide variety of backgrounds and cultural traditions. Living with each other can be difficult, but we work hard to find common ground and to communicate honestly with each other. God takes our imperfections and, in the mystery of Christ's body, makes us whole.

JUDE SSF
(Minister Provincial, assumed office May 2005)
THOMAS CAREY SSF *(Assistant Minister)*

Antonio Sato	Eric Michael	Richard Jonathan
Clark Berge	Ivanildo	Robert Hugh
(Minister General)	Jonathan Guthlac	*Novices:* 5
Derek	Joseph-Marie	*Postulants:* 3
Dunstan	Leo-Anthony	

Obituaries
24 Sep 2007 Jon Bankert, aged 62 years, professed 23 years

Community Publication: The Little Chronicle, four times a year, by donation. Write to: The Editor TLC, 573 Dolores Street, San Francisco, CA 94110, USA.

Guest and Retreat Facilities
There is a guest house at Little Portion Friary (Mount Sinai address), with twelve rooms, accommodating a maximum of sixteen guests. It is closed on Mondays. If there is no answer when telephoning, please leave a message on the answering machine.

Bishop Protector: in process of election

PAPUA NEW GUINEA PROVINCE
LAURENCE HAUJE SSF
(Minister, assumed office October 2008)

Anthony Kambuwa	Ham Kavaja	Philip Etobae
Charles Iada	Lester Meso	Robert Eric
Colin Velei	Lucas	Rodney Benunu
Dominic Ombeda	Nathaniel Gari	Selwyn Suma
Dudley Adia	Oswald Dumbari	Wallace Yovero
Gabriel Dominic	Owen Paul	Worrick*Novices:* 10

Obituaries
18 Dec 2008   Daniel Komota, in his second year as a novice
Addresses

All Saints' Friary	Saint Margaret's Friary	Martyrs' House
Dipoturu, PO Box 78	Katerada, PO Box 78	PO Box 78
Popondetta 241	Popondetta 241	Popondetta,
Oro Province, PNG	Oro Province, PNG	Oro Province, PNG
		Tel & fax: 3297 491
Saint Mary of the	Saint Francis Friary	
Angels Friary	Koke, PO Box 1103	Philip Friary
Haruro, PO Box 78	Port Moresby, NCD	Ukaka, PO Box 22
Popondetta 241	PNG	Alotau
Oro Province, PNG	*Tel & fax: 320 1499*	Milne Bay Province
Tel: 329 7060	*Email:*	PNG
	ssfpng@online.net.pg	

PROVINCE OF THE SOLOMON ISLANDS
GEORGE SSF
(Minister, assumed office October 2008)

Athanasius Faifu	Harry Atkin	Nathanael Volohi
Anderson So'oli	Hilcliff Tahani	Noel Niki
Andrew Manu	Hilton Togara	Patteson Kwa'ai
Anthony Huta Awao	Hudson Filiga	Peter Haga
Benjamin Tabugau	Ini Mumua	Samson Amoni
Caspar Gu'urou	Isom Waisi	Samson Gapu
Christopher Gegeo	John Kogudi	Samson Siho
Clifton Henry	John Rare	Selwyn Tione
Colin	Jonas Balugna	Steven Watson Hovu
Comins Romano	Lent J. Fugui	Thomas Hereward
Ellison Sero	Luke Manitara	Peleba
Ezekiel Kelly	Manasseh Birahu	Winston Paoni
Francis Christopher	Martin Tawea	
Hartman Dena	Matthew Melake	*Novices:* 14

Obituaries
30 Jan 2009   James Sou, professed 8 years

Brother Clifton Henry presiding at the Eucharist

Addresses

Patteson House
PO Box 519
Honiara
Guadalcanal
SOLOMON ISLANDS
Tel: 22386
Regional Office
    tel & fax: 25810

St Bonaventure Friary
Kohimarama
        Theological College
PO Box 519
Honiara, Guadalcanal
SOLOMON ISLANDS
Tel: 50128

Saint Francis Friary
PO Box 7
Auki, Malaita Province
SOLOMON ISLANDS
Tel: 40054

San Damiano Friary
Diocese of Hanuato'o
Kira Kira
Makira Ulawa Province
SOLOMON ISLANDS
Tel: 50031

Michael Davis Friary
PO Box 519
Honiara
Guadalcanal
SOLOMON ISLANDS

La Verna Friary/
            Little Portion
Hautambu
PO Box 519
Honiara
Guadalcanal
SOLOMON ISLANDS

Holy Martyrs Friary
Luisalo
PO Box 50
Lata
Temotu Province
SOLOMON ISLANDS

Bishop Protector: Rt Revd Richard Naramana, Bishop of Ysabel

Society of St John the Divine

SSJD

Founded 1887

Cottage 252
Umdoni Retirement
Village
PO Box 300
Pennington 4184,
Natal
South Africa

Tel: 039 975 9552

Emails:
maryevelyn
@polka.co.za

hil777
@telkomsa.net

**Angelus
& Morning Prayer**
8.15 am

**Angelus
& Midday Office**
12.15 pm

**Angelus
& Evening Office**
5.00 pm

Compline
7.30 pm

Prayer Time
8.30 - 9.00 pm

The Society has never been a large community, with just sixty professions over a century, and has always worked in Natal. Originally the community ran schools and orphanages. In 1994, after the death of the older Sisters, the four of us who remained moved to a house that was more central in Durban.

We moved to Umdoni Retirement Village in Pennington in 2003. Our involvement outside the village involves being on the Board of Governors of our school, St John's Diocesan Scool for Girls in Pietermaritzburg, and all our Associates, Friends and Oblates worldwide. Both Sisters Hilary and Mary Evelyn are Layministers and exercise their ministry within Umdoni.

Sister Mary Evelyn   Sister Margaret Anne
Sister Sophia   Sister Hilary

Oblates and Associates
These are people who are linked with us and support us in prayer.
Oblates: There is one, non-resident, and she renews her oblation annually.
Associates: There are over a hundred, some overseas. They have a Rule of Life and renew their promises annually.
Friends: They have a Rule of Life and like the Associates and Oblates meet with the Sisters quarterly, and they renew their promises annually.

Community Publication
One newsletter is sent out each year to Oblates, Associates and friends at Advent.

Community History and books
Sister Margaret Anne SSJD, *What the World Counts Weakness*, privately published 1987.
Sister Margaret Anne SSJD, *They Even Brought Babies*, privately published.

Community Wares
Crocheted girdles for clergy and lay ministers.

Bishop Visitor
Bishop Rubin Phillip, Bishop of Natal

Office Book
An Anglican Prayer Book 1989 (South African) for Morning & Evening Prayer.
Our own SSJD book for Midday Office & Compline.

Society of St John the Evangelist

(UK)

SSJE

Founded 1866

St Edward's House
22 Great College St
Westminster
London SW1P 3QA
UK
Tel: 020 7222 9234
Fax: 020 7799 2641

Email *(for superior):*
frpeter@ssje.org.uk

Website
www.ssje.org.uk

Mattins
7.00 am
(7.30 am Sun)

Eucharist
7.30 am
(8.00 am Sun)

Terce 9.00 am

Sext 12 noon

Evensong 6.30 pm

Compline 9.30 pm

A Registered Charity.

The Society of Saint John the Evangelist is the oldest of the Anglican orders for men, out of which the North American Congregation (and others worldwide) grew. We have been at the forefront of the Religious life since then, and have pioneered a new and more flexible way into the Community for the twenty-first century. New members first of all become 'Seekers' and then take simple annual vows as 'Internal Oblates' and live alongside us for a period of years before coming into First Vows. In this way, we escape the rigidity of the old system as people these days come from a much wider background than was formerly the case.

We seek to make use of their individual God-given talents as they seek to become what our Founder, Father Benson, envisaged: mission priests and lay brothers, based on their Community and its prayer life, but proclaiming Christ to the world. So we are engaged in running quiet days and retreats, both within and outside the House, counselling and spiritual direction. We look to befriend people whose English is limited and teach then as well as helping with students from overseas. We work in liturgics and preach and run parish missions. St Edward's House is a centre for private retreats and hospitality and is used by many religious and charitable groups for meetings, prayer etc.

FATHER PETER HUCKLE SSJE
(Superior, assumed office 7 March 2002)
BROTHER JAMES SIMON SSJE
(Assistant Superior and Novice Guardian)

Father Alan Bean　　　　Father Peter Palmer
Father David Campbell

Obituaries
6 Jan 09 Father James Naters, aged 88,
　　　　　professed 54 years, Superior 1991-2000

The Fellowship of St John
The Fellowship was completely revamped in 1998 and this is an on-going process. It seeks to become a group of members, lay and ordained, who, through the connection with SSJE, seek to deepen their own spiritual life through a number of simple obligations. It has its own committee and the Father Superior is the Warden.

There are members throughout the country: those in London and the South East meet regularly in St Edward's House. The Newsletter is sent out to some five hundred subscribers and organisations every month, including people in Australia, Canada, Europe, South Africa and New Zealand.

People wanting to be associated with SSJE in this way serve a year's probation and are then admitted. Further details may be obtained from the Contacts' Officer, Brother James Simon.

Community Publication
Newsletter, published monthly, editor c/o St Edward's House.
All enquiries to Brother James Simon (*Contacts Officer*). £6 per annum.

Guest and Retreat Facilities
There are Quarterly Quiet Days. Individual retreatants are welcomed and there are also facilities for Quiet Days. There are nineteen single rooms.
Email for guest master: guestmaster@ssje.org.uk

Most convenient time to telephone: 9.30 am - 8.30 pm

Bishop Visitor: Rt Revd Dominic Walker OGS, Bishop of Monmouth

---

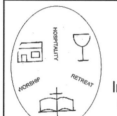

Society of St John the Evangelist

(North American Congregation)

SSJE

Founded 1866

The Monastery
980 Memorial Drive
Cambridge
MA 02138
USA
Tel: 617 876 3037
Fax: 617 876 5210
Email:
monastery@ssje.org

Website
www.ssje.org

Morning Prayer
6.00 am

Eucharist 7.45 am

Midday Prayer
12.30 pm

Evening Prayer
6.00 pm

Compline 8.30 pm

Office Book
BCP of ECUSA,
and the Book of
Alternate Services of
the Anglican Church
of Canada

The Society of St John the Evangelist was founded in the parish of Cowley in Oxford, England, by Richard Meux Benson in 1866. SSJE is the oldest Anglican Religious order for men. The presence of the Society in North America dates from 1870, when SSJE came to Boston. The brothers of the North American Congregation live at the monastery in Cambridge, Massachusetts, near Harvard Square, and at Emery House, a rural retreat sanctuary in West Newbury, Massachusetts. They gather throughout the day to pray the Divine Office, and live under a modern Rule of Life, adopted in 1997. The Rule of SSJE is now available on the community's website: www.ssje.org. At profession, brothers take vows of poverty, celibacy and obedience.

SSJE's guesthouses offer hospitality to many. Guests may come individually or attend a group retreat focused on some area of prayer and spirituality. SSJE brothers lead these retreats and programs in their own houses and throughout North America in parishes, dioceses and conference centers. SSJE brothers also serve as preachers and teachers, spiritual directors and confessors. One of the brothers, Thomas Shaw, is Bishop of Massachusetts. Several times a year, SSJE brothers serve as chaplains for pilgrimages in Israel/Palestine sponsored by St George's College, Jerusalem. In recent years, the brothers have been leading retreats and teaching in Anglican churches and seminaries in Kenya and Tanzania. Nearer to home, they are engaged in part-time in ministries to students and young adults, Asian-Americans, and those who live in poverty in the city of Boston.

CURTIS ALMQUIST SSJE
(*Superior, assumed office 13 May 2001*)
GEOFFREY TRISTRAM SSJE (*Deputy Superior*)
DAVID VRYHOF SSJE (*Assistant Superior*)

Paul Wessinger	Mark Brown
David Allen	Kevin Hackett
John Oyama (*in Japan*)	Robert L'Esperance
Bernard Russell	Timothy Solverson
Thomas Shaw	Bruce Neal
John Goldring	*Novices:* 4
Jonathan Maury	Andrew Gary
Eldridge Pendleton	Keith Nelson
James Koester	James Farrell
John Mathis	Jacob Kilda

Bishop Visitor: Rt Revd Arthur Walmsley

Associates
The Fellowship of Saint John is composed of men and women throughout the world who desire to live their Christian life in special association with the Society of Saint John the Evangelist. They have a vital interest in the life and work of the community and support its life and ministries with their prayers, encouragement and gifts. The brothers of the Society welcome members of the Fellowship as partners in the gospel life, and pray for them by name during the Daily Office, following a regular cycle. Together they form an extended family, a company of friends abiding in Christ and seeking to bear a united witness to him as "the Way, the Truth and the Life", following the example of the beloved Disciple. For further information, or to join the Fellowship, visit the Society's website: www.ssje.org.

Other address
Emery House, 21 Emery Lane, West Newbury, MA 01985, USA
Tel: 978 462 7940   Fax: 978 462 0285

Community History: This is now being written.

Community Publication
Cowley: for a subscription, write to SSJE at the Cambridge, Massachusetts, address. The suggested donation is US$20 annually. This publication is also available on the community's website (www.ssje.org).

Guest and Retreat Facilities
Monastery Guesthouse in Cambridge, MA
                    - sixteen rooms - US$75 per night/ US$40 for full-time students.
Emery House in West Newbury, MA
                    - currently unavailable to guests (through May 2010).

COWLEY PUBLICATIONS
Books published by Cowley Publications are obtainable from:
in the USA
          Website: www.cowley.org (connects to Rowman Littlefield Publishers,
                                        who now distribute Cowley books.)

in Canada
Anglican Book Centre, 80 Hayden Street, Toronto, Ontario M4Y 3G2, CANADA
          Tel: 416 924 1332   Fax: 416 924 2760
          Website: www.anglicanbookcentre.com
in the UK & Europe
Columba, 55a Spruce Avenue, Blackrock, Co. Dublin, IRELAND
          Tel: 1 294 2560   Fax: 1 294 2564
          Website: www.columba.ie
in Australia
John Garratt Bookroom, 32 Glenvale Crescent, Private Bag 400, Mulgrave, Victoria 3170, AUSTRALIA   *Tel: 300 650 878   Fax: 395 453 222*
          Website: www.johngarratt.com.au

Society of St Margaret

(Boston)

SSM

Founded 1855
(Boston Convent
founded 1873)

St Margaret's
Convent
17 Highland Park St
Boston
MA 02119-1436
USA

Tel: 617 445 8961
Fax: 617 445 7120
Email: ssmconvent
@ssmbos.com

Website
www.ssmbos.com

Morning Prayer
6.00 am

Eucharist 7.30 am

Noon Office
12 noon

Evening Prayer
5.30 pm

Compline 8.30 pm

Office Book
BCP
of the Episcopal
Church of the USA

The Sisters of St Margaret are an Episcopal Religious Order of women called to glorify God and proclaim the gospel of Jesus Christ through our worship and work, prayer and common life. Our commitment to God and to one another is expressed through vows of poverty, celibate chastity and obedience.

The Eucharist is central to our lives. From the center we go forth to celebrate the diversity, fullness and creativity of the people of God. We reverence all, seeking the living Christ in one another and in all creation. We strive for a spirit of fearlessness in Christian service, encouraged and empowered by the presence of the Spirit.

Our Sisters minister in many places: schools, prisons, parishes, nursing homes and homeless shelters. Our Houses offer hospitality to guests, retreatants, parish and civic groups, and all who long for a contemplative space in their lives. As a Community we will deepen our commitment to prayer, inviting others to join us in seeking greater intimacy with God. We live out our values in ministry with the poorest of the poor in Haiti; at the crossroads of urban life in lower Manhattan; and in Boston and its suburbs.

SISTER CAROLYN SSM
(Mother Superior, assumed office March 2002)
SISTER ADELE MARIE SSM *(priest)* *(Assistant Superior)*

Sister Bernardine	Sister Claire Marie
Sister Lucy Mary	Sister Mary Gabriel
Sister Catherine	Sister Adele
Louise *(priest)*	Sister Julian
Sister Jane Margaret	Sister Christine
Sister Rosemary	Sister Marie Therese
Sister Marjorie Raphael	Sister Brigid
Sister Marion	Sister Promise
Sister Mary Michael	Sister Grace
Sister Emily Louise	Sister Sarah Margaret
Sister Gloria	Sister Kristina Frances
Sister Marie Margaret	Sister Kethia
Sister Ann	

Obituaries

22 Mar 09	Sister Mary Eleanor *(priest)*, aged 69, professed 44 years
29 Apr 09	Sister Esther, aged 93, professed 69 years

Associates

Associates of one Convent of the Society of St Margaret are Associates of all. They have a common Rule, which is flexible to circumstances. They include men and women, lay and ordained. No Associate of the Society may be an Associate of any other community.

Addresses of other houses
St Margaret's Convent, Port-au-Prince, HAITI　　*Tel: 509 2222 2011*
　Mailing address:
St Margaret's Convent, Port-au-Prince, c/o Agape Flights, Inc., 100 Airport Avenue, Venice, FL 34285-3901, USA　　*Email: mariemargaretssm@yahoo.com*

Neale House, 50 Fulton Street, New York, NY 10038-1800, USA
Tel: 212 619 2672　　Email: sisters@trinitywallstreet.org

Community Publication: *St Margaret's Quarterly.*　For information, contact the Editor at the Boston Convent.　The subscription rate is $5.

Community History
Sister Catherine Louise SSM, *The House of my Pilgrimage: a History of the American House of the Society of Saint Margaret,* privately published, 1973.
Sister Catherine Louise SSM, *The Planting of the Lord: The History of the Society of Saint Margaret in England, Scotland & the USA;* privately published, 1995.

Community Wares: Haitian Gift Shop, with cards, crafts and altar linens for sale for the benefit of the Scholarship Fund for Holy Trinity School in Port-au-Prince. Available both at the Convent in Boston and in Port-au-Prince.

Guest and Retreat Facilities: All our houses have facilities for guests and retreatants. For costs and details of facilities, contact the house you are interested in.

Bishop Visitor: Rt Rev David Joslin, Assisting Bishop of Rhode Island

---

Society of
St Margaret

(Hackney)

SSM

Founded 1855
(St Saviour's Priory
1866)

St Saviour's Priory is one of the autonomous Houses which constitute the Society of St Margaret founded by John Mason Neale.　Exploring contemporary ways of living the Religious life, the community seeks, through a balance of prayer and ministry, to respond to some of the needs that arise amongst the marginalised in East London.　The Office is four-fold and the Eucharist is offered daily.　The Sisters' outreach to the local community includes: working as staff members (lay or ordained) in various parishes; supporting issues of justice and racial equality; supporting the gay community; Sunday Stall and Drop in Centre; Dunloe Centre for the homeless and alcoholics; complementary therapy; individual spiritual direction and retreats; dance workshops; art work and design. The Sisters also share their community building and resources of worship and space with individuals and groups.

St Saviour's Priory
18 Queensbridge
Road
London E2 8NS
UK
Tel: 020 7739 9976
Email:
ssmpriory@aol.com

Leader of the community
020 7613 1464

Guest Bookings
020 7739 6775
Fax: 020 7739 1248

(Sisters are not available on Mondays)

Website: www.
stsaviourspriory.
org.uk

Morning Prayer
7.15 am
(7.30 am Sun)
followed by
Eucharist
(12.15 pm on major feasts)

Midday Office
12.45 pm

Evening Prayer
5.00 pm

Night Prayer 8.30 pm

Office Book
Celebrating Common
Prayer

Registered Charity
No 230927

THE REVD SISTER HELEN LODER SSM *(priest)*
(Leader of the Community, assumed office 17 February 2001)
THE REVD SISTER JUDITH BLACKBURN SSM *(priest)*
& SISTER MOIRA JONES SSM *(Assistant Leaders)*
Sister June Atkinson
Sister Frances (Claire) Carter
Sister Elizabeth Crawford
Sister Pauline (Mary) Hardcastle
Sister Anna Huston
Sister Enid Margaret Jealous
Sister Sue Makin
Sister Pamela Radford
Sister Mary Michael (Lilian) Stokes

Associates and Friends
Associates make a long term commitment to the Society of St Margaret, following a Rule of Life and helping the Community where possible. An Associate of one SSM house is an Associate of all the houses. There are regular quiet days for Associates who are kept in touch with community developments.

Friends of St Saviour's Priory commit themselves to a year of mutual support and friendship and are invited to regular events throughout the year.

Community Publication
The Orient, yearly. Write to The Orient Secretary at St Saviour's Priory. Brochures about the Community are available at any time on request.

Community Wares: Traidcraft, South American Toybox, cards, books and religious items for sale.

Community History
Memories of a Sister of S. Saviour's Priory, Mowbray, 1904.
A Hundred Years in Haggerston, published by St Saviour's Priory, 1966.
Sister Catherine Louise SSM, *The Planting of the Lord: The History of the Society of Saint Margaret in England, Scotland & the USA*; privately published, 1995.

Guest and Retreat Facilities
Six single rooms for individual guests. Excellent facilities for non-residential group meetings.
Most convenient time to telephone: 10.30 am - 1.00 pm (Not Mondays).

Bishop Visitor
Rt Revd Dominic Walker OGS, Bishop of Monmouth

Society of St Margaret

(Uckfield)

SSM

Founded 1855

St Margaret's
Convent
Hooke Hall
250 High Street
Uckfield
East Sussex
TN22 1EN
UK
Tel: 01825 766808

Emails:
uckfieldssm
@hotmail.co.uk

egmotherssm
@hotmail.com

Matins 7.15 am
(7.30 am Sun & Wed)

Eucharist 8.00 am
(9.30 am Sun & 11
am Wed in the parish
church)

**Midday Office & Litany
of the Holy Name**
12.30 pm

Vespers
5.00 pm (4.45 pm Sun)

Compline 8.00 pm

Office Book
'A Community Office'
printed for St
Margaret's Convent,
East Grinstead

The Convent at Hooke Hall is one of the autonomous Convents which constitute the Society of St Margaret, founded by John Mason Neale. The Sisters' work is the worship of God, expressed in their life of prayer and service. They welcome visitors as guests and retreatants, and are involved in spiritual direction and parish work. At Chiswick they care for elderly people in a nursing home and have guests. There is a semi-autonomous house and a branch house in Sri Lanka.

MOTHER CYNTHIA CLARE SSM
(Mother Superior, assumed office 2 March 2000)
SISTER MARY PAUL SSM *(Assistant Superior)*

Sister Raphael Mary	Sister Lucy
Sister Mary Michael	Sister Barbara
Sister Rita Margaret	Sister Elizabeth
Sister Jennifer Anne	Sister Sarah

Obituaries
29 Dec 07   Sister Eleanor, aged 86, professed 45 years

Associates
Associates observe a simple Rule, share in the life of prayer and dedication of the community, and are welcomed at all SSM convents.

Other address: St Mary's Convent & Nursing Home, Burlington Lane, Chiswick, London W4 2QF, UK
Tel: 020 8 994 4641   Fax: 020 8995 9796

Community Publication: St Margaret's Chronicle, Newsletter twice a year. Write to the Editor at St Margaret's Convent. £4.00 per annum, including postage and packing.

Community History
Sister Catherine Louise SSM, *The Planting of the Lord: The History of the Society of Saint Margaret in England, Scotland & the USA;* privately published, 1995.

Pamela Myers, *Building for the future: A Nursing History 1896 to 1996 to commemorate the centenary of St Mary's Convent and Nursing Home, Chiswick,* St Mary's Convent, Chiswick, 1996.

Doing the Impossible: a short sketch of St Margaret's Convent, East Grinstead 1855-1980, privately published, 1984.   Postscript 2000.

Guest and Retreat Facilities
There are six beds, primarily for individual retreats. Day retreatants are welcome: both individuals and groups of

Bishop Visitor
Rt Revd John Hind,
Bishop of Chichester

Registered Charity:
No. 231926

St Margaret's
Convent
157 St Michael's
Road
Polwatte
Colombo 3
SRI LANKA

Bishop Visitor
Rt Revd
Duleep de Chickera,
Bishop of Colombo

to twelve people. Some Sisters are available for support in these retreats. Donations appreciated. Quiet afternoons are arranged on a regular basis.

Most convenient time to telephone:
10.00 am - 12 noon, 7.00 pm - 8.00 pm.

SEMI-AUTONOMOUS HOUSES OVERSEAS

The Sisters run a Retreat House, a Hostel for young women, a Home for elderly people, and are involved in parish work and church embroidery.

SISTER CHANDRANI SSM
(Sister Superior, assumed office 2006)

Sister Lucy Agnes   Sister Jane Margaret
Sister Mary Christine

Other address
A children's home:
St John's Home, 133 Galle Rd, Moratuwa, SRI LANKA

Society of St Margaret

(Walsingham)

SSM

Founded 1855
(Walsingham Priory founded 1955)

The Priory of Our
Lady
Bridewell Street
Walsingham
Norfolk   NR22 6ED
UK
Tel: 01328 820340
(Revd Mother)
Tel: 01328 820901
(Sisters & guests)

In January 1994, the Priory of Our Lady at Walsingham reverted to being an autonomous house of the Society of St Margaret. The Sisters are a Traditional Community whose daily life is centred on the Eucharist and the daily Office, from which flows their growing involvement in the ministry of healing, and reconciliation in the Shrine, the local parishes and the wider Church. They welcome guests for short periods of rest, relaxation and retreat, and are available to pilgrims and visitors. They also work in the Sacristy, shop, the Education Department and the Welcome Centre of the Shrine. One sister is involved with a new Youth Project, which is being set up in the locality.

MOTHER CAROLYNE JOSEPH SSM
(Revd Mother, assumed office April 2009)

Sister Mary Teresa	Sister Wendy Renate
Sister Joan Michael	Sister Phyllis
Sister Christina Mary	Sister Mary Joan
Sister Alma Mary	Sister Mary Clare
Sister Francis Anne	Sister Jane Louise
Sister Columba	

Emails:
Revd Mother: mothercarolyne@ssmargaret.com
Bursar: bursar@ssmargaret.com

**Readings
& Morning Prayer**
7.00 am
(6.30 am Thu)

Mass
9.30 am (7.10 am Thu)
(No Mass on Sun in
Sisters' Chapel)

Midday Prayer
12.45 pm

Evening Prayer
5.00 pm

Night Prayer
8.45 pm

Office Book
The Divine Office

Registered Charity
No . 25515

Associates
There are Associates, and Affiliated Parishes and Groups.

Community Publication: Community booklet, *Wellspring*, published annually in the autumn. Write to the Priory for information. £3.50, including postage.

Community History:
Sister Catherine Louise SSM, *The Planting of the Lord: The History of the Society of Saint Margaret in England, Scotland & the USA;* privately published, 1995.

Community Wares: Cards (re-cycled) and embroidered; books; Breviary and Missal markers; Religious objects (statues, pictures, rosary purses etc); wire-wrapped rosaries (made to order).

Guest and Retreat Facilities: St Margaret's Cottage, (self-catering) for women and men, families and small groups. One single room (bed sit, ensuite) on the ground floor, suitable for a retreatant, and three twin rooms upstairs.
Most convenient time to telephone: 10.30 am - 12.30 pm; 2.30 pm - 4.30 pm; 6.30 pm - 8.30 pm.

Bishop Visitor: Rt Revd Peter Wheatley, Bp of Edmonton

Society of
St Paul

SSP

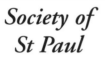

Founded 1958

2728 Sixth Avenue
San Diego
CA 92103-6397
USA
Tel: 619 542 8660
Email: anbssp@
earthlink.net

Bishop Visitor
Rt Revd
James R Mathes,
Bishop of San Diego

The Society of St Paul began in Gresham, Oregon in 1958. Early ministry included nursing homes, a school, and commissary work in the Mid-East and Africa. In 1959, SSP was the first community for men to be recognized by the canons of ECUSA. The brothers live a life of prayer and are dedicated to works of mercy, charity and evangelism. In 1976, the order moved to Palm Desert, California, providing a retreat and conference center until 1996. In 2001, the brothers moved to St Paul's Cathedral in San Diego. In particular, we are involved at St Paul's Senior Homes and Services, the Uptown Faith Community Services, Inc., Dorcas House, a foster home for children whose parents are in prison in Tijuana, Mexico, and St Paul's Cathedral ministries.

THE REVD CANON BARNABAS HUNT SSP
(*Rector, assumed office 1989*)
THE REVD CANON ANDREW RANK SSP (*Associate Rector*)

Fellowship of St Paul
The Fellowship of St Paul, our extended family, is an association of Friends, Associates and Companions of the Society of St Paul, who live a Rule of Life centered on the Glory of God.

Society of the Sisters of Bethany

SSB

Founded 1866

7 Nelson Road
Southsea
Hampshire PO5
2AR
UK
Tel: 02392 833498
Email: ssb@
sistersofbethany.
org.uk

Website: www.
sistersofbethany.
org.uk

Mattins 7.00 am

Mass 7.45 am
(8.00 am Sun; 9.30 am
Wed & alternate Sats)

Terce 9.15 am

Midday Office
12.00 noon

Vespers 5.00 pm

Compline 8.00 pm

Office Book
Anglican Office book
with adaptations

Registered Charity:
No. 226582

By prayer and activity, the Sisters seek to share in the work of reconciling the divided Churches of Christendom and the whole world. At the heart of each Sister's vocation is a call to prayer. Praying in the Spirit which unites us all to Christ and in Christ, for the wholeness of broken humanity, for the integrity of creation, for the peace of the world and for the Kingdom of God.

The Community prays daily for the unity of Christians. The intention of the Eucharist every Thursday is for Unity and is followed by their Office for Unity. On Fridays a three-hour Prayer Watch is kept in Chapel, and in addition each Sister has her own special intentions.

Each Sister makes the offering of herself in the hidden life of prayer within the Community, in the belief that God desires and accepts that offering. They are encouraged to persevere by some words of Abbé Paul Couturier with which he concluded one of his letters to the Community: "In Christ let us pray, pray, pray for Unity."

By simplicity of life-style, the Sisters try to identify with those for whom they share in Christ's work of intercession in the power of the Holy Spirit. The work of the Sisters includes giving hospitality for those seeking spiritual or physical refreshment and arranging retreats and quiet days. Some Sisters also give spiritual direction, lead quiet days and help in parishes. From time to time they are engaged in missions and cathedral chaplaincy work.

The Community motto is: 'Silentium et Spes' - In Quietness and Confidence - Let us pray to the Lord [Isaiah 30:15].

MOTHER GWENYTH SSB
(Reverend Mother, assumed office 1 November 1994)
SISTER MARY JOY SSB *(Assistant Superior)*
SISTER RITA-ELIZABETH SSB *(Novice Guardian)*

Sister Christina Mary	Sister Ann Patricia
Sister Katherine Maryel	Sister Constance Mary
Sister Ruth Etheldreda	Sister Joanna Elizabeth
Sister Florence May	
	Novices: 1

Obituaries
16 Sep 2007   Sister Margaret Faith,
                               aged 95, professed 58 years

Associates
The Associates are a body of close friends who unite their life of prayer to that of the Community and who are accepted as members of an extended Community

family. They live in their own homes and accept a simple rule of life which is the expression of a shared concern to love and serve God and one another after the example of Martha, Mary and Lazarus.

Community Wares: Cards.

Community Publication: Associates' magazine, July and December

Guest and Retreat Facilities: Six guest rooms (1 twin-bedded). Individual retreatants can be accommodated. Closed at Christmas.

Most convenient time to telephone: 9.30 am - 11.45 am, 1 pm - 4 pm, 6 pm - 7.45 pm

Bishop Visitor: Rt Revd Trevor Willmott, Bishop of Basingstoke

Some Other Communities in the Anglican Communion

AFRICA

Community of St Paul CSP) Maciene, MOZAMBIQUE

ASIA

Sisters of St Francis (SSF)
206 Eoamri, Miwonmyeon, Cheongwongun, Chungcheonbukdo 363-872, REPUBLIC OF KOREA   *Tel: (043) 225 6856*

AUSTRALASIA AND THE PACIFIC
Congregation of the Sisters of the Visitation of Our Lady (CVL)
Convent of the Visitation, Hetune, Box 18 , Popondetta,
Oro Province, PAPUA NEW GUINEA

EUROPE
Society of the Franciscan Servants of Jesus and Mary (FSJM)
Posbury St Francis, Crediton, Devon EX17 3QG, UK

Society of Our Lady of the Isles   (SOLI)
Lark's Hame, Aithness, Isle of Fetlar, Shetland ZE2 9DJ, UK   *Tel: 01957 733303*

NORTH AMERICA & THE CARIBBEAN
Order of St Anne   (OSA)
Convent of St Anne, 1125 North LaSalle Boulevard, Chicago, IL 60610-2601, USA
Tel: 312 642 3638

Order of the Teachers of the Children of God   (TCG)
5870 East 14th Street, Tucson, AZ 85711, USA
Tel: 520 747 5280   Fax: 520 747 5236   Email: smltcg@aol.com

Society of Our Lady St Mary   (SLSM)
Bethany Place, PO Box 762, Digby, Nova Scotia BOV 1AO, CANADA

SINGLE CONSECRATED LIFE

One of the earliest ways of living the Religious life is for single people to take a vow of consecrated celibacy and to live in their own homes. This ancient form of commitment is also a contemporary one with people once again embracing this form of Religious life.   Some may have an active ministry whilst others follow a contemplative lifestyle.

In 2002, the Advisory Council (for Religious communities in the Church of England) set up a Personal Vows group in response to enquiries from bishops and others to advise those who wish to take a vow of consecrated celibacy. The Sub Group now provides support for those who have professed this vow and arranges an annual gathering.   In the Roman Catholic Church, this form of living the consecrated life was affirmed by Vatican II, which re-established the order of consecrated Virgins (OCV) and now an order of Widows is also emerging.

People exploring this call should be single, mature Christians (men or women) already committed to a life of prayer and willing to undertake a period of discernment before taking a temporary vow which may precede a life vow.   An appropriate spiritual director and support from a Religious community or through the single consecrated life network is important to ensure adequate formation.

The vow is received by a person's bishop. The bishop (or his appointee) becomes the 'guardian of the vow' and the act of consecration is registered with the Advisory Council.   Further information may be obtained from this address: *The Single Consecrated Life*, c/o St John's House, 652 Alum Rock Road, Birmingham B8 3NS.

Directory
of
dispersed
Communities

In this section are communities that from their foundation have lived as dispersed communities. In other words, their members do not necessarily live a common life in community, although they do come together for chapter meetings and other occasions each year.
Like traditional communities, they do take vows that include celibacy.

Oratory of the Good Shepherd

OGS

Founded 1913

Website
www.ogs.net

Bishop Visitor
Rt Revd Jack Nicholls

The Oratory of the Good Shepherd is a society of priests and laymen founded at Cambridge (UK), which now has provinces in North America, Australia, Southern Africa and Europe.

Oratorians are bound together by a common Rule and discipline; members do not generally live together in community. The brethren are grouped in 'colleges' and meet regularly for prayer and support, and each province meets annually for retreat and chapter. Every three years, the General Chapter meets, presided over by the Superior of the whole Oratory, whose responsibility is to maintain the unity of the provinces.

Consecration of life in the Oratory has the twin purpose of fostering the individual brother's personal search for God in union with his brethren, and as a sign of the Kingdom. So through the apostolic work of the brethren, the Oratory seeks to make a contribution to the life and witness of the whole Church.

In common with traditional communities, the Oratory requires celibacy. Brothers are accountable to their brethren for their spending and are expected to live simply and with generosity. The ideal spiritual pattern includes daily Eucharist, Offices, and an hour of prayer. Study is also regarded as important in the life. During the time of probation which lasts one or two years, the new brother is cared for and nurtured in the Oratory life by another brother of his College. The brother may then, with the consent of the province, make his first profession, which is renewed annually for at least five years, though with the hope of intention and perseverance for life. After five years, profession can be made for a longer period, and after ten years a brother may, with the consent of the whole Oratory, make his profession for life.

Companions and Associates
The Oratory has an extended family of Companions, with their own rule of life, and Associates. Companionship is open to men and women, lay or ordained, married or single.

Community History
George Tibbatts, *The Oratory of the Good Shepherd: The First Seventy-five Years*, The Almoner OGS, Windsor, 1988.

Obituaries
2 Mar 2009   Siboniso Bhengu, age 37, professed 9 years

CARLSON GERDAU OGS
(*Superior, assumed office August 2005*)
Apt 19 A/N, 60 Sutton Place South, New York, NY 10022, USA
Tel: 212 421 6942   Email: cgerdau@ogs.net

The Community in Australia
TREVOR BULLED OGS   (*Provincial, assumed office 2002*)
Holy Trinity Rectory, Box 1220, Fortitude Valley, Brisbane,
Queensland 4006, AUSTRALIA
Tel: 73852 1635   Email: tbulled@ogs.net

Michael Boyle	Barry Greaves	Kenneth Mason
Robert Braun	Charles Helms	Geoffrey Tisdall
Michael Chiplin	Ronald Henderson	Richard Waddell
Keith Dean-Jones	Roger Kelly	*Probationers: 1*

The Community in North America
PHILIP HOBSON OGS   (*Provincial, assumed office August 2005*)
151 Glenlake Ave, Toronto, Ontario, M6P 1E8, CANADA
Tel: 416 604 4438   Email: phobson@ogs.net

Troy Beecham	William Derby	Edward Simonton
David Brinton	Robert MacSwain	
Gregory Bufkin	Wally Raymond	

The Community in Southern Africa
BARRY ROBERTS OGS   (*Provincial, assumed office 2008*)
Apartment E192, Musgrave Park, Old Kendal Road, Diep River, Cape
Town 7800, SOUTH AFRICA
Tel: 021 712 7549   Email: broberts@ogs.net

Thami Masekani	John Salt	*Probationers: 6*
Thanda Ngcobo	Thami Shangi	
Douglas Price	Mark Vandeyar	

The Community in Europe
PETER FORD OGS   (*Provincial, assumed office April 2005*)
Calle Montevideo 2-7, 35007, Las Palmas de Gran Canaria, SPAIN
Tel & Fax: 928 267 202   Email: pford@ogs.net

Peter Baldwin	Peter Hibbert	John Ruston
Michael Bartlett	David Johnson	John Thorold
Alexander Bennett	David Jowitt	Lindsay Urwin
Michael Bootes	Brian Lee	Dominic Walker
Michael Bullock	Michael Longstaffe	
Nicholas Gandy	Christopher Powell	*Probationers: 3*

SNEATON CASTLE CENTRE
WHITBY YO21 3QN

The ideal venue for your Parish Weekend,
Church Outing, PCC Away Day or Retreat.
For B&B, Holidays, Pilgrimages and Conferences
All types of Day and Residential events.

Standard and en-suite accommodation for up to 120 guests

Ring 01947 600051 or visit
www.sneatoncastle.co.uk

Directory of acknowledged Communities

In this section are communities that are 'acknowledged' by the Church as living out a valid Christian witness, but whose members do not all take traditional Religious vows. Some communities expect their members to remain single whilst others may include members who are married: some have both members who remain celibate and those who do not. The specific vows they take therefore will vary according to their own particular Rule. However, all communities in this section have an Episcopal Visitor or Protector. Some are linked to communities listed in section 1, others were founded without ties to traditional celibate orders.

In the Episcopal Church of the USA, they are referred to in the canons as 'Religious communities' as distinct from those in section 1, which are referred to as 'Religious orders'. However, this distinction is not used in other parts of the Anglican Communion where 'communities' is also used for those who take traditional vows.

There are an estimated 3,500 members of acknowledged communities in the Anglican Communion.

Brotherhood of Saint Gregory

BSG

Founded 1969

Brotherhood of
Saint Gregory
PO Box 57
White Plains
NY 10602
USA

Email:
Servant@
gregorians.org

Website
www.
gregorians.org

Office Book
The Book of Common
Prayer (1979)

The Brotherhood of Saint Gregory was founded on Holy Cross Day 1969, by Richard Thomas Biernacki, after consultation with many Episcopal and Roman Catholic Religious. The first brothers made their profession of vows in the New York monastery of the Visitation Sisters. Later that year, Bishop Horace Donegan of New York recognized the Brotherhood as a Religious Community of the Episcopal Church.

The community is open to clergy and laity, without regard to marital status. Gregorian Friars follow a common Rule, living individually, in small groups, or with their families, supporting themselves and the community through secular or church-related employment.

The Rule requires the Holy Eucharist, the four Offices of the Book of Common Prayer, meditation, theological study, Embertide reports, the tithe, and participation in Annual Convocation and Chapter.

The postulancy program takes a minimum of one year; novitiate at least two years, after which a novice may make first profession of annual vows. Members are eligible for life profession after five years in annual vows.

Gregorian Friars minister in parishes as liturgists, musicians, clergy, artists, visitors to the sick, administrators, sextons, and teachers. A number serve the diocesan and national church. For those in secular work the 'servant theme' continues, and many are teachers, nurses, or administrators.

Community Publications
The Brotherhood produces a quarterly newsletter titled *The Servant*. Subscription is US$8.00 per year. An order blank is available by mail or via our website.

Community Wares
There are a number of Brotherhood publications - please write or visit our website for further details regarding placing an order.

Associates
There are currently one hundred and fifty-eight associates of the Brotherhood. Please write or visit our website for further information.

Bishop Visitor
Rt Revd Rodney R Michel,
                    assisting Bishop of Pennsylvania

BROTHER RICHARD THOMAS BIERNACKI, BSG
(Minister General and founder, assumed office 14 September 1969)

Brother James Teets
Brother Luke Antony Nowicki
Brother William Francis Jones
Brother Stephen Storen
Brother Tobias Stanislas Haller *(priest)*
Brother Edward Munro *(deacon)*
Brother Donovan Aidan Bowley
Brother Christopher Stephen Jenks
Brother Ciarán Anthony DellaFera
Brother Richard John Lorino
Brother Ronald Augustine Fox
Brother Maurice John Grove
Brother Charles Edward LeClerc
(deacon)
Brother Virgilio Fortuna
Brother Gordon John Stanley *(deacon)*
Brother Karekin Madteos Yarian
Brother William David Everett
Brother Thomas Bushnell
Brother Thomas Mark Liotta *(deacon)*

Brother James Mahoney
Brother Robert James McLaughlin
Brother Peter Budde
Brother John Henry Ernestine
Brother Francis Sebastian Medina
Brother Aelred Bernard Dean
Brother Joseph Basil Gauss
Brother Mark Andrew Jones
Brother Emmanuel Williamson *(priest)*
Brother Richard Matthias
Brother William Henry Benefield
Brother Nathanael Deward Rahm
Brother Thomas Lawrence Greer
Brother Enoch John Valentine
Brother Ron Fender
Brother Michael Elliott *(priest)*
Brother David Luke Henton

Novices: 4
Postulants: 3

Obituaries

9 Oct 2007   Brother Damian-Curtis Kellum, aged 75, professed 17 years

Community of St Denys CSD

Founded 1879

St Denys Retreat Centre
2/3 Church Street
Warminster
BA12 8PG
UK
Tel: 01985 214824
(Warden of the Retreat House)

Email: stdenys
@ivyhouse.org

Website
www.ivyhouse.org

(Contact for Sisters only)
Revd Sister
Frances R Cocker CSD
Flat 7
St Nicholas Hospital
St Nicholas Road
Salisbury SP1 2SW
UK
Tel: 01722 339761

Office Book
CCP;
& CW (as appropriate)

Bishop Visitor
Rt Revd
David Stancliffe,
Bishop of Salisbury

Registered Charity
No 233026

The Community was founded in 1879 for mission work at home and overseas. We now fulfil our calling as a dispersed community engaged in parish work, spiritual guidance, retreat work, and hospital chaplaincy. CSD's members include Sisters, and men and women committed to a Rule of Life. The revised constitution has been recognised by the Advisory Council, and the community is now an 'acknowledged community' (10 June 2004). The Sisters live in individual accommodation. All enquiries should be sent to the Leader c/o the Retreat House or the deputy leader at her Salisbury address.

REVD CANON ALAN GILL (*priest associate CSD*)
(*Leader, assumed office 9 October 2005*)
1 Cheshire Close, Salisbury SP2 9JT
MRS JUNE WATT (*Oblate CSD*) (*Deputy Leader*)
57 Archers Court, Castle St, Salisbury SP1 3WE, UK

Committed members: 38
among whom the professed sisters are:

Sr Margaret Mary Powell
Sister Phyllis Urwin

Sister Frances Anne Cocker (*priest*)
Sister Elizabeth Mary Noller (*priest*)
Sister Theresa (*temp. vows*)

Obituaries
6 Aug 2008 — Sister Carol Ham, aged 95, professed 60 years
11 Dec 2008 — Sister Gladys Henbest, aged 92, professed 58 years

Fellowship: CSD has a fellowship (i.e. friends).

Community Publication
Annual *Newsletter* and quarterly prayer leaflet. Write to the Secretary of the S. Denys Fellowship, 2/3 Church St, Warminster, Wiltshire BA12 8PG, UK. The suggested donation is £5.00 per annum.

Community History: CSD: The Life & Work of St Denys', Warminster to 1979, published by CSD, 1979.

Guest and Retreat Facilities
ST DENYS RETREAT CENTRE is available for various types of retreat and parish conferences. Guests are also welcome. It has twenty-two rooms, six of which are double. The Centre is closed at Christmas. The Members lead Quiet days, Individually-Guided Retreats and traditional preached Retreats, both in Warminster and elsewhere. Apply to the Retreat Secretary for further details.
Most convenient time to telephone: 9am-1pm

Companions of St Luke, OSB

Founded 1992

Abbey of
St Benedict
2288 220th Street
Donnellson
Iowa 52625
USA

Tel: 319 837 8421
Email:
abbotmichael
johnaustin
@yahoo.com

Website:www.
holythoughts.org

Matins
7.00 am
followed immediately
by the Mass

Noonday Prayer
12 noon

Vespers
5.00 pm

Compline
8.00 pm

Bishop Visitor
Rt Revd Dean Wolfe,
Episcopal Diocesan
of Kansas

The Companions of St Luke is a Benedictine community founded on the Rule of St Benedict incorporating both traditional and contemporary aspects of Religious life. The Companions of St Luke is a community who honours the rich tradition and wisdom that has been passed down to us through the ages, yet knows that if Religious life is to prosper into the 21st century that it must be open to the movement of the Holy Spirit and the windows of opportunity that it might bring. The Companions are a hybrid reflecting the best of what 'Orders and Christian communities' offer.

The Companions of St Luke is about making choices. Members are given choices of living at the Abbey or living their life in mission in the larger community. Members may choose to follow the traditional model of living as a single person or in a married state, both requiring a chaste life. The Community is a blend of male and female.

Vowed members take vows of: obedience, conversion of life, and stability; Oblates take corresponding promises of the same.

Michael-John Austin was consecrated Abbot at Conception Abbey (Roman), Missouri, in 2004. Since then, the Abbot Primate of the Roman Catholic Church has invited Michael-John to participate in the gathering of the Abbots of the Americas, representing Anglican tradition. Michael-John is also a member of the National Association of Episcopal Christian Communities.

MICHAEL-JOHN AUSTIN
(Abbot, founder 1992)

Brother Thomas Ferrell
Brother Raymond Owens
Brother Matthias Smith
Sister Monica Ruth Mullen
Brother Chad-Anselm Gerns
Sister Anna Grace Madden
Sister Catherine Unterseher
Sister Clare Benedicta Myers
Brother Paul Howard
Sister Vincent-Marie
Rittenhouse
Brother David-Vincent
Cotton
Sister Cecilia Lamoy
Brother Luke Doucette

Sister Mary Catherine
Christopher
Sister Hannah Sophia
Korver
Sister Mary Francis Deulen
Sister Sophia
Stevenson Holt
Brother Aidan Maguire
Brother Bede Leach
Brother Timothy Titus Lunt
Brother Gregory Kingsley
Sister Bernadette Barrett
Brother Simon DiNapoli

Novices: 6
Postulants: 6

Oblates and Companions

The Companions of St Luke has an Oblate program. Oblates are considered by this community to have a 'full and authentic' vocation deserving its own formation. Oblates sit with their vowed counterparts in the Office, have voice and seat in Chapter.

The Companions of St Luke also offers a 'Companion Associate' affiliation. These are individuals who desire to be affiliated with the Community and grow in their own understanding of what it means to live an intentional life grounded in baptism.

Office Book

The Office Prayer Book. This prayer book is unique to the charism of the community and incorporates part of the Rule of St Benedict, as well as antiphons taken from the Gospel of Luke and Acts. The prayer book also includes the Eucharist, Rite II setting from the BCP.

Community Publication

The Community has a quarterly newsletter called 'The Bridge'. This may be mailed, or downloaded from the website: www.holythoughts.org.

Guest and Retreat Facilities

The Abbey of St Benedict dedicated Phase One of its building projects in August 2008. The three buildings are able to accommodate fifteen individuals, all with private bathrooms and independent heating and air-conditioning. Each building has common areas and hospitality.

Most convenient time to telephone

The Abbey welcomes calls at all times. If someone is not near the phone, an answering system will take the message.

(Society of the) Community of Celebration

SCC

Founded 1973

The Community of Celebration is a life-vowed, contemporary residential community whose roots stretch back to the renewal of the Church of the Redeemer, Houston, Texas, in the 1960s. Today the Community resides in Aliquippa (near Pittsburgh), Pennsylvania. Members are women and men, single and married, adults and children, lay and ordained. Following the Rule of St Benedict, members live a rhythm of prayer, work, study, and recreation.

Our ministry is to be a Christian presence among the poor, responding to the needs around us by offering safe, affordable housing; wellness programs to women in the county jail; serving with neighborhood organizations concerned with the revitalization of Aliquippa, and providing hospitality, retreats, sabbaticals, and conferences. We provide various chaplaincies, supply clergy, liturgical consultants, worship leadership and speakers for conferences.

809 Franklin Avenue
Aliquippa
PA 15001-3302,
USA
Tel: 724 375 1510
Fax: 724 375 1138

Email: mail@
communityof
celebration.com

Website
communityof
celebration.com

Morning Prayer
8.00 am

Noonday Prayer
12.30 pm

Evening Prayer
5.30 pm

Compline
9.00 pm

Conventual **Eucharist**
is celebrated on
Saturday evenings at
5.30 pm, and Saints'
days as applicable.
Monthly service Taizé
worship.

Office Book
Book of Common
Prayer

Bishop Visitor
Rt Revd
C. Christopher Epting

BILL FARRA
(Primary Guardian, assumed office 1995)
MAY McKEOWN *(Guardian for Vocations)*

Mimi Farra   Joe Beckey
Revd Steven McKeown   Revd Phil Bradshaw
James von Minden   Margaret Bradshaw

Associates
Companions of the Community of Celebration follow the
Rule of Life for Companions.

Other address: Celebration UK Branch house, c/o Revd
Phil Bradshaw, 35 Cavendish Road, Redhill, Surrey RH1
4AL, UK

Community Publication
News from Celebration - twice a year. Contact Bill Farra for
a free subscription.

Community books
W Graham Pulkingham, *Gathered for Power*,
                    Hodder & Stoughton, London, 1972
Michael Harper, *A New Way of Living*,
                    Hodder & Stoughton, London, 1972
W Graham Pulkingham, *They Left their Nets*,
                    Hodder & Stoughton, London, 1973
Betty Pulkingham, *Mustard Seeds*,
                    Hodder & Stoughton, London, 1977
Maggie Durran, *The Wind at the Door*,
                    Kingsway Publications/Celebration, 1986
David Janzen, *Fire, Salt, and Peace*,
                    Shalom Mission Communities, 1996

Community Wares
Music and worship resources, psalms, anthems, books
and recordings - see website store.

Guest Facilities
We offer a chapel, meeting and dining spaces, and
overnight accommodation for 13-17 people (one guesthouse can be self-catering for 4-5 people). We welcome
individual retreatants and groups, men and women.
For further information contact Celebration's hospitality
director by mail, telephone or email.

Most convenient time to telephone:
                    9.00 am - 5.00 pm Eastern Time (Mon-Fri)

Company of Mission Priests

CMP

Founded 1940

Website
www. missionpriests.org

Warden's address:
99 Hilfield Avenue
Crouch End
London N8 7DG

Email: fathertimpike @hotmail.com

Office Book
The Divine Office (Vincentian calendar)

Community Publication
Occasional Newsletter

Associates
Laymen closely associated with the Company in life and work may be admitted as Associates of the Company.

Bishop Visitor
Rt Revd
Lindsay Urwin OGS,
Bishop of Horsham

The Company of Mission Priests is a dispersed community of male priests of the Anglican Communion who, wishing to consecrate themselves wholly to the Church's mission, keep themselves free from the attachments of marriage and the family, and endeavour to strengthen and encourage each other by mutual prayer and fellowship, sharing the vision of Saint Vincent de Paul of a priesthood dedicated to service, and living in a manner prescribed by our Constitution, and with a Vincentian rule of life. For many years the company, although serving also in Guyana and Madagascar, was best known for its work in staffing 'needy' parishes in England with two, three, or more priests who lived together in a clergy house. Although this is rarely possible nowadays, because of the shortage of priests, we encourage our members who work in proximity to meet as often as practicable in order to maintain some elements of common life. The whole company meets in General Chapter once a year, and the Regional Chapters more frequently.

We were among the founding members, in AD 2000, of the Vincentian Millennium partnership, which works 'in accordance with the principles established by St Vincent de Paul, to support and empower those who are poor, oppressed, or excluded.

FATHER TIMOTHY PIKE CMP
(Warden, assumed office 2005)

Michael Whitehead	Mark McIntyre
Anthony Yates	Alan Watson
Allan Buik	Simon Atkinson
Brian Godsell	Peter Bostock
John Cuthbert	Kevin Northover
Peter Brown	Peter Bolton
Beresford Skelton	Alan Parkinson
Michael Shields	Jonathan Kester
David Beater	Robert Martin
Michael Gobbett	Christopher Buckley
John Vile	Kevin Palmer
Ian Rutherford	Antony Homer
Andrew Collins Jones	Philip Meadows
James Geen	Andrew Welsby
Robert Page	Derek Lloyd
Colin Patterson	Anthony Moore
Philip North	*Probationers: 1*
Mark Elliott Smith	*Aspirants: 1*

Little Sisters of Saint Clare

LSSC

Founded 2002

Mother Guardian
Dorothy-Anne
Kiest, LSSC
Franciscan House of
Prayer
408 9th Ave N.
Edmonds
WA 98020
USA
Tel: 425 776 8182

Email:
motherguardian
@gmail.com

Website
www.
stclarelittlesisters.
org

Office Books
BCP, SSF Office for
Franciscan saints,
Lesser Feasts & Fasts

Episcopal Visitor
Rt Revd Sanford
Z K Hampton, *retd*

Our primary mission is the same as that of other Franciscan orders: To make our Lord known and loved through the land. Secondly, it is our desire to bring the contemplative spirituality of St Clare out of the cloister and into our churches, being grounded in the roots of the past, while finding wings for the future.

We take seriously the original call to St Francis as he was praying before the cross in the ruins of the little church of San Damiano in Italy. In that spirit and with the greater freedom and equality between men and women of this age, we encourage one another to work in our respective churches, according to our individual abilities. We strive always to be mindful of our vocation to contemplative life and intercessory prayer, carefully maintaining the difficult balance between secular and Religious life.

SISTER DOROTHY-ANNE KIEST, LSSC
(Mother Guardian, assumed office October 2006)

LSSC Sisters:
Abbess Gloria-Mary Goller
   Founder (retd), PCLS
Mary-Agnes Staples
Mary-Louise Sulonen
Marie-Elise Trailov
Jeanne-Marie Williamson

Mary-Frances Yanagihara
Kathryn-Mary Little

Companion LSSC:
Tovi Andrews

Novices: 1
DedraAnn Bracher

Obituaries
27 Nov 2008   Sister Marion-Hilda Lofgren, LSSC,
                             aged 94, with LSSC since 2002

Associates LSSC:
Pam Bedford
The Rev Dr
   Sandra Bochonok
Laura Carroll
Grace E Grant
Nancy Jones
Judith Kenyon

Joan Lindall
Marie McAnally
The Rev Bridget Moore
Mary Beth Peterson
Patricia Roberts
Judith Mary Rose
Mary Sherman
Olivia M. Stalter

Associates
The Ecumenical associate membership is open to women both clergy and laity, who seek an active affiliation with the little sisters of St Clare. They take their life of prayer seriously and feel the need to be helped in their commitment by an accountability which is one of the features of a rule as established by a Religious order. They also desire to be associated with the life and work of the

Sisters, whether through prayer or through active involvement. Associates will want to support the Little Sisters of St Clare through prayer and alms as they may be able. Associates may attend our meetings but if, for matters of health or distance, may be unable to attend regular meetings. If two or more Associates live in one area, they may be recognized as a fellowship, getting together to pray and observe whatever part of the rule is practical for them, at least monthly. The Sisters in turn pledge their support and hospitality whenever possible.

Other Addresses
Tovi Andrews,Comp/LSSC   *(Secretary)*
25732 Pioneer Way NW, Poulsbo, WA 98370, USA   *Tel: 360 779 2610*

Sister Mary-Louise Sulonen, LSSC *(Formation Director)*
16300 State Hwy 305 #32, Poulsbo, WA 98370, USA   *Tel: 360 779 3662*

Guest and Retreat Facilities
Limited. Call Mother Guardian 425 776 8182, spiritual direction and personal retreat ministry.

Most convenient time to telephone:
Pacific Time, USA : 9.00 am - 11.30 am , 2.00 pm - 4.00 pm

Order of the Community of the Paraclete

OCP

Founded 1971

PO Box 61399
Seattle
WA 98141
USA

Website
www.
theparacletians.org

Monthly gathering at
St George's Episcopal
Church,
2212 NE 125th Street,
Seattle, WA

Eucharist, meal, study
and fellowship, every
third Saturday
5.30 pm - 9.00 pm

The Community of the Paraclete is an apostolic community offering an authentic Religious life of prayer and service. We were recognized by the Episcopal Church in 1992. The Paracletians are self-supporting women and men, lay and ordained, who have committed themselves to live under the Paracletian Rule and constitution. Our vision: we are a network of Paracletian communities learning how to grow spiritually and exercising our gifts in ministry.

BROTHER JOHN RYAN OCP
(Minister, assumed office June 2009)

Tel: 206 363 6773   Email: rjhbro@mac.com

Brother Douglas Campbell
Sister Ann Case
Sister Susanne Chambers
Sister Suzanne Elizabeth Forbes
Brother Carle Griffin
Sister Barrie Gyllenswan
Sister Patricia Ann Harrison
Brother Timothy Nelson
Sister Martha Simpson
Brother Marvin Taylor

Friends and Associates
FRIEND:
any baptized Christian, with the approval of chapter.

ASSOCIATE:
confirmed Episcopalian, active member of an Episcopal parish, or church in communion with the Episcopal Church or the Episcopal See of Canterbury; six months' attendance at local chapter, and the approval of chapter.

Community Publication
Paracletian Presence, distributed free

Office Book
Book of Common Prayer

Bishop Visitor
Rt Revd Nedi Rivera, suffragan Bishop of Olympia

The Third Order, Society of Saint Francis

TSSF

The Third Order of the Society of Saint Francis consists of men and women, ordained and lay, married or single, who believe that God is calling them to live out their Franciscan vocation in the world, living in their own homes and doing their own jobs. Living under a rule of life, with the help of a spiritual director, members (called Tertiaries) encourage one another in living and witnessing to Christ. The Third Order is worldwide, with a Minister General and five Ministers Provincial to cover the relevant Provinces.

THE REVEREND DOROTHY BROOKER TSSF
(Minister General, assumed office September 2005)
16 Downing Avenue, Pirimai, Napier,
Aoteoroa-New Zealand
Tel: 7 345 6006   Email: dmbrook@clear.co.nz

KENNETH E NORIAN TSSF
(Assistant Minister General)

Founded
1920s (Americas)
1930s (Europe)
1975 (Africa)
1959 (Australia)
1962
(Aoteoroa-New Zealand)

Statistics for the whole community

	Professed	Novices
Americas	436	63
Europe	1820	177
Australia	283	60
Africa	96	17
NZ-Aoteoroa	176	57
Total	**2811**	**374**

PROVINCE OF THE AMERICAS

KENNETH E NORIAN TSSF *(Minister Provincial)*
45 Malone Street, Hicksville, NY 11801, USA
Tel: +1 917 416 9579   Email: ken@tssf.org
Website of Province: www.tssf.org

Office Book
Third Order Manual
The Manual includes a form of daily prayer called 'The Community Obedience'. Members are encouraged to use this in the context of Morning or Evening Prayer.

Statistics of Province
Professed: 436; *Novices:* 63; *Postulants:* 35

Associates of the Society of Saint Francis: Welcomes men and women, lay or clergy, single or in committed relationships, young and old, to join us as Associates in our diverse Franciscan family.

Provincial Publication
The Franciscan Times.
Available online at www.tssf.org/archives.shtml

Bishop Protector General
The Most Reverend Roger Herft, Archbishop of Perth, Western Australia

Bishop Protector: The Right Reverend Gordon P Scruton, Bishop of Western Massachusetts

EUROPEAN PROVINCE

THE REVD JOANNA CONEY TSSF *(Minister Provincial)*
4 Rowland Close, Lower Wolvercote, Oxford OX2 8PW, UK
Tel: +44 1865 556456
Email: ministertssf@franciscans.org.uk

Administrator (temporarily held by Provincial Secretary):
JOHN MORRISON TSSF
Foxdown, Neals Place Road, Canterbury, Kent CT2 8HX, UK
Email: jpm_480540@hotmail.com
Website of Province: www.tssf.org.uk

Statistics of Province: *Professed:* 1820; *Novices:* 177

Provincial Publication
The Chronicle (twice yearly) & Third Order News (quarterly) - available on website.
Contact: Alan Williams TSSF, Communications Coordinator
Email: williams.a.r@btopenworld.com (New Co-ordinator to be appointed)

Bishop Protector: The Right Reverend Michael Perham, Bishop of Gloucester

AUSTRALIAN PROVINCE

REVD TED WITHAM TSSF *(Minister Provincial)*
Novacare Lifestyle Village, 139 / 502 Bussell Hwy, Broadwater,
Western Australia 6280
Tel: +61 (0)8 9751 1288   Email: provincial.minister@tssf.org.au
Website of Province: www.tssf.org.au

Statistics of Province: *Professed:* 265; *Novices:* 83

Deaths since last Year Book:

11 Jul 2006	Bartholomew Yababana	14 Jul 2007	Champion Siburewa
2 May 2007	Frank Lomax	5 Mar 2008	Anne Johnson
	4 May 2008	Thory Bonsey	
	4 Oct 2008	Edna Mary Dale, professed 54 years	
	4 Mar 2009	Dorothy Bolton, professed 34 years	

Provincial Publication
Quarterly Newsletter - available on request from the Provincial Secretary, David White TSSF, or from the website www.tssf.org.au/Newsletter/
Email: provincial.secretary@tssf.org.au

Community History
Denis Woodbridge TSSF, *Franciscan Gold: A history of the Third Order of the Society of St Francis in the Province of Australia, Papua New Guinea and East Asia : Our first fifty years: 1959-2009.* Available from the Provincial Secretary.
Bishop Protector: The Most Reverend Roger Herft, Archbishop of Perth

AFRICAN PROVINCE

REVD DAVID BERTRAM TSSF *(Minister Provincial)*
PO Box 579, Hoedspruit 1380, South Africa
Tel: +83 299 3388 (mobile)   Fax: +86 542 5513
Email: polo.dave@yahoo.com

Statistics of Province
Professed: 96   *Novices:* 17

Provincial Publication
Pax et Bonum (published three times a year)
Available free of charge from the Provincial Publications Officer:
Alan Rogers TSSF   *Email: AlanR@mcgind.co.za*
or the Newsletter Editor: Neil Heslip   *Email: nheslip@medunsa.ac.za*

Associates
The African Province includes a small number of Companions who are associated
with, and pray for, the First Order, but are in the Third Order address list.   The
Secretary of the Companions is:
Mrs Joyce Gunston, 2 Swannack Gardens, Vonkehouse, Lourensford Road,
Somerset West 7130, SOUTH AFRICA   *Tel: 021 21 852 1830*

Bishop Protector: The Right Reverend Merwyn Castle, Bishop of False Bay

NEW ZEALAND PROVINCE

REVD JOHN HEBENTON TSSF *(Minister Provincial)*
15 Farm Street, Mt. Maunganui, NEW ZEALAND
Tel: 07 575 9930 (home); 07 574 0079 (work); 021679202 (mobile)
Fax: 07 574 0079
Email: jbheb@clear.net.nz   or   aynf.tp@clear.net.nz

Website of Province: www.franciscanthirdorder.godzone.net.nz

Statistics of Province:
Professed:	New Zealand: 94	Melanesia: 78
Novices:	New Zealand: 11	Melanesia: 46

Provincial Publication:
TAU; Available from the Provincial Secretary: Anne Moody *Email: anne@ix.net.nz*

Community History
Both these booklets are by Chris Barfoot:
Beginnings of the Third Order in New Zealand 1956-74
Peace and Joy : Part 2 of the History of the Third Order, SSF, in New Zealand

Bishops Protector
The Right Reverend Philip Richardson, Bishop of Waikato
The Right Reverend Richard Naramana, Bishop of Ysabel *(for Melanesia)*

The Worker Sisters and Brothers of the Holy Spirit

WSHS & WBHS

Founded 1972 in the Diocese of West Missouri (Sisters) & 1979 Brothers, and the community expanded to Canada

Contact address:
Sr Catherine Marie
WSHS
Executive Director
1125 Prescott Lane
Crystal Lake
Illinois 60014
USA
Tel: 1 815 455 0347
Fax: 1 815 455 0796
Email:
sr.catherine.marie@
gmail.com

Website: www.
workersisters.org
& www.
workerbrothers.org

Office Book
Book of Common
Prayer

The Worker Sisters and Brothers of the Holy Spirit is a Covenant Community which seeks to respond to God's call through the power of the Holy Spirit, participate in Jesus Christ's vision of unity, become his holy people, show forth Fruit, and in obedience to his command, go forth into the world. It offers women and men, regardless of marital status, a path for individual spiritual growth through a life commitment to a Rule which provides an opportunity to experience prayer, worship, becoming, discovery, belonging, relating, commitment and mission. Membership is made up of:

First Order: Sisters - Lay Workers and Lay Sisters;
Second Order: Brothers - Lay Workers and Lay Brothers;
Third Order: Clergy Sisters and Clergy Brothers;
Companions: Lay and Clergy Persons;
Friends: Lay and Clergy Persons

The first three Orders are bound together under a Life Commitment to a common Rule which is Benedictine in orientation. Companions make a Life commitment to a Rule of Life. Friends share in the prayer and spiritual journey of the community. Members do not live together, yet are not separated by geographical boundaries.

SISTER CATHERINE MARIE WSHS
(Executive Director, assumed office April 2006)

SISTER DEBORAH WSHS *(Canadian Director)*
SISTER CHRISTINE WSHS *(American Director)*

Members: 157
Postulants: 6

Other Address
Sister Pam Raphael WSHS, Director of Admissions, PO Box 658, St Helena Island, South Carolina 29920, USA

Obituaries
24 Jun 2007   Brother Denis James WBHS,
                          professed 29 years
23 Jan 2008   Sister Evelyn Paul WSHS,
                          professed 32 years
1 Feb 2009   Sister Joyce Abraham WSHS,
                          professed 35 years

Community Ecclesiastical Visitor
UNITED STATES, HAITI: Rt Revd Barry Howe, Friend WSHS/ WBHS - Diocese of West Missouri, USA

Obituaries

Brother Bernard SSF
(1929-2007)

Michael Apps was born in Birmingham, UK, the son of a successful business man, and attended King Edward VI School in Edgbaston, Pembroke College, Cambridge, and Cuddesdon Theological College, before ordination and a curacy at Spalding. In 1958, he followed a long-standing call to the Franciscans and, after the novitiate, served in Plaistow (East London), in Brisbane (Queensland, Australia), and at Hilfield Friary in Dorset, UK, as Guardian of each successively.

Bernard was gifted by God as a leader, a preacher, and a spiritual guide in the ways of prayer; he had in addition a wonderful sense of fun and great personal warmth, which sometimes came across more as heat!

His last active years were spent in the house in Halcrow Street, Stepney, in London, to which his many 'directees' found their way. He occupied the back room on the ground floor next to the chapel which was the scene of a ministry whose value became apparent both at the funeral in Dorset, and the Requiem at St Paul's, Bow Common. Those whom he guided were truly meeting a wounded healer, who had experienced in his own life much in the way of frustration, disappointment, and matter for penitence - and was therefore a master in the discernment of what in their lives, they kept concealed from themselves.

His final months were overshadowed (for his brothers as for him) by a mental senility which confused and distressed him, but, thanks to the faithful ministry of the Hilfield community, he was able to remain at home almost until the end.

May he rest in peace, and rise in glory.

Sister May Elizabeth CMM
(1926-2008)
Reverend Mother Superior 1968-71

Born in the village of Machite in the Tanzanian diocese of Masasi in 1926, Sister May Elizabeth was brought up in the families of her uncles, as her mother had died soon after her birth. Educated at St Mary's Anglican School, Ndwika, she joined a new venture in the Religious life at Kwa Mkono, Tanga region, being first professed in 1949. Her life vows in Chama Cha Mariamu Mtakatifu (Community of St Mary of Nazareth and Calvary) followed in 1957. She continued her studies whilst testing her vocation and she qualified as a teacher. From 1952, she taught English and Mathematics at a girls' school in Newala, Masasi, then run by the Community of the Sacred Passion.

As one of the founders, she undertook administrative work in the Community and was Sister-in- charge at the time the CSP sisters decided to give independence to CMM. She was elected its first Reverend Mother Superior in 1967 and held office until 1971, during which time she opened the house in the remote village of Liuli.

In the 1970s and 1980s, she taught in schools and Sunday schools, attached to St Nicholas parish, in the Ilala district of Dar es Salaam, and was Sister-in-charge of the house. In 1998, she transferred to Mtwara in the south of the country, but the following year had to return to the Mother House as her health required her to receive more care.

She had always been a leader in the agricultural work of the Community, looking after chickens and especially the cats and dogs, necessary to keep pests at bay. All the years of hard work were perhaps responsible for the crippling arthritis, which confined her to a wheel chair in the last three years of her life.

Her courage and commitment were notable. It is to May Elizabeth and the other founding Sisters that we owe the existence of the vibrant CMM Community today. She died on 25 July 2008. All who knew her loved her and she will be remembered by the special name given to her: Bibi Upendano (Grandmother of Love).

Sister Philippa SSJD (1922-2008)

Sister Philippa was born Dorothy Watson in Winnipeg on 21 December 1922. Her parents had emigrated from Aberdeenshire in Scotland, and took both her and her sister back there to be baptised. Philippa remained very proud of her Scottish heritage throughout her life, and was toasted by a piper on her Golden Jubilee.

After completing her degree in Winnipeg in 1944, she attended Library school in Toronto. There she came to know the Sisterhood and entered as a postulant in 1949, being clothed the following year and then professed on 11 June 1953.

Philippa worked at the St John's Convalescent (later Rehabilitation) Hospital, run by SSJD, in her novitiate, and returned there in 1954 as the assistant to the Administrator, Sister Vera. It was the beginning of forty-three years of service to the hospital. She succeeded Sister Vera in 1969. The title of the post changed through the years - at her retirement in 1996 she was the President and CEO - but the responsibilities of running and developing the facilities for patients remained the same. She sat on many boards and committees at the hospital and in the healthcare field; in 1992 she was awarded the Order of Ontario in recognition of her contribution.

She was also an enthusiastic organizer of social events, the Burns Night every January, Scottish country dancing, the June Garden Party, and events for Hallowe'en and Christmas. Even in her later years of declining health, she wanted to be a part of everything that happened at the Convent. She loved people and opportunities for conversations and visits. Her wonderful sense of humour will be missed but most especially her loving and prayerful presence.

Revd Alan Harrison
(1920-2008)

Born in Stafford in 1920, Father Alan felt a vocation to the priesthood from the age of ten but he was called up for service in the Royal Navy, so his response to the calling was delayed. After the war his training at the Hostel and College of the   Resurrection, Mirfield, brought him into a living contact with the Religious life which remained with him throughout his ministry - as a Benedictine oblate, then as a member and later Warden of the Company of Mission Priests, and then in work with Religious communities in the UK and overseas.

His ordained ministry began at St Mary's, Wellingborough in 1951. He next served as a mission priest in what is now Belize in Central America (1955-61) where his practical abilities in furniture-making, boatbuilding, and making vestments came in very handy. On his return to England he served in Winchester Diocese at St Francis' Bournemouth and then in Eastleigh. Increasingly, he felt a call to the ministry of healing and deliverance which sprang from work as a confessor and spiritual director and was Chaplain of the Guild of Health 1972-76.

In 1973 his long-standing connections with the Religious life led him to Ham Common where he became Chaplain to the Sisters of the Church until 1976 when he entered upon a decade as Secretary to the Advisory Council on the Relations of Bishops and Religious Communities, in parallel with his work as Secretary to the Communities' Consultative Council.   This was a time of change and upheaval in Anglican Religious life, in the wake of Vatican II and a dearth of vocations and diminishing numbers. Father Alan offered support and wise counsel that was both profound and practical, and filled with wit and humour. He was confessor and spiritual guide to the Sisters of the Love of God (Fairacres) and

a member of the Economic Commission supporting Anglican and Roman Catholic contemplative communities.

He retired in 1986 and spent his last sixteen years at Morden College, Blackheath where he died from cancer on 6 October 2008, aged 88. Tom Butler, Bishop of Southwark, presided at the Solemn Requiem at All Saints', Blackheath - the church at which Father Alan had assisted.

To the end he was irrepressible, loving, and laughing. Who knows how many individuals, communities, groups and organisations he had helped during his long life, with his God-given talents of spiritual insight, his devout but unostentatious Christian faith and practice in which humour and profundity both flourished?

Sister Mary Adela CSC (1912-2008)

Mary Adeline Carthew was born March 15, 1912, at Moorefield near Palmerston, Ontario, Canada. Graduating from Hamilton General Hospital in 1932, she became the school nurse at St. Mildred's College, Toronto in 1936. She entered the Community of the Sisters of the Church in 1938 and was professed as Sister Mary Adela on September 28, 1943. She held several positions of authority in the Community in Canada, and was in charge of two schools: St Mildred's College, Toronto, from 1954 to 1960 and the Lightbourn School in Oakville from 1964 to 1967. In later years, Sister lived in St Elizabeth Village, a retirement complex in Hamilton, and then from 2001 until her death on November 14, 2008, she was lovingly cared for in the infirmary of the Sisterhood of St John the Divine in Toronto.

Her Requiem Mass at the Church of St Mary Magdalene, Toronto, sung by the Ritual Choir and the Schola Magdalena reflected her deep love of music both polyphonic and plainchant. From early childhood until her last days, she enjoyed playing the piano and listening to others perform. She was a gifted artist in a variety of media - pencil, watercolour and oils - though she was her own severest critic. Her writing, both prose and poetry, made her a regular contributor to the CSC Newsletter.

Her widespread ministry of correspondence endeared her to alumnae, family, Sisters, friends and Associates. She was a letter-writer of the 'old school' and had written her Christmas letter just days before she died. Her letters, full of warmth and interest, were treasured by the recipients, whilst her handwriting was firm and clear to the end. Her international telephone ministry was also greatly valued, reflecting as it did her great love of, and interest in, people in all walks of life.

Organizations

Africa

Council for the Religious Life (in Southern Africa)

All Religious communities in the Church of the Province of Southern Africa come under the Council for the Religious Life. The superiors of all communities are members. The officers of the executive are:

The Rt Revd Merwyn Castle
The Most Revd Njongonkulu Ndungane, Archbishop of Cape Town *(ex officio)*
Sister Thandi CJC *(Chair)*
Sister Erika OHP *(Vice-Chair)*
Father Mark Vandeyar OGS *(Bursar)*
Mrs V M Rogers TSSF *(Secretary)*

Australia

Advisory Council for Anglican Religious Life in Australia

The Council consists of:
Rt Revd Godfrey Fryar, Bishop of North Queensland *(chair)*
Rt Revd Peter Danaher, Assistant Bishop of Bathurst
Ann Skamp, Diocese of Grafton
Revd Michael Jobling, Diocese of Melbourne *(Secretary)*
Email: hjjandmjj@bigpond.com

Brother Robin BSB	Sr Josephine Margaret CHN	Sister Patricia SI
Mother Rita Mary CCK	Brother Wayne LBF	Sister Eunice SSA
Sister Jean CSBC	Father Trevor OGS	Br Alfred Boonkong SSF
Sister Linda Mary CSC	Abbot Michael King OSB	Father Matthew SSM

Observers from New Zealand:
Mother Keleni CSN   Sister Anne SLG
Most Revd David Moxon, Bishop of Waikato *(liaison bishop)*

Europe

Advisory Council on the Relations of Bishops & Religious Communities (commonly called 'The Advisory Council')

Rt Revd David Walker, Bishop of Dudley *(Acting Chair)*
Rt Revd Humphrey Southern, Bishop of Repton
Rt Revd John Pritchard, Bishop of Oxford
Rt Revd Anthony Robinson, Bishop of Pontefract
Rt Revd Andrew Burnham, Bishop of Ebbsfleet *(co-opted)*
Rt Revd Dominic Walker OGS, Bishop of Monmouth *(co-opted)*

Communities' elected representatives (elected November 2005 for five-year term):

Sister Anita CSC	Sister Mary Stephen OSB
Mother Ann Verena CJGS	Father Peter Allan CR
Father Colin CSWG	Sister Rosemary CHN
Brother Damian SSF	Abbot Stuart Burns OSB
Sister Mary Julian CHC	

ARC representative: Father Jonathan Ewer SSM
Roman Catholic Observer: Sister Catherine McGovern OSF
Pastoral Secretary: Revd Preb Bill Scott   *Tel: 020 7024 5576 or 020 7930 9996*
                                               Email: william.scott@royal.gsx.gov.uk
Acting Administrative Secretary: Jonathan Neil-Smith,
Central Secretariat, Church House, Great Smith Street, London SW1P 3NZ
Tel: 020 7898 1373   Fax: 020 7898 1369   Email: jonathan.neil-smith@c-of-e.org.uk

Conference of the Leaders of Anglican Religious Communities (CLARC)

The Conference meets in full once a year, usually in June.
Steering Committee 2009
(dates indicate the year that the member's elected term ends)

Mother Ann Verena CJGS	Father Peter Huckle SSJE (2010)
(administrative assistant)	Brother Simon OSB (2010)
Sister Dorothy Stella OHP (2009)	Mother Monica Jane CHN (2011)
Mother Elizabeth CAH (2009)	Father Jonathan Ewer SSM (2011)
Sister Joyce CSF (2009)	Mother Cynthia Clare SSM (2011)
Brother Stuart OSB (2009)	

General Synod of the Church of England

Representatives of Lay Religious

Sister Anita OHP	(Elected 2006)
Brother Desmond Alban SSF	(Elected 2008)

Representatives of Ordained Religious

Revd Sister Rosemary CHN	(Elected 2002, re-elected 2005)
Revd Thomas Seville CR	(Elected 2005)

Anglican Religious Communities in England (ARC)

ARC supports members of Religious communities of the Church of England. Its membership is the entire body of professed members of communities recognised by the Advisory Council *(see above)*.

ARC holds an Annual Conference in the first week of September each year when members can come together both to hear speakers on topics relevant to their way of life and to meet and share experiences together. A news sheet is regularly circulated to all houses and ARC represents Anglican Religious life on various bodies, including the Vocations Forum of the Ministry Division of the C of E, The Advisory Council and the *Year Book* editorial committee. Some limited support is also given to groups of common interest within ARC who may wish to meet. Its activities are co-ordinated by a committee with members elected from Leaders, Novice Guardians, General Synod representatives and the professed membership. The committee normally meets three times a year.

Sister Anita CSC, Father Jonathan Ewer SSM & Father George Guiver CR
(representing Leaders)
Sister Anita OHP *(representing General Synod Representatives)*
Sister Rita-Elizabeth SSB *(representing Novice Guardians)*
Brother Colin Wilfred SSF, Sister Jane Louise SSM, Sister Mary Catherine OSB,
Sister Pam OHP, Sister Pamela CAH & Brother Steven CR
(representing professed members)
Sister Christine James CSF *(Administrative Secretary)*

More information about Anglican Religious Life (in England) or about ARC itself, may be obtained from: The Anglican Religious Communities Secretary, c/o Jonathan Neil-Smith, Secretary to the House of Bishops, Central Secretariat, Archbishops' Council, Church House, Great Smith Street, London SW1P 3AZ
Email: info@arcie.org.uk   *Website: www.thekingdomisyours.org.uk*

North America

Conference of Anglican Religious Orders in the Americas (CAROA)

The purpose of CAROA is to provide opportunities for mutual support and sharing among its member communities and co-ordinate their common interests and activities, to engage in dialogue with other groups, to present a coherent understanding of the Religious Life to the Church and to speak as an advocate for the Religious Orders to the Church. CAROA is incorporated as a non-profit organization in both Canada and the USA.

Father Gregory Fruehwirth OJN *(President)*
Brother Jude Hill SSF *(Vice-President)*
Sister Marguerite Mae Eamon CSC *(Secretary-Treasurer)*

The Revd Dr Donald Anderson *(General Secretary)*
PO Box 99, Little Britain, Ontario K0M 2C0, Canada
Tel: 705 786 3330   Email: dwa@nexicom.net

House of Bishops Standing Committee on Religious Orders in the Anglican Church of Canada

The Committee usually meets twice a year, during the House of Bishops' meeting. Its rôle is consultative and supportive.

Rt Revd James A J Cowan, Bishop of British Columbia *(chair)*
Most Revd Fred J Hiltz, Archbishop & Primate of Canada
Rt Revd George Elliot, Suffragan Bishop of York-Simcoe, Diocese of Toronto
Rt Revd Linda Nicholls, Suffragan Bishop of Trent-Durham, Diocese of Toronto
The Superiors of CSC, OHC, SSJD & SSJE
Revd Dr Donald W Anderson, General Secretary of CAROA
The Ven Paul Feheley, Principal Secretary to the Primate *(Secretary)*

General Synod of the Anglican Church of Canada

Religious Synod members:
Sister Marguerite Mae Eamon CSC   Sister Elizabeth Ann Eckert SSJD

National Association for Episcopal Christian Communities (NAECC)

The NAECC is an inclusive association that shares and communicates the fruits of the Gospel, realized in community, with the church and the world.   It is primarily a forum for those who are living or exploring new or continuing models of religious commitment within the context of community.

Brother Bill Farra SCC *(Chair)*
Brother Ken Murphy OP *(Recorde)*
Brother James Mahoney BSG *(Treasurer)*

Website: home.earthlink.net/~naecc/index.htm

ECUMENICAL & INTER-DENOMINATIONAL

Conference of Religious (CoR)

The Conference of Religious is open to all Roman Catholic Provincial leaders of Religious Congregations in England and Wales.   The leaders of Anglican communities may be Associate members, which, apart from voting rights, means they receive all the same benefits and information as the Roman Catholic leaders. CoR is run by an executive committee, elected from its members, which meets every two months.   It deals with matters affecting men and women Religious, and various matters of interest to them. There is particular emphasis on peace and justice issues.

CoR Secretariat, P.O. Box 37602, The Ridgeway, London NW7 4XG
Tel: 020 8201 1861   Fax: 020 8201 1988   Email: confrelig@aol.com

Glossary
and
Indices

Glossary

Aspirant
A person who hopes to become a Religious and has been in touch with a particular community, but has not yet begun to live with them.

Celibacy
The commitment to remain unmarried and to refrain from sexual relationships. It is part of the vow of chastity traditionally taken by Religious. Chastity is a commitment to sexual integrity, a term applicable to fidelity in marriage as well as to celibacy in Religious Life.

Chapter
The council or meeting of Religious to deliberate and make decisions about the community. In some orders, this may consist of all the professed members of the community; in others, the Chapter is a group of members elected by the community as a whole to be their representatives.

Clothing
The ceremony in which a postulant of a community formally becomes a novice, and begins the period of formation in the mind, work and spirit of the community. It follows the initial stage of being a postulant when the prospective member first lives alongside the community. The clothing or novicing ceremony is characterised by the Religious 'receiving' the habit, or common attire, of the community.

Contemplative
A Religious whose life is concentrated on prayer inside the monastery or convent rather than on social work or ministry outside the house. Some communities were founded with the specific intention of leading a contemplative lifestyle together. Others may have a single member or small group living such a vocation within a larger community oriented to outside work.

Enclosed
This term is applied to Religious who stay within a particular convent or monastery - the 'enclosure' - to pursue more effectively a life of prayer. They would usually only leave the enclosure for medical treatment or other exceptional reasons. This rule is intended to help the enclosed Religious be more easily protected from the distractions and attentions of the outside world.

Eremitic
The eremitic Religious is one who lives the life of a hermit, that is, largely on his or her own. Hermits usually live singly, but may live in an eremitic community, where they meet together for prayer on some occasions during each day.

Evangelical Counsels
A collective name for the three vows of poverty, chastity and obedience.

Habit
The distinctive clothing of a community. In some communities, the habit is worn at all times, in others only at certain times or for certain activities. In some communities, the habit is rarely worn, except perhaps for formal occasions.

Novice
A member of a community who is in the formation stage of the Religious Life, when she or he learns the mind, work and spirit of the particular community whilst living among its members.

Oblate
Someone associated closely with a community, but who will be living a modified form of the Rule, which allows him or her to live outside the Religious house. Oblates are so-called because they make an oblation (or offering) of obedience to the community instead of taking the profession vows. In some communities, oblates remain celibate, in others they are allowed to be married. A few oblates live within a community house and then they are usually termed intern(al) oblates. The term oblate is more usually associated with Benedictine communities.

Office/Daily Office/Divine Office
The round of liturgical services of prayer and worship, which mark the rhythm of the daily routine in Religious Life. Religious communities may use the services laid down by the Church or may have their own particular Office book. The Offices may be called Morning, Midday, Evening and Night Prayer, or may be referred to by their more traditional names, such as Mattins, Lauds, Terce, Sext, None, Vespers and Compline.

Postulant
Someone who is in the first stage of living the Religious life. The postulancy usually begins when the aspirant begins to live in community and ends when he or she becomes a novice and 'receives the habit'. Postulants sometimes wear a distinctive dress or else may wear secular clothes.

Profession
The ceremony at which a Religious makes promises (or vows) to live the Religious Life with integrity and fidelity to the Rule. The profession of these vows may be for a limited period or for life. The usual pattern is to make a 'first' or simple profession in which the vows are made to the community. After three or more years a Life Profession may be made, which is to the Church and so the vows are usually received by a bishop. In the Anglican Communion, Life Professed Religious can usually be secularized only by the Archbishop or Presiding Bishop of a Province.

Religious
The general term for a person living the Religious life, whether monk, nun, friar, brother, sister etc.

Rule
The written text containing the principles and values by which the members of a community try to live. The Rule is not simply a set of regulations, although it may contain such, but is an attempt to capture the spirit and charism of a community in written form. Some communities follow traditional Rules, such as those of St Benedict or St Augustine, others have written their own.

Tertiary/Third Order
This term is usually associated with Franciscan communities, but is used by others

too. A Third Order is made up of tertiaries, people who take vows, but modified so that they are able to live in their own homes and have their own jobs. They may also marry and have children. They have a Rule of Life and are linked to other tertiaries through regular meetings. In the Franciscan family, the Third Order complements both the First Order of celibate friars and sisters and the Second Order of contemplative Religious.

Vows
The promises made by a Religious at profession. They may be poverty, chastity and obedience. In some communities, they are obedience, stability and conversion of life.

Index of Communities by Dedication or Patron Saint

Index by location

Index of Community Wares
& Services for Sale

Community of the Servants of the Will of God, UK   81
Korean Franciscan Brotherhood, Korea   91
Order of St Benedict, Broad Marston, UK   107
Order of St Benedict, Camperdown, Australia   110

INCENSE
Alton Abbey, UK   52
Order of the Holy Cross, USA   100
Order of St Benedict, Broad Marston, UK   107
Order of St Benedict, Camperdown, Australia   110

MUSIC & WORSHIP RESOURCES
Community of the Resurrection, UK   54
Community of St Mary the Virgin, UK   75
Society of the Community of Celebration, USA   165

PRINTING
Community of St Clare, UK   60
Order of St Benedict, Camperdown, Australia   110

WINE
Christa Sevika Sangha, Bangladesh   33
Society of the Holy Cross, Korea   126

Index of Communities by Initials

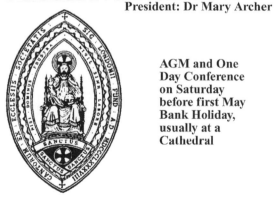

Notes and Amendments

Notes and Amendments

Notes and Amendments